HERE WE GO GATHERING CUPS IN MAY

HERE WE GO GATHERING CUPS IN MAY

Liverpool in Europe – the Fans' Story

by

Nicky Allt, Tony Barrett, Jegsy Dodd, Peter Hooton, Dave Kirby, John Maguire and Kevin Sampson

CANONGATE

Edinburgh · London · New York · Melbourne

First published in Great Britain in 2007 by
Canongate Books Ltd, 14 High Street,
Edinburgh, EH1 1TE

This paperback edition first published in 2008 by Canongate Books

1

British Library Cataloguing-in-Publication Data
A catalogue record for this book is available
on request from the British Library

Every effort has been made to contact copyright holders where appropriate,
but please contact the publisher if there are any errors or omissions.

ISBN 978 1 84767 167 7

Typeset by Palimpsest Book Production Ltd,
Grangemouth, Stirlingshire

Printed and bound in Great Britain by Clays Ltd, St Ives plc

www.canongate.net

It goes without saying that this book is dedicated to the 96 . . .

And to Mrs Shankly and Mrs Paisley for supporting their husbands' fierce allegiance to turning Liverpool from an overgrown Anfield superloo into a streamlined footballing superpower.

The four people above allied to raw Scouse passion became our Alchemy.

And finally: to a Bootle lady, Mrs Margaret McDonald –
For gathering a needle, a thread, and a line from her head,
Before waving her son off to follow the Red.
Mrs Mac – A seven-writer salute goes out just to you
xxxxxxx

It would be eight, but the eighth writer . . . it was you.

ABOUT THE AUTHORS

Nicky Allt: author and playwright, born and bred on the banks of the Mersey, dreamed of being a Docker or Seaman but ended up running wild around Kirkby as a pre-teen, Europe as a youth and the world as an adult. Falling out of love with football once divvy players' wives started wearing knickers that cost a docker's yearly wage he decided to do what his Irish English teacher at school told him he was born to do: write. Not listening to that shout for twenty years at least gave him a million stories to tell. In here lie two of them.

Tony Barrett has been a Liverpool fan all his life and has been an Anfield regular since the age of five, and a Kop season ticket holder for twenty-one years. A veteran of countless domestic away games and European trips, Tony, thirty-one, works as a feature writer with the *Liverpool Echo* newspaper. He grew up in Fairfield in Liverpool but recently moved a couple of miles up the road to Broadgreen because 'it's the ideal place to get a lift from and to away games'. Tony credits his dad, Eddie, with making him a Red and is forever grateful that he didn't follow in the footsteps of his mum, Monica, by becoming a Blue. His favourite players past and present are Jamie Carragher and King Kenny Dalglish.

Jegsy Dodd is a practising heterosexual who lives on the Wirral and drives a taxi. His first album for almost twenty years, *Wake Up and Smell the Offy*, produced the surprise No. 1 track on the prestigious Radio 1 Festive Fifty in 2005. At the time of going to press he is recording a new album, has an extremely fit girlfriend called Hema and a slight pain in his right shoulder. His vital stats are 40-40-34. Star player: Ian Rush. Bevvy: beer – lots of it. He continues to have opinions. More info: www.jegsydodd.com.

Peter Hooton's dad took him to his first away match to Old Trafford in the 1973/1974 season and he was hooked from then on. He has been to hundreds of matches at home and away ever since. During the 1980s he co-edited *The End*, an underground satirical magazine that was sold at Liverpool games. Later on he became the singer/songwriter in The Farm, had a UK number one album with them in the early '90s and toured extensively. But football remains his first love. Peter is a season-ticket holder in the Kop.

Dave Kirby was born in Liverpool in 1959 and grew up in Kirkby, a vast council overspill north of the city. His away journeys began in the early 1970s; occasionally hitch-hiking before progressing to the infamous football-special trains. A builder for twenty-three years, he now writes full-time and can often be found on the after-dinner circuit with ex-Liverpool legends, performing his terrace verse LFC poetry.

John Maguire, from Bootle, spent seven years working in a steel yard on the Dock Road before getting fed up and going to university to study to become a social worker. He enjoys nothing more than having a bevvy with his mates and watching his beloved Redmen. He is a keen follower of the local music scene in Liverpool and loves any type of creativity in the community. He thinks Michael Head (Shack) is a musical genius and his favourite scran is Three Meat Curry, Fried Rice (no onions).

Kevin Sampson is the author of seven novels, including the best-selling *Awaydays*, *Powder* and *Outlaws*, along with a horribly funny account of Liverpool FC's worst season in recent times, *Extra Time*. His favourite player ever is John Barnes and, thanks for asking, his tipple is Becks with a Jameson's chaser.

CONTENTS

FOREWORD

Standing on the pitch at the Olympic Stadium in Rome, 1977, was one of the proudest moments of my life. I scanned the massed ranks of red and white, hoping to see a few mates or my two brothers, Frank and Dave, who were amongst the 26,000 that travelled over. It was an incredible sight. It seemed a far cry from the days when we used to get the number 86 bus, then the 27, to Anfield. Like most young scousers back then I served my time in the 'Boys' Pen' watching great players like Peter Thompson, Ian Callaghan and my hero, Tommy Smith. At every home game we'd try and bunk out of the pen into the Kop. We'd wait till the copper moved away from the fence, then bail over and join the swaying crowd and deafening noise. Over the years I travelled home and away to places like West Brom and Walsall – fitting the match around my job as an apprentice spark and my amateur football career.

While at South Liverpool I was spotted by Tom Saunders and, after a two-week trial, agreed to sign as a semi-pro. I'd play two mornings a week at Melwood then head straight to a building site in the afternoon. Most of my mates off the sites went to the match. It was a welcome diversion away from a tough job with poor pay and poor conditions – following Liverpool could do that; take you away from it all. I finally made my debut in April '75. It was a fantastic feeling being named alongside Toshack and Keegan. I ran out in front of the packed Kop where I'd stood for so long. The raw passion and pride that they felt was a natural part of me; there was no way I was going to let them down. Two years later – on that incredible night in Rome – I stared at the red masses who had gone to unbelievable lengths to make the journey. If things had turned out differently, I know for a fact that I'd have been right there in the middle of them waving a chequered flag. That's how it is when you're a fanatic – you'd do anything and travel anywhere to watch Liverpool. I'd have died for those fans that night. I knew exactly how they felt because they were me – I was them.

Jimmy Case, Liverpool 1972–1981

INTRODUCTION

Walking the atmospheric boulevards of old Marseilles, eventually reaching dockside, I found the bar where I'd sat and spoken to a wizened old Frenchman all those years ago. Presuming he'd be part of the incoming tide by now, I never bothered to ask the owners of his whereabouts. Patrick Le Duveneh, Marseilles fisherman, had told me among many pearls of wisdom that he'd have his ashes scattered at sea the next time I visited his Southern French port. Yeah, that's what he called it: *his;* like he was the yacht-owning, wrinkly Popeye version of the southern King of France.

Almost thirty years since I last breathed the intoxicating whiff of Gauloise smoke, sea air and Gallic streets, I let the scenery, sounds and a sprinkling of Mediterranean salt water wash over me. Noisy ocean waves crashed into boats and rocks with a densely defiant thud that proclaimed, 'I am the sea'. Like Patrick, I too loved everything about the ocean. Along with old briny, I also loved these rough and ready portside settings – bit like Naples, bit like Hamburg, bit like Liverpool. The rougher the setting, find the right people and, warmer the welcome.

Thinking how I'd gotten here last time, penniless after another European trek, myself, Fast Eddie and Joey O' had started out at William Hill's betting office outside Liverpool's Lime Street Station. With no *real* intention other than to pass time and see what Fast Eddie could do with his just-cashed giro cheque, we talked about the buzz of hitting the road. Arriving back from places like Amsterdam, Geneva and Cologne, story-laden, hungry for more, with a travel bug nipping away at toes and backsides that made sitting or standing still for five minutes seem like a life sentence, we badly wanted off.

Small, blue, betting-office pens between teeth, nervously biting at the over-chewed tops, we talked of where we'd like to take off to, there and then, if a big pools win came in (pipe dreaming, as we didn't do the pools), or, if wrinkly Lester Piggott romped home on a decently priced filly to put a nice, fat, bundle in your back bin. You know, as a dreamer does, as a kid does, as you do. Fast Eddie, pinpointing Monaco as his beloved destination, grinned to himself, tearing another betting slip from the metal container on the wall. Asked why he'd chosen a rich mans dining table as the place he'd cash his chips, he replied, 'If all those tax-dodging fruit-cakes were spending money there, and the place was riddled with gambling casinos, I'd be aboard glistening yachts, rolling dice under the stars every night with pop stars and princesses.'

A long-winded answer by our own in-house gambling fiend, his mid-afternoon dream got sliced when Joey O', countered, 'Who are you kidding, Betting-Office Balls? On yachts! You only have to bunk the Royal Iris ferry across the Mersey to Birkenhead and you're spewing your ring soon as the engines kick in!'

He was right about Eddie's seafaring legs, but it was only a harmless dream. Defending the lad's answer, I responded, 'Well, where would you choose then, Joey the rock-hard pirate?

'I'd get right off to the Caribbean. Money goes a long way there. It's sunny, there's loads of cricket and, there's a thousand black beauties to wine and dine and take to those boss reggae clubs!'

Loving cricket in school, since getting tuned into Bob Marley's 'Exodus' by a calypso Scouser, he listened to nothing but reggae music. I understood his choice, till Fast Eddie butted in: 'Ha! Cricket's a load of shit! Sitting there, bored off your skull with a big bag of money to spend!'

'Yeah, he's got a point there with the cricket,' I offered.

'Nah, you've got no culture, youse two. Crickets a game for lords. I'd be a lord in the Caribbean. Yeah, Lord Joseph of Trinidad, or Barbados or Jamaica, that'd do for me.'

'Kingston is in Jamaica . . . isn't it?' I quizzed.

'Yeah . . . why?' asked Joey.

'Cos Kingston is one seriously rough gaff and you'd be mugged, battered and robbed within a week.'

Clocking me for a moment, he asked 'Alright smartarse where would you go then?'

Without a thought I snapped back, 'Marseilles!'

'Marseilles?' Joey O' goes, 'that's even rougher than Kingston!'

Wanting to be different, not choosing the obvious glitter-paved tinseltown, I'd been reading a book about the mystical French port, something with *French Connection* similarities and uttered the first thing that came to mind.

'And your reasons?' enquired Joey O'.

'Well, it sounds like a mad dockland place full of gangsters and molls, and you could shoot into Monaco for a blast like Eddie said, but live with real people and not all those phoney rich pricks when you needed to get your head together.' He looked at me for the briefest, turning to Eddie for opinion. Eddie had grown disinterested, already studying the riders for the next giddy-up ride. 'Marseilles, yeah, that's where I'd go right now – no passport, no bags, nothing!'

'Right now, yeah, you'd go right now?' Eddie had rejoined the chinwag, speaking through teeth still clenched around a small, blue plastic pen, his eyes glued intently to the TV screen above. 'Well, if this wins, let's go, right now, yeah? The Monaco Grand Prix is on this week and I've always fancied a bet on those nutcase car drivers. Anyway, it's Lester Piggott in the next and, guess what, the skinny little fucker's not even favourite!'

Killing to hit the road, I didn't think he had the bottle. Off the cuff was usually me, but noting the seriousness in his voice I sat up. I hated horse racing, but if it could take me to Marseilles and the Monaco Grand Prix, then maybe it wasn't such a nags 'n' moneybags sport after all. Wanting the same commitment, Eddie asked for whatever change sat in our pockets. Holding back a pound for bus fares home, in case Lester had an off day, we raised almost twenty-nine pounds and watched as Eddie wrote out the race time, the name of horse and the amount that, in my mind, we were about to squander. Under starter's orders I asked Joey O' if the horse had a chance. Replying that with Lester you always had a chance, I took his words discerningly.

Soon as the race gun sounded, Piggott hit the front and, that's where he stayed right to the finishing line. At 7–1 our own race to the Station was up and out of the blocks, as the lady behind the counter paid the readies. Bouncing outside, Eddie asked if we wanted a quick scoff. Answering for the two of us, I said, 'No, fuck all that, let's hit the road!'

With nothing except a tightly wound bundle of notes (two hundred pound) and three well-chewed biros, we jumped the first London train to Victoria, had a free nosebag in west London, where we left the restaurant faster than Lester's horse, hopped aboard the night train to Dover, then Calais, bunking the boat from the white cliffs to the welcoming northern French port, and caught the overnight express to Marseilles, changing once in Paris. Reaching our destination, we were bedraggled yet, as happy as Eddie in Monaco, Joey O' in the Caribbean, and me, in . . . well, Marseilles.

First impressions: it looked rough as Ken Dodd's teeth on a no-toothbrush diet of Blackpool rock – even when it was dark. Booking into the shabbiest B&B, we jumped a taxi, telling the puzzled driver to take us to the nightlife. The first boozer we drank at we met Patrick Le Duveneh. Finding he spoke good English, we regaled him with our betting-office tale of Lester Piggott and the Grand Prix, and how and why we'd reached his Marseilles. Warning us it was a crazy place full of crazy characters, he added we were crazy so deserved to be there.

Next day Patrick sailed his small boat around the rugged hills and beaches of coastal southern France. Knowing a berthing friend, once our boat was tied-up among the many poseurs' yachts docked at Monaco marina, we clambered the steep urban hills of the small city full of Machiavellian moneymen in search of a decent speck to view the show. Patrick told Eddie his permanently being sick over the side simply wasn't worth the hassle: racing cars were cars that went by fast.

Thinking we'd fight for space on a hill full of anorak car

mechanics to watch snazzy motors whizz past, we ended up on an apartment balcony of one of Patrick's female acquaintances, Gypsy Francine. Here the cars did boringly fly by, and me and Joey O' got drunk trying to look up Francine's lacey skirt as she purposely stretched out her bronzed sprinter's legs. The gold chain that lay upon her lovely brown melons looked like she was keeping it warm for the Lord Mayor of Monaco, till later she left it in the bathroom and we sussed it was a home-made set of curtain rings with an imitation gold medal holding a picture of Elvis in the middle.

We could've slept with the alley cats and well-fed Monaco rats and still thought we'd beamed down to the land of exotica. The fact we had some francs, a decent flock for the night, and were in the company of two real locals made it feel like we were Romany wanderers visiting the seaside on one leg of a lifetime journey. Though we were three young Liverpudlians, I knew moving about in an alien environment with what were to me, totally foreign people using strange mannerisms and language, made me happy as a well-fed Aborigine in the Australian bush. Coming from a city by the sea made any place with an ocean backdrop seem all the more alluring. Feeling like Hunter S. Thompson in *Fear and Loathing in Las Vegas*, set free and on the road to somewhere yet nowhere, confronting strange moments and characters on an hourly basis, meant not only mind-broadening education was taking place, but also an addiction to hitting the road was being fostered that I still turkey for to this day.

Returning to Marseilles next morning, Patrick showed us his treasured city. Listening intently, he told of Marseilles legend and fable, mainly originating from the boulevards and dock fronts. So many in fact that, I almost got collared and cuffed while bunking the train that ran the full length of France back to Calais, next day. My head, still chokka-block-full of travelling stories, almost stopped me travelling some more, as I failed to concentrate on the bunk-in-hand. Staring dreamily out the window, comparing my home town, Liverpool, to Patrick's Marseilles, the French guard, opening the carriage door, asked for my *billet* (ticket) as I pretended to be sick by running past him to the stench-riddled toilet clutching my guts. Tailing me, he waited outside for fifteen minutes, till the train stopped at some lone-scarecrow Gallic town. Hearing him step from the rattler, shouting instructions to platform workers, I seized the chance to break out of my bog cell, legging it to the engine part of the train. For five or six hours, with the train rattling through central France, we played rail-track cat and mouse. Eventually chugging into Calais, I sped from the station with Inspector Clouseau bang on my case. Losing him in passenger traffic, I also lost my mates, not seeing them till ensconced back in Liverpool the following evening.

It didn't matter. If anything, it was easier bunking long distance alone. And, listening to the engine mechanisms of the boat and train without the constant idle banter that young lads are prone to, allowed me time to devise a plan for my next jaunt and destination. Coming from Liverpool, it had to be football linked. Born and reared in a dockside city full of Footy Fanatics, it became my one-way ticket, my passport, my justification to hit the road. Having an Alan Whicker-sized hankering for voyage, they were football expeditions that always turned the ignition at Stony-Broke Street. Being a fanatic who required road trips as much as football, I defied the Jaffa Cake crumbs that lined my pockets to stop me from venturing out to see the world – especially when there was a scarlet-red jersey in town.

Truth be known, I must've bunked my way around the world, then tried the other route just in case I missed a stadium or two. Nothing to do with bragging or bravado, but the old Scouse cockiness definitely came in handy when boarding a plane to Germany with no passport or tickets at hand. Thinking of Bill Shankly and how he said he loved the Liverpool swagger made me think, like the Queen of Motown, that, ain't no mountain high enough that you can't climb, no country too far to reach and, in my own individual way, no stadium un-bunkable. Even when I had brass in pocket those pathetic allocations handed out by nepotistic, suit-wearing officialdom meant a ticket was always gold dust anyway. I had to take the pain of Cup final rejection away somehow. Having a jibbing-in skill honed over the most successful football seasons any team or its supporters has ever seen, meant that that skill, habit, or whatever you want to call it, was always going to come in handy for a fervent footy kid like me. No, not born of bravado, born of a need of drug-addict proportion to see how the other half lived, twinned with just as strong an addiction to be in attendance if a tiny white Liverbird was taking stage. In other words: a creature of my environment, born of necessity. If Shankly had said that, 'Tommy Smith hadn't been born, he'd been quarried', then his words, the Mersey, the music, the city streets and the enormous wealth of Liverpool characters I'd grown up with had helped quarry me. And, I wouldn't change a single thing about any of it.

Though the other writers here may never have shared my perpetual bunking habit, I know they all love to travel – how else could you follow Liverpool FC? – and are every bit as proud of their city as I am. Who knows? Maybe because the city was built by migrants from all over the planet, remains the reason why so many Scousers get ants in their pants and feel a need to see the world. Anyway, ask Dave Kirby, ask Jegsy Dodd, ask Peter Hooton or Kevin Sampson, or the younger John Maguire and Tony Barrett what they would change about their privileged Red upbringing. I'm sure they'd answer in unison: 'Nothing!'

Breathing in the aura of the boulevards and scented harbour *la rues* of old Marseilles once more, I thought of Patrick and Francine, I thought of the glory of Rome '77, and gay Paree '81, of heady nights in Munich and Dusseldorf, of drunken nights in Blankenburg and Antwerp, of opportunist nights in Zurich and Prague, of wonderous nights in Barcelona, Bilbao and Lisbon, of truly brilliant . . . forget it! I followed and follow the Liverbird; you know the dance. I'd have to write the 3000-page A–Z of a true football loon so, that's a whole lot of dancing. See, I'm on my way to Athens and to sit down and decipher some of those streets that have been pickled by sing-songs, Stella and glory, I'd only end up mixing streets in Vienna, Madrid and Moscow with lanes in Budapest, Basle and Belgrade. To untangle thousands of miles of rail track, paved walkways and salty sea would take years of solitude and contemplation and I'm still too busy travelling.

It was a few years ago, in Marseilles, while looking for Patrick's café bar near the sea front that I first thought of how I'd love to read about our European Cup escapades and all the things that get thrown into the mix to make it a trip of legend – a trip of dreams. I thought I'd like to stick to two or three clear-cut years: some abiding memories and football folklore. Then I thought I'd be hogging the limelight and how it might become repetitive hearing me fare-dodging and turnstile and players-entrance-swerving my way to seven European Cup Finals. Then I thought of how refreshing it would be for other Reds, including me, to hear other supporters' gory-glory stories. So, clocking the class scribblers on offer, that's why we're here.

The book title came about when I remembered one of my favourite old Liverpool banners and searched in vain for its maker and owner. After giving up on finding him, or her, a lad came up to me at Manchester City's new stadium and introduced himself as John McDonald, telling me he was the owner of the banner and about its illustrious history. John hailed from the Waterloo area of Liverpool and was a face I instantly recognized as a long-gone Red fanatic like myself. He went on to tell me that his brilliantly talented mother, Margaret, had ingeniously come up with the slogan, then the needle and thread, before the banner started its journey to the Cup finals of our dreams. Back in '77, John and his mates, John Melia and Peter Davies, all wanted something a little distinctive to carry to the final (Scousers eh, always wanting to be different!). John mentioned this to his mum, and the rest, as they say, is history. For Mrs Mac (1924–97) her legacy lives on through the title of this book and through John's daughter and her grand-daughter, Hannah, who now travels everywhere with the Reds as she has since being a Mersey munchkin. Written by the fans for the fans, the banner was carried from the loft by those same supporters, washed and ironed, and will soon be making a bid for a space in Liverpool Football Club's museum. Noted for their literary wit, Liverpudlians will no doubt acknowledge Margaret and her saying as a truly poetic one of our own.

Well . . . with the goose pimples in evidence I'm rattling now, so, with the rattler being a favoured mode of transport, it seems good a place as any to step aboard for Rome '77: a steaming, sweating, overcrowded football train from hell – get me – from hell, not to hell. As the passengers like Dave Kirby will testify, this train took you on a Swiss Alp'd, water-dry, ghost ride to the thirst-quenching glory that was Rome. But, how were they to know it had been brought back from Hell's scrapyard to make one last grimy pilgrimage to the holy Roman city. Who knows . . . maybe a few on-board demons might be exorcised for good; maybe a few wheels might remain intact for the full 3000-mile journey; and maybe, just maybe, if it gets there in one piece, Emlyn Hughes, Liverpool's captain, might take that big-eared silver beauty down to the supporters to sip from, because from what Dave's told me, it was the only cup in Rome big enough to quench the thirst of each individual who stepped aboard at Lime Street's platform 9. If that train now sits in some Rusty Rattler graveyard, it would no doubt tell a tale or two. Listen, I'm parched just talking about it. Win, lose or draw, I'm off to Athens for a bit of who's who with the Ouzo. See you if it gets there!

Nicky Allt, May 2007

Rome, 1977

DAVE KIRBY

European Cup Final, 25th May 1977
Stadio Olimpico, Rome
Attendance: 60,000

Liverpool FC   3–1   **Borussia Moenchengladbach**
McDermott (28')   Simonson (52')
Smith (64')
Neal (82', pen.)

Substitutes: David Fairclough, Peter McDonnell,
David Johnson, Alan Waddle, Alec Lindsay

Manager: Bob Paisley

Borussia Moenchengladbach: Wolfgang Kneib (1), Berti Vogts
(2, captain), Hans Klinkhammer (3), Hans-Jürgen Wittkamp (4), Winfried
Schäfer (5), Horst Wohlers (6), Herbert Wimmer (7), Uli Stielike (8),
Rainer Bonhof (9), Jupp Heynckes (10), Allan Simonsen (11)

Substitutes used: Wilfried Hannes, Christian Kulik

Manager: Udo Lattek

Spring 2007

Friday morning, 25th May, 2007 wasn't great. I'd jetted back from Athens the night before so was still feeling a bit fuzzy and pissed off . . . though not about the result. I woke up despising the suits that run football after just being treated like the shit on a UEFA official's shoe.

I tried to blank things out – took the kids to school, stuck the kettle on, warmed up me laptop ready for a day's graft – but me head just wasn't right. Then a text message came through from me brother: 'Five out of seven isn't bad, kid. Happy Rome anniversary, 30 years today.' From that moment me morning was wiped out. I sat on the couch supping me tea trying to remember what it was like to be eighteen and wondering where the fuck thirty years had gone. Half an hour later me laptop was switched off and I was climbing up a loft ladder heading for me footy box.

You know the type of box I'm on about: ticket stubs, scarves, stuff like that. I sat under the loft light and looked inside it. After a few minutes I was gone, totally gone . . . you know the score.

I rummaged past all sorts – St Etienne scarf, Brugge flag, a Real Madrid hat – then I saw it.

It was in a clear plastic wallet clipped to the inside page of Liverpool's first European Cup final programme; two cockerels fighting . . . beside them the words:

Coppa finale Dei Campioni. Curva Nord.

Above them:

Roma, 25 Maggio, 1977. Stadio Olimpico.

To this day it remains the best match ticket I've ever seen.

This is just one of the 26,000 stories.

Money Troubles and Trebles

It was mid-March when a mate of mine, Big Dave Coogan, got me a start as a pump attendant in a garage on the East Lancs Road. It was an absolute shithole. The kiosk where we worked from was like a corporate box at Goodison – just ten foot x four foot with caged windows and no heaters. The outside bog was seriously bum-damaged, and the petrol pumps were like rusty daleks. But it was better than traipsing through mud and shite on freezing-cold building sites. All me mates went the match. None of us had season tickets; it was all queues and pay at the turnstiles back then. Going to work was a tortuous head-wrecking daily ritual, but it was the only way to finance my ale, clobber and, more importantly, my footy . . . you know the score.

Liverpool had reached the last eight of the FA Cup, but everyone's thoughts were focused on another quarter-final . . . the big one. French champions St Etienne were coming to town in the European Cup. The Reds were also looking good in the league, so people were starting to whisper about a unique Treble – the first in British history. One of the shift workers at the garage was a Bluenose. There was always banter. One day he said to me and Big Dave, 'If you get to Rome, youse'll blend in nice, cos Italy's full of shithouses.'

Dave came back with, 'The last time you crossed the Channel with Everton, the ship had fuckin' cannons on it.'

The St Etienne match was cash on the gate as usual. We got there about five o'clock and couldn't believe the crowds. The back of our queue for flagpole corner was up by the Annie Road. Mounted bizzies edged us along Kemlyn Road inches at a time. Their horses kept dumping all over the place, just missing fellas' shoes. Loads of shouts were going off. 'Stick a nosebag on its fuckin' arse' was one I remember, though by the time we reached the flagpole it was us who were shitting ourselves, listening to turnstile bells going off by the minute (full to capacity).

About seven o'clock I was wedged half in and out of a turnstile when the school-bell sound went off. There was loads of pushing, shouting and swearing. I held me arm out to a bizzie inside and let out a harrowing Oscar-winning scream: 'Ahhh, me legs.' He panicked and pulled me through, then the door slammed behind me. (I still say a prayer of thanks to this day.) Every button on me Wrangler shirt had popped, and I'd lost a shoe, but I was in. An arl fella gave me a woollen scarf to tie round me foot. After a while I didn't notice me shoe was missing. To be honest, knowing what I know now I'd have stood barefoot on broken glass in there because like everyone else I was about to sail, float, then drown in the greatest atmosphere on the greatest ever night at Anfield.

When Fairclough slotted the third, I bounced from near the back of the Kop to the Kemlyn Road corner flag. My clobber was stuck to me; I was soaked to the skin and drunk on adrenalin. There were 55,000 inside Anfield that night, mainly raucous, working-class Scousers, and apart from the frog firm in the corner of the Annie Road every single person in the ground was bouncing up and down singing 'We shall not be moved'. I've never seen anything like it before or since. I levitated out of the Kop after that game with me foot-scarf trailing behind me. There was still a semi-final to play, but deep down everyone who experienced the phenomenon that night knew that nothing could stop us from getting to Rome. As some fella said on the bus going home, 'I can smell the fuckin' pasta.'

I was still floating three days later when bang . . . a two-till-ten shift on FA Cup quarter-final day shot me out the sky. It was a bad comedown. My Kop that day was a minty kiosk with a burst chair and an oily floor, the only atmosphere being the noisy traffic on the East Lancs. My lifeline was a poxy little battery radio in the kiosk. I'm not kidding: finding Radio City on it was like trying to crack a fuckin' safe. I listened to the Boro game with it held to me ear. Somewhere between the hissing and crackling I heard us win 2–0. That meant two semis. The Treble really was looking on.

The entire month of April was a permanent rush, and I don't mean drug-induced. In fact there were no heavy drugs around at that time, just pot, and even that was seen as a sweaty hippy thing to do . . . 'love and peace' and all that shite. At home in the league we beat Leeds, Man City, Arsenal and Ipswich and drew away at Stoke to virtually seal the First Division title. In the FA Cup we beat the Bluenoses after two semis at Maine Road, and in the European Cup we steamrollered FC Zurich twice to nail our place at the Olympic Stadium in Rome. You hardly had time to get the ale out your system before the next colossal game. I must've gone through about twenty packs of Rennies that month. Treble talk was rampant. What started off as a hopeful Kop whisper had steadily built into a Red roar that engulfed the entire city. Every street corner, every shop, bus stop, alehouse, radio chit-chat, the patter was all about the ultimate three-in-the-bed.

Town's Travel was blitzed after the second Zurich game. By noon next day 2000 fans had booked package flights to Rome costing between ninety-three and a hundred and thirty-three quid (including match ticket). It was out of my price league. I told me ma and da I was going, but I didn't have a clue how I was gonna get there.

Gordon Lee, the Everton manager, was at the Zurich home match. Radio City spoke of the 'ecstasy and agony at Anfield'. The ecstasy was obviously ours, while the agony was for Lee, whose wallet was dipped outside the main entrance. 'A consid-erable amount' was mentioned. It was tough luck on old Skeletor. He reckoned that the person who did it would have no luck in the future: 'He will end up paying for behaviour like this,' he said. But I don't know about that, because I wouldn't mind betting that the Scouse Fagin who zapped him was in Town's Travel next day booking a flight to Rome.

The two semis against Everton were in everyone's price range: one pound fifty for a ground ticket and one pound fifty on the special. I'll never forget the first game for a couple of reasons – not the exquisite chip from Terry Mac or the iffy Clive Thomas decision; I'm talking about a Mario Lanza song from the film *Seven Hills of Rome* and an incident that epitomises Scousers at the time.

For someone like me who was into stuff like Floyd and Deaf School, the thought of listening to some operatic tit singing 'Arrivederci, Roma' was ridiculous. But boy was that about to change. I'd heard rumblings of the song at Anfield when we beat Zurich, though the words were vague. Then, three days later at Maine Road, the song echoed with clarity across the Kippax like a Vatican choir. To this day the song never fails to take me back to that spring:

> We're on our way to Roma
> On the 25th of May
> All the Kopites will be singing
> Vatican bells they will be ringing
> Liverpool FC we'll be singing
> When we win the European Cup.

Something else happened that day. We were on one of the seventeen specials into Manchester Victoria; Reds and Blues together. There was usually murder outside that station – remember these were the days when trouble was a big part of footy culture – but we weren't arsed that day, with fifty-odd thousand Scousers heading in. United were playing Leeds at Sheffield in the other semi, so quite a few Mancs were mooching around. We heard chants of 'United', then they charged at the people in front, forcing them back. It was literally only a minute till the Red and Blue masses spilled out the station and chased them down the street. As far as trouble goes it was an absolutely nothing incident, but it was the catalyst to what happened next and the thing that's stayed with me. As we set off in a police escort, the entire special (about 500 people) tied their scarves together and held them aloft. The confused expression on bizzies' faces sticks in the mind. Shoppers looked just as stumped. Buses and traffic slowed . . . all staring at the ranks of entwined red and blue and white marching down Deansgate in the pissing-down rain, singing:

> Merseyside, la la la
> Merseyside, la la la.

It was a natural and genuine show of Scouse solidarity – a moment of pride that means more to me now than it did then because it captures the Liverpool that I grew up in; a time before 'banter' was replaced by the word 'bitter'.

Sunday afternoon, 1st May: I can see meself now . . . kicking an oily ball at the diesel pump in a deserted garage, waiting to change shifts with Lol (the Bluenose). My head was up me arse around that time. British Rail had announced that they were putting on trains to Rome with match ticket included and were taking name and address reservations with payment at a later date. Like most I took a chance and booked not knowing how I'd get the wedge together. I was seriously skint, and back then skint meant skint. If you wanted to travel, you had to get off your arse and do a bit of independent, creative head-working, usually without tank or ticket.

We were due to face the Mancs at Wembley, but all I could think about was Rome. Getting around Britain wasn't an issue. If you couldn't afford a train or coach, you'd just thumb it. Loads of footy journeys began with me left thumb at the East Lancs/Kirkby junction, including a trip to Stoke that spring with me mate Gary (Smigger) hiding in the boot of a coach that we opened and dived into at Kirkby traffic lights, taking turns to hold the boot closed. But Rome was different. Europe at that time for me was uncharted territory. I'd never set foot outside the country. Like most Scousers, the only holidays I knew were in caravan parks in North Wales, the highlight of the week being a day out to the Everton stronghold of Rhyl.

Every time the ball hit the diesel pump, it made a hollow clanging sound. Lol walked across the forecourt to take over shifts. First thing out of his mouth was, 'Are y' goin' to Rome?'

I hoofed the ball at the diesel pump . . . clang! 'Yeah, if I get the money,' I said.

Then he goes, 'It's fifty-nine quid on the train, isn't it?'

I stopped, put one foot on the ball, then booted it again . . . clang!

I was chocka. Fifty-nine quid doesn't sound much now, but for me then it was nearly a month's wedge. April's wage cheque was owed out, courtesy of five massive league games and the European and FA Cup semis. The endless sequence of big matches had forced me into dipping the odd fiver out the till. I asked the area manager if I could have May's pay cheque in advance, but he wasn't having it. I was tempted to do a 'Tom, Tom, the piper's son' with the till (stick it under me arm and run like fuck), but everything would've went pear-shaped – bizzies and all that lark . . . you know the score.

I dipped enough out the till to get the special to QPR (six pound fifty) and Coventry (four quid). We drew both games, paving the way to win the title at home on the Saturday to West Ham. The league was boxed off. One down, two to go. I celebrated big time that weekend but also had a serious sweat on. Rome was just eleven days away, and all's I had saved was seventeen quid. Time was running out.

On Wednesday 18th May I was on the verge of phoning the Samaritans. The reserved train and match tickets for Rome were going on sale at Lime Street next day at an increased price of seventy quid per ticket. The extra eleven quid came about because the French were having a national strike. It meant a detour through Belgium, Germany and Switzerland and an extra twelve hours on the journey, but to be honest everyone was so paranoid about getting to Rome that no one was arsed about the extra mileage. They could've taken us through Spain, Morocco, Algeria, Tunisia and came in through fuckin' Sicily for all we cared . . . just as long as we got there.

By that afternoon the temptation to rob the till was at fever pitch – it looked like the only option. Every time I opened it, I almost grew horns, a pointy tail and started laughing like Vincent Price. The irritation and frustration of handling bank notes when you're desperate for wedge is mental torture. A few more hours and I'm convinced that I would've swooped and took off like an Olympic sprinter. But then something happened.

Through frustration I'd been volleying the ball at the diesel pump. The front panel fell off a few times and the pump made a weird gurgling noise . . . like a washing machine. I thought nothing of it until a transit van rolled up. The driver asked for a fiver's worth, and we stood there watching the digits spin round. It got to about three quid, then for some unknown, fateful, beautiful, life-defining reason, the digits jammed. I stopped and stared at the seized numerals. Believe me I may as well have been looking at a 7777 jackpot on a fruit machine. I pressed the pump trigger again and nearly burst into tears of joy. The diesel was gushing out but not registering.

Over the next two hours I made nearly two weeks' wages but was still short of me Rome money. I was racking me brains trying to think of anyone with a diesel van or wagon . . . then it hit me: Kirkby Cabs! The phone call was terrible. For some reason me voice went dead shady and deep . . . like a Red Indian chief: 'All right. Half-price diesel . . . East Lancs Garage . . . now.'

Minutes later a black hackney turned up, and I filled it for a fiver. The driver couldn't believe it and radioed the office. Nothing could've prepared me for what was about to happen. It started off slow – two or three cabs, then a few more, till there were about fifteen in the queue. I was just guessing how much to charge – mostly between five and seven quid. As one cab left, another three would turn up. I started panicking, filling tanks while looking over me shoulder at the queue, which was backing up onto the East Lancs. Most had containers with them. Diesel was splashing all over the bastard place, blowing back out the tanks and containers all over me. After half an hour it went mental. A convoy of black cabs stretched from the diesel pump out the garage, along the Lancs, past the lights and down Moorgate road into Kirkby. It looked like the annual taxi charity day out to Southport. I was like a headless chicken, running from cab to cab filling tanks and containers quicker than Edward fuckin' Scissorhands. I was shitting meself in case the bizzies got onto it or the area manager turned up; no blag in the world could've got me out of that one.

An hour later I slid into the kiosk chair. My right hand was stinging and the rest of me was minging – the smell was pure diesel. If I'd lit a ciggy, I think they'd have heard the explosion in Rome. I locked the garage up early and got a cab to take me home. My pockets were bulging with cash. I emptied it onto me bed, then lashed me fuming jeans out the window.

Straightening and counting those scrunched up, diesel-stinking notes is one of the most satisfying things I've ever done. The final count was three hundred and twenty-eight quid. I walked into the kitchen in just me boxer shorts and threw fifty green one-pound notes up in the air. 'You can have that, Ma,' I said. She looked at me like I was soft. It was a great feeling, getting me Rome trip sorted and boxing me ma off. It made me realise what a load of bollocks that old saying is: 'Money's not everything'. I know it can't buy health, but take it from me, it's just a blag spread round by rich bastards . . . you know the score.

Next day Lime Street was chocka with Roman Reds. I was used to travelling away so knew what a footy-special train ticket looked like. But I honestly thought British Rail would make an effort for the big journey abroad. They didn't; just the usual little cheapo pink card, only this time enriched with the magic words 'Rome and back'. We got our photos done in the booth at the station, then got our six-month passports at the post office . . . job done; I was Rome bound.

It was like little Italy in the alehouse that night. Four of us were making the trip. One was on the taxis, one on the dole, our kid was hitting the sick and I was taking a week's leave without pay – an easy decision after you've just sexually assaulted a diesel pump. Someone suggested we all get a Liverpool FC tattoo done for the occasion. I was well up for it and arranged to meet them next day at Sailor Jack's hut under the bridge in Tuebrook. There was so much Italian talk going on that the FA Cup final was almost forgotten about. When one of the lads mentioned it, the conversation instantly shifted from European-holiday mode to a more domestic, moody feel – the type that was the norm then, especially when playing the Mancs, like how many Scousers were going, potential trouble, stuff like that. Twelve of us were heading down in a transit van on the Friday night; just two with tickets, and I wasn't one of them.

I was buzzing when I finished me shift that Friday. It was sunny; I had tank; I was getting a Liverpool tattoo done; I was going to Wembley that night; and at home under me mattress I had a train and match ticket for Rome: life couldn't get sweeter. Only one of the lads turned up at Sailor Jack's for a tattoo. It cost us twelve quid each to get branded with the old Liverpool badge. It looked superb – full of colour. But it didn't half hurt.

United in Grief

It was well after midnight when thirteen of us left St Lawrence's club in Kirkby in a Brookhire transit van filled with old cushions that we used as seats. The extra passenger just tagged along after singing Liverpool songs in the club with us. By the time he sobered up, we were at Keele service station. He kept saying 'I shouldn't be here'. There were loads of United around, so we just swooped on a load of sarnies, then out.

In the car park a dozen or so Mancs had sussed the 'Merseyside Truck Rental' logo on the side of our van and started singing 'We hate the Scousers'. Luckily we had a fearless leader with us. Gerry was a seriously hard lad. It was a boost and a great relief when you knew he was travelling away. If trouble came, he'd be first in and last away. He walked towards them: 'Ee-arr, we're the fuckin' Scousers yer hate . . . do something about it,' he shouted. We spread out behind. It did the trick. They started filtering towards the cafe. Lads like Gerry were priceless in those violent '70s. He saved our arses on numerous occasions. The lad who tagged along started again: 'I shouldn't be here.'

I had a feeling that incident was just a dress rehearsal for what was coming. I was right. We parked half a mile from Wembley at about half six in the morning. Our van logo attracted a gang of about twenty Mancs who'd seen us drive past. They waited at the top of the street where we parked, then all walked towards us. Most of our lads probably felt like I did – a kind of nervous churning, the type you get when you know a situation's on top. But Gerry was made different. He told us to spread out and keep moving towards them, then he jogged ahead, rolling his sleeves up and giving the Mancs the come on, shouting to them, 'Come on, keep fuckin' walking.' It spooked the Mancs. Most of them stopped. They could obviously see he was game. Our inevitable roar and charge scattered them . . . saved by Gerry again.

Half an hour later we met Kirkby, Gilly and about thirty of his mates in the car park outside Wembley. We thought things were mellowing when a coach full of decent Mancs asked us if we fancied a game of footy. Next thing there's a big match going on. Everything was sound until a mob of around 200 other Man U came from underneath the Wembley Way flyover.

Give the Mancs who were playing footy their due. They tried to stop them, but you could see that these other, snarling septics weren't having any of it. Cue Gerry: 'Come on, we'll fuck these,' he said. The odds were ridiculous, but he led a charge that backed them off . . . though only for a couple of minutes. They came back big time. We all ran towards Wembley, apart from Big Dave, who ran the opposite way. I don't know why they all went after him. They cut him off and were breathing down his neck, closing in from both sides. He had absolutely nowhere to go, apart from towards a twelve-foot-high corrugated fence. As long as I live, I'll never know how he scaled it. He escaped with just a cut head. The mob turned towards us. The straggler was next to me. 'I shouldn't be here,' he said again.

The Mancs piled up the Wembley steps, bombarding us with all sorts. We headed for a high wooden fence that led to a railway embankment. Bricks bounced off it, making a noise like a drum solo. Gerry stayed till the last again, throwing stuff back at them. I was on top of the fence when I saw something out the corner of me eye and instinctively put me hand up for protection – a broken bottle hit me palm. The pain was instant; the blood followed. My hand was in a bad way, but I was lucky – I'd nearly had me face and me Rome dream shattered.

It was a crazy start to the day. Eight o'clock in the morning and I was heading back down Wembley Way in an ambulance with our kid and two of the lads. I beat Big Dave's stitch count by four and still bear the scar to this day. In the space of eighteen hours I'd been branded for life twice: once with a tattoo and the other with a bottle. In other words once by a needle prick and the other by a Manc prick.

We stocked up with cans, then got the bus back to Wembley. Take it from me, tetanus injections and lager definitely don't mix. We stood at the bottom of Wembley Way waiting for the Scouse cavalry to emerge from Wembley Park off the twenty-five specials that left Lime Street that day. Four cans each later we were still waiting, watching wave after wave of Mancs streaming out the station. Scousers were outnumbered by about two to one. At times it felt like four to one. We were taking 26,000 to Rome the following Wednesday – the biggest mass departure across the Channel since D-Day – so understandably a lot of Reds chose to sack the mediocre Mancs for the mighty Munchen.

At every block entrance around Wembley there were tall, revolving turnstiles that the bizzies used as ejector gates, so bunking in was always worth a go. If you got collared, all they did was lash you out again. Bunking has always been rife at Cup finals – a situation brought about by leeches and hangers-on getting tickets before passionate, zealous fans. Some Scousers had it down to a fine art. I'm not talking about just booting gates down; I mean using your head to breach the castle walls. Two of Gilly's mates climbed over the gates at six o'clock that morning and hid in a ladies' bog for nearly seven hours. A lad I know from Wavertree walked through the main entrance with the brass band and blagged it (in a Scottish accent) that he was a band reservist. The same fella couldn't play the fuckin' spoons.

To front that kind of situation, you had to have confidence and composure. But they're two qualities that don't surface when Heineken and tetanus are speeding through your veins faster than a footy special. I was absolutely polluted. Four times I got lashed out. They have to go down as my worst-ever bunking-in attempts.

There was no keeping a low one or being cagey. I may as well have had a sandwich board on saying 'Get out me fuckin' way!' The final desperate effort was a drunken, mazy run, then a big belly-flop over the turnstile. All's I remember is laying face-down on the floor with me foot trapped in the stile and all sorts of laughter going on around me. I think the bizzies were even laughing as they dragged me away. My head was spinning faster than the ejector gate, which I was thrown back through with a full-on warning that if I got collared again I'd be nicked. Next thing I'm on a little wall opposite our end, squinting in the sun and thinking that I'd have half an hour's kip then try again. I curled up by the wall . . . bang . . . gone!

I'm sure you've all been there: waking up in a strange place, thinking, 'Where the fuck am I?' I focused on the deserted Wembley steps that were now in the shade with litter everywhere. All the gates were open, so I ran up and into the ground. It's still vivid: emerald-green pitch and an empty stadium dotted with yellow jackets brushing the terraces. I shouted to a sweeper near me, 'What score was it, mate?' I could tell by the blank look on his kite that he was a beaut: mouth open, wet bottom lip . . . you know the score, a bit like a Wigan fan. He shrugged his shoulders (don't know). At least he could tell the time. It was ten past six.

I started jogging back, paranoid about the result and missing me lift. When I got to the car park, the jog slowed to a concerned trot, then a sickly stroll. Coaches were still pulling away, mostly full of jubilant Mancs. It cut me in half. A bizzie confirmed the score. I felt me stomach drop, then that sickly feeling. The Treble dream was over, I'd missed my lift home and me bandaged hand was throbbing more than me head. I managed to thumb a lift on the North Circular road – off a Manc! He turned out to be a dead sound fella. We stopped for a pint and a nosebag in Walsall, then he went miles out of his way down the East Lancs and dropped me at the lights at Kirkby. There's Mancs and there's Mancs . . . you know the score. I got in about midnight and told me ma that I'd got me hand caught in the van door.

Next morning she woke me up, concerned that our kid still wasn't back. The others had stopped for a pint in London and ended up in a club full of Man U cockney Reds. There were a few arrests for drunk and disorderly. One of them was the driver, so the lads had to kip in the transit van overnight.

The sun was blazing again that Sunday. The only sound in the house was Rod Stewart playing low on the kitchen radio. It felt like he was taking the piss, singing about how he didn't wanna talk about it, how somebody had broken his heart. The song was number one at the time. Me da switched it off. 'Jammy bastards,' was all he said. It was like a wake. Me ma said that me younger brother had locked himself in the bathroom for hours after the match and his mate had gone home in tears. It made me glad that I'd slept through it.

The Brookhire van finally turned up, and the lads emerged like a gang of spud pickers. Big Dave had done the same as me and slept through the match in the back of the van. Of the others just two had managed to bunk in. It had been a bad trip, especially for the poor bastard who'd tagged along. He'd ended up ripping his jeans on the fence, losing his watch, getting locked out the ground and being charged with drunk and disorderly. 'I shouldn't be here, your honour,' was one shout.

By mid-afternoon the gloom was beginning to lift. If the FA Cup final had been the usual end-of-season showcase, then the stench of defeat would have clung for weeks. But the phone went a couple of times . . . all Rome talk. 'What time are yer going?' 'Have yer changed your money?'

Later on I lifted me mattress and looked at me Rome gear. It was all there: sterling, lire, passport and that superb ticket. Just eyeballing it was enough to exorcise the red devils from the day before. They'd managed to steal the Cup with a lucky smash-and-grab raid, but opportunist thieves can never steal pride, passion or pedigree. By Sunday night nobody in Liverpool gave a fuck about the FA Cup. Small platoons of Scousers were already on their way to Italy. The train legions, including me, were due to follow on the Monday. That Sunday night I was like a kid on

Christmas Eve, too excited to sleep, not realising at the time that Santa was coming three days later – dressed in red with a gift that I'd treasure for life.

The Leaving of Liverpool

If I was going on a five-day trip abroad next week, I'd pack a small case or a hefty sports bag with five pairs of undies and socks, a few changes of clobber, toothbrush, paste, shampoo, razor, foam, a bit of aftershave and some books to read . . . you know the score. At around half three on Monday 23rd May, me and our kid left me ma's carrying two little plastic Co-Op bags with six sarnies and an apple each . . . and that was it. Honest to fuck, not even a comb. And the only reason we took apples is because our kid said, 'They'll clean our teeth.'

When we met the others, they had similar bags. Peter, the lad on the dole, only had crisps and Coke. It was a mixture of foreign-trip inexperience and couldn't-give-a-shit attitude. Our kid summed it up: 'It'll do till we get to the boat.'

Standing at the bus stop outside the Park Brow pub in Kirkby was special. I really felt like somebody. We were all decked out in scarves and hats, and our kid and Peter had flags draped around them. Every car that passed blew their horn. On the bus we were treated like royalty. The driver didn't charge us, and people on the top deck offered us ciggies and talked about the mass exodus. One fella said that his brother-in-law raised his trip money by selling his Ford Capri then telling his bird that the car had been robbed. There were all sorts of stories like that. Peter sold his entire record collection – about forty LPs and sixty singles. Our kid's mate funded his trip by packing in his job as a sheet-metal worker so he could get his hands on the severance pay. The pawn shops got absolutely battered with hocked jewellery . . . in many cases unbeknown to the wives or girlfriends. Odd-job men were at an all-time high. Everywhere you looked, there were houses getting painted and gardens being mown.

I remember a Kopite who was always in Church Street playing

a classical acoustic version of 'You'll Never Walk Alone', with a bucket that said 'Busking for Rome'. The *Echo* ran a story about a lad from Speke who did a sponsored run dressed as a Roman gladiator, with all monies (after his fare) going to charity.

There were also more dodgy ways. Scrapyards put the price of copper down after hundreds of empty houses and flats around the city were stripped clean. A few Reds I knew from Huyton financed their trip by travelling round the north-west blowing water into fruit machines with a straw till the machines went haywire and paid out for any sequence. They also mastered the art of taping up ten-pence pieces with electricians' tape then using them as fifty-pence pieces in ciggy machines.

Two brothers who drank in the Kingfisher in Kirkby got their trip sorted in one weekend after going to Blackpool and snaffling sets of chrome wheel trims from parked coaches (sixty quid per set). They'd never stolen a thing before that and have never done since. A well-known Kopite from Netherley got his fare together by going round putting people's electricity metres on the fiddle for a pound a time. Then there were the famous Scottie Road shop hoisters who, in the spring of '77, were lifting more shirts than Freddie Mercury and Elton John put together. It was a case of getting to Rome by any means without harming anyone. Everyone seemed to rally round and help each other out. I gave a lot of my diesel money away. I didn't want it back; that's just the way it was. Don't get me wrong, there were a few no-marks and arseholes in the city, like everywhere else. But they were few and far between. There weren't so many people with 'I'm all right, Jack' or 'fuck-thy-neighbour'-type attitudes. These were the days before rag-heads, bag-heads, scag-heads and fuckin' Thatcher. Harmless scallywags, yeah; scumbags, no . . . you know the score.

When we got to town, it was bouncing. The streets and bars around the station were wall to wall. Some of the costumes were fantastic: ten-gallon hats, top hats, bowler hats, red jumpsuits, white boiler suits, rosettes as big as sunflowers. The excitement and buzz was like nothing I'd ever experienced. Fellas were getting off buses and out of taxis then punching the air through gritted teeth before shaking hands with anybody. Some even hugged like the Reds had just scored a goal. It was obvious that this was something special. All together, 5000 of us were making the journey on twelve specials. One left early afternoon; the rest of us were due out in the evening.

Flags were draped inside pub windows – mostly home-made. There wasn't enough room to roll a ciggy in the Crown, the Yankee bar and the Big House. Round in Casey Street a giant conga was snaking up and down singing 'Let's all go to Roma, let's all go to Roma, na na na na'.

The 'Arrivederci, Roma' song had lads stopping women in the street and dancing slowies with them – all the birds happily obliged. A bearded tramp wearing a red and white plastic bowler hat was dancing around singing 'Ee ay addio, we won the Cup'. I don't know if he'd had a premonition or if he was just blagging it, but it did the trick – loads poured ale in his glass and filled his hat with loose change.

One of me mates, Vinnie, was gonna try and bunk the train. He was meeting us in the Star and Garter boozer at the front of St John's precinct. The singing in there was deafening: 'Liverpool are magic, Liverpool are magic, na na na na'. It took us about fifteen minutes to get from the entrance stairs to the bar. Our plastic carrier bags were a nuisance. It was all 'Hold that while I go the bar', or 'Mind that for us while I go for a piss'. Ninety per cent of Reds had one.

Some lad had it sussed. He'd threaded and tied his carrier-bag handles through a belt-loop on the front of his jeans while he pretended to play the guitar solo in the Liverpool FC team song 'We Can Do It', which blasted from the jukebox. Soon everyone was walking round with plastic bags bouncing off the front of their kecks. Most sounds on the jukebox were drowned out by LFC songs, apart from one hilarious five minutes when everyone sang along and did the bump to Joe Tex's 'Ain't Gonna Bump No More With No Big Fat Woman'. There was definitely a few squashed sarnies after that one.

For someone who had to look inconspicuous to bunk a train, Vinnie was as loud as fuck. He turned up in a white Liverpool hat, white T-shirt and white jeans. Peter was right on it. 'Where's your paintbrush?' he said. The choice of outfit seemed even crazier when Vinnie said he was gonna buy a platform ticket then run across the lines and board a Rome special. All's he had with him was a bag of sarnies and a tenner – no passport, no match ticket and no Italian lire. We didn't believe him, but he was serious. 'I don't care. I'm having a go,' he said.

By the time we walked over to the Crown on Lime Street, we were all half-gassed. There were just as many people outside the boozer as in it, mostly drinking their own gear. Davey and Eddie Mac from Breck Road passed me a bottle of Strongbow cider. Like a beaut I necked most of it – big mistake! It was the start of one of those phases where a simple trip to the shithouse becomes a major expedition. The occasional flashbacks I get are of me in the Yankee bar rabbiting to a gang of fellas from Park Road. Fuck knows why I went there or how long I was gone, but when I got back to the Crown I couldn't see the lads. I looked inside: no sign. Star and Garter: no sign. It was no big deal. Getting split up from your mates was a massive and totally accepted part of footy culture then. If ten of you went the game, you'd be lucky to see eight of them till after the match at a prearranged meeting point – usually a pub. That's why I wasn't arsed when I couldn't find them, especially in the atmosphere that was around Lime Street. The word 'stranger' doesn't exist when you're travelling to your first European Cup final. I had 5000 mates that night. Every bastard was talking to any bastard . . . you know the score.

We all had an itinerary with designated train numbers and times, but loads were just getting on any. About half eight I walked up past the Punch and Judy cafe with three dead funny lads from Halewood. One of them had a Roman laurel on his head made from privets, and a T-shirt that said 'Julius Scouser'. There were some great T-shirts knocking about. A few I remember are 'Tommy Smith is Spartacus', 'The Pope is from Gerard Gardens' and 'Is Hadrian taking brickies on?'.

The singing inside the station had a Pied Piper effect. I followed it to the side of platform nine, where hundreds were queuing up. I bumped into Vinnie. He told me that our kid and the others thought I'd jumped on a train, so they'd done the same. 'Your Mick said if I see yer, to tell yer they'll see yer at Folkestone.'

Vinnie's platform-ticket plan had gone pear-shaped. Platform tickets were just tuppence each and were for waving goodbye only. He said there were about twenty-five Scousers trying the same thing. They were all smiling and waving to strangers on the London train as it pulled away. 'They must've thought we were all on a day out from the fuckin' loony bin,' he said. Bizzies and train guards were well onto it and moved in. There were still a few specials due to leave, but the odds of him bunking on one looked impossible. 'I'm gonna try the ladder,' he said, meaning coming in via a fixed metal fire-escape ladder that led into the station from Skelhorne Street – a known bunker's route that brought you out further down platform nine. His parting words were 'God loves a trier', then he passed me his sarnie bag. I watched him go, knowing deep down that he had no chance.

The next half-hour in the queue was heart-pumping stuff. I joined in the singing: 'Tell me ma, me ma, I don't want no tea, no tea, we're goin' to Italy, tell me ma, me ma'. Adrenalin diluted the ale inside me and replaced it with nervous butterflies. This was it. Five weeks of scrimping, saving, stealing, fiddling and dreaming was within touching distance, and the way I felt at that moment every single second of worry and struggle had been worth it. Passing through those gates onto platforms eight and nine was like being liberated.

I boarded the train and right away bumped into three Kirkby pissheads: Mick and Gilly Stewart and Ged Wainwright. They were all wearing white jeans, which were bang in fashion for the trip; hundreds had them on. Mick pulled a piece of coal out of his jeans pocket . . . the others did the same. I was snookered till they told me the score. Years ago, during the War, it was tradi-tion for loved ones to pass coal to soldiers before they set off for battle – 'Keep the home fires burning for a safe return' – so Mick's nan had given them a piece each.

It sort of captured the feeling and spirit of the whole thing. It was as if we were all going on a war crusade to some foreign land and the people had come in their droves to see us off. The scenes as we pulled out of Lime Street still give me goosebumps. Bodies and flags waved from every window to the deafening sound of cheers and applause from women, kids and well-wishers in the station. I've never felt as proud or as much a part of something in my whole life. It was a touching and unique Scouse send-off.

Train and Boats and Pains

Anyone who ever travelled on a footy special in the 1970s will understand the meaning of the word 'rough' – and boy am I talking rough. They carried 400–500 people in conditions that nowadays wouldn't be fit for a robber's dog to travel in. The carriages were ramshackle – some with compartments, some with tables, all with the kind of seats that had your arse begging and pleading for a cushion. Most of the time they were laid up, festering in the sidings at Edge Hill station, skulking in the shadows, hiding from the scrap-man before being dragged out screaming every Saturday to transport footy fans around the country with all the grace and comfort you'd expect from being pulled over cobblestones for hundreds of miles in a rickshaw.

The one I boarded was the table type: four seats facing each other with a table in the middle, similar to today's trains. But let's get this right: similar only in design. I wandered through it in case our kid and the lads were on board. The buzz inside the carriages drowned out the eardrum-bursting racket of the moving train. It looked and sounded like the wine lodge on a Saturday night: people standing up, loads of laughter and loud talking. It was supposed to be a dry train, but everyone seemed to have a drink in their hand. We hadn't passed Edge Hill when some fella in his mid-50s handed me a can of McKeown's Export. 'Wet your whistle, son,' he said. I stayed with him and his mate while I drank the can. They were both Shankly fanatics who'd seen action at Anzio during the War. One had been shot and injured. 'Last time I was in Italy, the Germans battered us. It'll be the other way round on Wednesday,' he said.

They were great to listen to. Anyone their age on a footy train nowadays could only reminisce about battles at away games. But those old Shankly boys were the real deal. The likes of them made the trip possible. They were the reason why the train guards weren't wearing jackboots or the trains themselves weren't gonna be shelled or blitzed in Europe – although, saying that, I think by the time we got to Rome it looked like they had been.

In every carriage, plastic bags were stacked up on tables alongside jumpers, cardies, scarves and rolled up flags. More gear was stuffed underneath. It took ages to weave my way through. I was surprised how many women were on board, mainly older ones dressed in red fancy-dress costumes and hats, singing their heads off in that whining old pensioner's voice – the type that'd shatter a glass from fifty yards. The whole train was rammed. The only empty spaces were in the no-man's-land between carriages where the bogs and train doors were situated, and where the racket of the train was deafening. Those places were always freezing and were often referred to as 'mingebag alley' because of the minges you'd see there having a sly smoke to save them flashing their ciggies around. But this trip began like a Red Cross mission. By the time I got to the end of the train, I'd been given a can of ale, a bag of crisps and a packet of beechnut chewies. The exuberance was so full on that even tight-fisted bastards were acting like Mother Teresa.

Our kid and the lads weren't on board, so I made me way back down the train, scanning round for a seat. The five-hour stint to Folkestone was only the first leg of a 3000-mile round-trip, so I badly needed to park me arse. It was starting to get a bit nippy, which was nothing new on a special, with the heaters always being fucked. They were a waste of space. To be honest, the only time I was ever roasting on a footy special was when some bastard set fire to the next carriage on the way home from Leicester in '75. But bringing a coat to Rome was unthinkable. Of the 26,000 who went, I was one of the 25,999 who didn't have one. I took me chances with a black V-neck jumper over a white T-shirt, a pair of Levi's (Lionel Blairs) and a pair of Clarks boots.

By about half ten things had settled down. The singing had fizzled and the wine-lodge buzz had faded to backdrop, replaced by the racket of the moving train. Halfway through a carriage I heard 'All right bollocks!', then saw a couple more Kirkby heads. There was an empty seat by them. Wardy was wearing one of those floppy Liverpool hats and was grinning, with a can of ale in his hand. It was a sight I'd get well used to over the next few days and how I'll always remember him. Jimmy had the same hat as me and thousands of other Reds – the thin-nylon peaked type with red and white quarters. My abiding memory of him is of a fella permanently blitzed. His raw, croaky voice sounded like he'd been inhaling smoke from a bus exhaust. He passed me a can: 'Ee-arr, swallee that,' he said.

I 'swalleed' it with three cheese sarnies. My food supply was half-gone, but I knew I had Vinnie's as backup. A fella on an overloaded table opposite started moaning about the lack of baggage space. Wardy reassured him: 'At least it won't be like this in Europe. I believe the trains over there are brilliant.' As far as statements backfiring go, that has to be on a par with Neville Chamberlain's 1938 'Peace in our time' speech, when he waved that white paper and said that Hitler was a great fella. To be fair to Wardy, at that time nobody knew what the rail networks on the other side of the Channel had in store for us – thank fuck.

By midnight the carriages were quiet. We were catching a ferry in the early hours, so we all needed some kip. The cold woke me a few times. I remember curling up on the seat and wishing I'd brought a flag to wrap around me. When Wardy woke me at Folkstone Harbour station, I was completely zombied. 'Come 'ed, it's D-Day,' he said, grinning, with a can in his hand. Jimmy was sprawled across the table, using his plastic bag as a pillow. One side of his head was matted with sweat.

I was surprised how big the ferry was. I'd only ever sailed over the Mersey on the Royal Iris. As we boarded, everyone had their beige cardboard passports ready, but no one asked to see them or even bothered checking our tickets. The boat was chocka. A lad called Ammo told me that our kid and the others had got the earlier ferry: 'Your Mick said if I see yer, to tell yer they'll meet yer by the Colosseum somewhere.'

Below deck the bar area seemed as big as Anfield. It was a mixed scene. Loads were sitting or lying around shattered. Some slept while others drank noisily. Jimmy moseyed over with two full, dripping pints: 'The bar's shut. Everyone's filling their boots.'

I stood on a chair and saw about six Reds behind the bar passing pints over into a forest of waving arms. Any other time and I'd have been right over there, but lack of kip, ale, cheese sarnies and ciggies had set fire to me gullet, so I popped a Rennie and got me head down.

It was about half eight when Wardy woke me up at Ostend . . . grinning, with a can in his hand. Jimmy was sprawled over a chair as if he'd been shivved. There was a huge queue to get washed, so we decided we'd wait till we boarded the Belgian train, thinking it'd be a modern, state-of-the-art job. At Ostend no one checked our passports or tickets again. I couldn't help thinking how easy it would've been for Vinnie or anyone else bunking. We waited on a chilly platform at Ostend station for half an hour, then this minty old train rolled up. The buzz simmered down. The looks of concern said it all. 'This bastard better not be ours,' Jimmy said. It was what we were all thinking. A steward confirmed the worst. Wardy put it in a nutshell: 'It looks like the fuckin' thing they used in *The Railway Children*.'

The interior was similar to an English footy special: sliding-door compartments that held eight, with roped luggage racks above the seats and a sliding window. Further down . . . the carriages changed to just seats with no tables. A steward told us it was because the carriages were half-Belgian and half-French. We sat in the French half (just seats). The entire train smelt musty and felt crusty, but because we were still in adventure mode we just got on with it. All that mattered was that we were well on our way. .

The first couple of hours were weird. People in the Belgian half of the train kept coming into our half saying 'It's fuckin' freezing down there'. The crazy scenario was that the heaters only worked in the French half. Then, as morning warmed up and the sun got going, we kept going down the Belgian end saying 'It's fuckin' roasting up there'. A steward eventually turned the heating off, though it was still stifling. The air conditioning was just a simple case of opening the windows.

The tannoy system was on a par with the train. Before any announcement you'd hear a few seconds of crackling, like an old wartime radio broadcast. A few mimicked Lord Haw-Haw: 'Germany Calling'. Most messages were in broken English, the clearest being a warning not to drink the water on board because of contamination. That isn't something you wanna hear when your throat feels like you've been gargling sand. I had nothing at all to drink, and Wardy and Jimmy only had ale. The situation led to an announcement that the buffet car was giving away free cans of soft drinks. When I got there, they'd all been snaffled. My salvation came when a few lads walked through our carriage carrying bags filled with drinks. They'd had a can whip-around on the train and were handing them to people who were thirsty, which I thought was a great Scouse touch.

It was boiling hot that afternoon. The open windows played havoc with any card games. It was as if there was a poltergeist in the carriage – cards flying all over the place. Plenty of yawning was going on. The initial hit of travelling on foreign soil had well worn off. The countryside seemed endless, flat and boring. Jimmy put his own geographical slant on it: 'It looks like them fuckin' cornfields at the back of Kirkby.' I must admit I still laugh at that.

I wolfed me last three butties, then gave Vinnie's sarnies to Wardy. His face was an absolute picture when he took them out

the bag. The tomatoes on them had blown. They were like dripping porridge in his fingers. It was the only time I saw his grin
disappear. His kite resembled someone holding his breath under-
water as he lashed the lot out the window.

I don't think anyone noticed that we'd crossed over into
Germany.

It looked exactly the same, apart from the occasional six-foot-
five, blond tit-head you'd see on a platform. Slowing and passing
through stations were the best parts of the day. All the red and
white colours would come out the windows, and the singing would
start. You could tell that the Belgians and Krauts had never
witnessed anything like it. Most of them stood gaping at the train
with constipated expressions. In one station we all started throwing
English coins and sweets to people on the platform. They were
holding their hands out and pushing each other out the way to
get at the booty. Any neutral observer would've seen it as a gesture
of good will from one culture being warmly embraced by another.
Jimmy's piss-holed eyes saw it differently from the train window.
'Yer fuckin' tramps,' he shouted.

As we got further into Germany, the countryside got more lush
and picturesque, while the scene on the train became uglier. The
Lord Haw-Haw voice announced that the buffet car was out of stock
and that the handbasins and toilet flushes had run out of water.
Now I'm no prude . . . but there was no way I was going anywhere
near shithouse pans that were chock-a-block with King Eddies.
They were gruesome. Don't ask me what the poor women on
board did, but most lads ended up having a burst in the handbasins. When we got to Strasbourg, scores bailed off the train
unofficially and stampeded to the bogs. Others swarmed the cafe-
teria, where there were more problems. Staff wouldn't accept
Italian lire or sterling. Back on the train they announced that
there'd be a fresh water supply at Basle. It was a blag. When we
got there, Swiss rail staff refused to fill the water tanks.

By the time we reached Zurich station early on Tuesday
evening, the state of play wasn't good. Swiss bizzies lined the platform and wouldn't let us off, because one of the starving trains

ahead had cleaned out the cafe, and for some reason the Swiss rail authorities still wouldn't refill the water tanks. There were some thirsty, hungry, irritated Scousers on board. People were desperate. Everyone's sarnies had been eaten or had fallen apart, and any dregs of juice that were left over were warm. The water shortage was so bad that a few lads from Wallasey near us used a big bottle of warm Kia-Ora orange to get washed with. Stewards partly restocked the buffet car, and we took off again, but you couldn't get within two carriages of it. After half an hour it was all gone again. I had to make do with a drink of warm, flat bitter off Wardy, who passed me it . . . grinning, with a can in his hand.

The stewards got serious earache about the water and sanitary situation. The bogs were starting to smell like Widnes. We'd have been well within our rights to start a mutiny. Then, as if by magic, the moody atmosphere mellowed when the Swiss Alps came into view. It was mid-evening, and the sunshine bounced off the snow peaks, lighting up the mountains in a stunning amber-white. Everyone was hanging out the windows, blown away. To put it blunt, it was fuckin' awesome. Jimmy's ale-blurred vision even saw the beauty. 'Imagine sliding down one of them on a piece of cardboard,' he said.

At one of the highest points, we stopped at a scenic little station; the views were spectacular. Then, from the Belgian end of the train, someone yodelled out the window in a high-pitched voice: 'Yodel-a-e-dee.' The echo it made was amazing. Next thing a deeper yodel came from the French end: 'Yodel-a-e-dee.' Everyone got onto it. After a few minutes the sound of hundreds of yodelling Scousers echoed round the Alps. It was hilarious to listen to. Just before we left, Wardy handed me a few coins and said, 'Do us a favour. Go and get us an *Echo*.'

The water tanks were finally refilled at a place called Chiasso, which is on the border with Italy. It was a big relief in more ways than one, especially for the women. There was a bird in our carriage called Jackie. She was a bit heavy on the make-up but was as fit as a butcher's dog – white blouse, skimpy red shorts and little white socks. Every time she walked past, at least twenty heads would lean over and follow her arse down the aisle. I had fantasies about her dragging me into one of the bogs . . . then I pictured the bogs, and the fantasy was fucked.

We didn't see anything of Milan or Parma – it was dark when we passed through them. I went for a walk to stretch me legs. The train was shitted up good style. There were no rubbish bins, just English plastic carrier bags all over the place, over-spilling with shite. A couple of carriages looked like a grenade had gone off in them. Cans and empty bottles rolled round floors full of playing cards, crisp bags, ripped magazines and Monday's news-papers. In one of the bogs there was a small, smashed up choco-late vending machine, which must've been dragged on at Strasbourg. Its moneybox wasn't touched, just the chocolate gone. I bummed a couple of squashed ciggies off a lad in the Belgian half. Every compartment I passed had bodies crashed out in the criss-cross-roped luggage racks. They looked more like torture racks. I had to make do with another sit-upright kip. I took the knock somewhere around Bologna with me legs entwined with Jimmy's, using the cold window as a pillow.

On the Wednesday morning I opened me eyes about 60 km north of Rome. The dawn hadn't long broken, and already the sun was on about gas mark four. The fields were baked dry, and everything was calm. You just knew we were in for a scorcher. Jimmy was half-awake, staring out the window, and Wardy was still asleep . . . grinning, with a can in his hand. It was early, and I was buzzing. It was a mixture of match excitement and relief that I was finally getting off the train. It felt strange. This was the run in – just a rag-arse kid from Kirkby ready to enter the Eternal City. It was a place that working-class lads weren't expected to get to – a city I'd have probably never seen in me life if it wasn't for Liverpool Football Club.

On the outskirts of the city the poverty was in your face – run-down blocks of flats with washing hanging from verandas and graffiti everywhere. It definitely wasn't what I'd seen in the Mario Lanza film. Jimmy broke the silence. 'It's a fuckin' dump,' he shouted, which got a big laugh. We crawled along for the last mile, then finally, after thirty-seven hours of backache, arse-ache, heartburn, thirst, hunger and sweat, we pulled into Rome's main Termini station.

The Siege of Rome

In 1944 a young Bob Paisley rode into Rome on a tank when the city was liberated. In ancient history it was the Etruscans and the Gauls who flooded in and took over. In the year AD 1977 it was the turn of the Scousers. To say that the Romans were worried is an understatement. English clubs' rep abroad was well dodgy. Tottenham fans had rioted in Rotterdam at the '74 UEFA final, and Leeds fans went berserk and wrecked the Parc des Princes in Paris during the '75 European Cup, both with only a fraction of the fans we had in Rome. The I-ties were so paranoid about the situation that they had 4000 bizzies on duty that day, including crack sections of the Carabinieri (military bizzies) plus riot squads and anti-terror units. It was the biggest-ever police operation in Italy for a footy match. The Olympic Stadium owners weren't taking any chances either. They actually took out extra insurance cover of seventy thousand pounds, in case we ransacked the stadium. I suppose the hysteria was understandable, but if they'd have done their homework, they could have all sat back with a big fat Italian cigar. Because we weren't English; we were Scousers . . . you know the score.

'Oh, we're the greatest team in Europe and we're here in Italy . . . Italy . . . Italy' was the song that greeted Rome as we came out the station. The sun was now on about gas mark seven. The heat hit us like a flame-thrower. I reckon I can honestly say that not one of the 26,000 had sun lotion. Nobody went abroad on holidays back then, and at home the sun was like a UFO, so suncream was unheard of. Some beaut on the train was telling everyone that if it got too hot, the best thing to use was olive oil. The soft bastard must've ended up barbecued. Buses were laid on to take us through the city, but we headed straight for a cafe over the road and sat under a parasol. Jimmy had the

Italian waiter fucked: 'D'yer sell bitter, mate?' The waiter just stood there.

Wardy's attempt sounded African, like Idi Amin. 'Bitter . . . beer,' he said. The waiter came back with three lagers. Wardy raised a toast to Rome . . . grinning, with a bottle in his hand. We savoured the moment, watching hundreds of Reds pour out the station; dozens had criss-cross red marks on their backs from the luggage racks.

The I-ties had warned us all via the *Echo* to beware of pickpockets, Rome being the dipping capital of Europe. It was a big talking point amongst Reds. The bullshitters were in their element. One lying bastard by the cafe said that 200 people off our train were dipped as they came out the station. 'D'yer mean by the same fella?' Wardy said. Everyone absorbed the warnings, but by the time we got to Rome it'd become a source of pisstaking. The main prank on the day was sliding your hand into one of your mate's pockets and watching his paranoid reaction. I had Jimmy spinning round like a gunslinger all day. If the dippers were rubbing their thieving hands waiting for 26,000 middle-class English tourists (the only folk who travelled those days) then they must've got a big shock when they saw the rough, unwashed hordes emerge from the station. We looked more destitute than them. One of the best shouts was from a white-haired old Scouser sitting by us outside the cafe. He said, 'The coppers have just arrested a dipper. They emptied his pockets and found 150 giros and 200 sick notes.'

After a few cold beers and an oily ham cob we moseyed, not knowing or caring where we were going. We followed what sounded like a fox hunt to a street around the corner. It could've been any street in Liverpool. Hundreds were sitting outside bars, drinking and reading Tuesday night's *Echo*. They were mainly from the airborne battalions that'd been winging in all night and morning blowing little trumpets they'd bought at Speke airport for a quid. A total squadron of sixty-eight planes had touched down since the weekend – the biggest airborne assault on Europe since the battle of Arnhem. For 99 per cent of Red passengers it was their first-ever flight. Some loved it, some hated it and some were so arse-holed that they probably still don't remember it. A gang of lads told us about a couple of stowaways who hid on their plane at Speke. They almost pulled it off but were smoked out after being sussed sneaking across the runway.

Fleets of orange trams kept passing with dozens of Reds hanging off them holding up fat green bottles of ale and singing the 'Arrivederci, Roma' song. It was only early, but already our heads were starting to get fuzzy. We wised up and decided to shoot back to the station for a swill, then try and see a few sights: Colosseum, Vatican, Trevi Fountain and all that lark.

I got some weird looks from locals in the station bogs when I started using the bandage on me hand as a toothbrush. The bandage was decomposing by the hour. It had ale and orange-juice stains on it and was coming in handy as a sweatband. There were about fifteen toilet cubicles in there. They were the first bogs we'd ever seen with just a hole in the floor. We couldn't believe it. Jimmy was pushing doors open saying, 'Where's the pans?' I wouldn't have minded, but the holes in the floor were tiny. We just had to get on with it. Quite a few Scousers were dotted about in the other cubicles. There was loads of laughing and shouting going on. 'This is like *The Golden Shot*' got a laugh. Someone came back with 'Y'mean The Golden Shit'. Wardy got a giggle with 'I've just gone in off the post'. Jimmy's voice was unmistakable: 'I think I've just hit the fuckin' corner flag.' It was a good grin but without doubt the most awkward, uncomfortable Barry White I've ever taken, especially with my bandaged right hand out of use. I was like a fuckin' contortionist.

The phone boxes only took special coins with grooves cut into them. Jimmy's translation was quality: 'All right, mate. Have y'got any of them phone coin things . . . lire for the blower?' It descended into sign language, with Jimmy holding an imaginary phone to his ear saying, 'Hello . . . hello.' He got two coins, and we headed for a phone box. Jimmy put his in first and dialled just the normal seven digits, like you do at home. 'It's dead,' he said.

I thought I knew the score and, like a tit, said, 'You forgot to dial 051 from outside Liverpool.' Jimmy lashed his coin up the street. I've still got mine.

By two o'clock the sun had hit gas mark ten. I was down to my T-shirt, with me jumper tied round me waist. Wardy had done the same, and Jimmy was down to his skin. We bumped into a gang of Netherton Reds who were swigging from impressive, big, vase-looking wine bottles with basket handles. Wardy inspected one closer. 'Fuckin' ell, is there a genie in this?' he said. They told us the bottles only cost two thousand lires each (about one pound fifty). Our sightseeing plans were about to be vinoed into touch.

We wandered the streets with our genie bottles. Every swig took our eyes up the walls of tall, baroque buildings that lined the roads and piazzas. The whole city was like a 3000-year-old museum. We passed an old tramp sprawled in a doorway with a flea-bitten dog tied to his wrist with string. Some Scouser had obviously walked past him earlier, because there was a piece of cardboard hanging off the tramp's neck with the words 'Gordon Lee' written on it. We buzzed and threw a few thousand lires in his begging bowl. Whoever did it didn't realise that it'd earn the tramp a tidy few bob off every Red who went past.

One bar we passed looked like something from *The Godfather*. Around three of its tables Reds were sprawled on chairs, all asleep in different positions like they'd been sprayed in a drive-by shooting. There was a huge cheer when a Manweb van drove past with Liverpool flags hanging out the windows. Someone said that the two lads in it were on sick leave and had sneaked the van out of the yard in Bootle.

By mid-afternoon the sun felt like it'd just been retubed. The official temp was 87°F, but in the suntrapped streets and piazzas it was easily around 100. In one street a Scouser dressed in a toga and wearing a blond Roman wig kept passing in a taxi . . . standing up in the sunroof waving to us like royalty. He went past about eight times shouting 'Hail, Scousers'. We'd all shout it back, then bow.

The I-ties were all smiles and handshakes. In one hotel chefs and waiters waved down from windows. We waved our genie bottles back. Within seconds they were lowering bottles of wine and champagne down on long cords. Jimmy couldn't stop blowing kisses up to them. Every I-tie who walked past was greeted with Red respect. The birds were stunners. There were a few bad attempts at chatting them up. The pick of the day was outside a packed bar, where Jimmy curtsied to a gorgeous brunette, held her hand and said, 'D'yer take it up the Tex Ritter?' I nearly choked. Boy was Rome the place to be that day.

By the time our genie bottles were empty, we were blowing bubbles. The train journey, the wine and the intense heat finally rugby tackled us. We crashed out in the shade of an ancient church and kipped on the pavement. In the hours that we slept, the siege of Rome continued. Every fountain and pool in the city had a pair of Scouse feet in it. One fountain we'd passed looked like Queens Drive baths. The elaborate Trevi was crawling with Reds. Though the bizzies weren't keen on anyone bailing in, loads did. A few lads I knew from Gerard Gardens made the trip. One was Franny Carlyle, who was Scouse/I-tie so knew a bit about Rome. His mates didn't have a clue. Shortly after they arrived, Franny said to them, 'Listen, boys, we can't leave Rome without goin' the Colosseum.' One of the lads genuinely and sincerely asked, 'Is it a late bar?'

Thousands descended on that ancient old ruin, draping it with banners and playing footy outside. Others swarmed to gaffs like the Pantheon, St Peter's Square and the Sistine Chapel – a place that me old buddies Stevie and Tony Riley described as 'Nearly as beautiful as the Kop'. The day was a mixture of football fervour and cultural education. Everyday life for a lot of Reds was seeing graffiti-ridden walls and derelict flats on run-down estates, but here they were feasting their eyes on grandiose architecture, mosaic-covered courtyards and wall frescoes by fellas like Botticelli and Perugino. And let's be honest, who could fail to be bowled over and gobsmacked by Michelangelo's incredible ceiling! It definitely beat stipple or swirl Artex. For many this trip was where the first seeds of cultural awareness were planted. LFC weren't just broadening our trophy cabinet; they were broadening our horizons and minds.

Wardy was grinning as usual when he woke us up at about five o'clock. I still owe him for that. Missing the FA Cup was a blessing, but if I'd have slept through the Rome game I'd have topped meself. Jimmy's head was torched. He'd slid out of the shade and into the sun – his kite looked like it had been cheese-grated. We panicked and checked our pockets . . . it was all there. How the I-tie dippers didn't have us off is a complete mystery.

We walked down a jigger into a proper back-street cafe. Wardy turned African again: 'Food . . . spaghetti.' When it came, it was full-on Italian. We stared at it, amazed at seeing white spaghetti. 'What the fuck's that?' Jimmy said. 'Ask them have they got any Heinz.'

It was our first hot meal in three days; we didn't come up for air. I've been seriously hooked on bolognese ever since.

The match was kicking off at quarter past eight, which meant a taxi to the Olympic Stadium. On the way there the Colosseum flashed past the taxi window. By the time Jimmy said 'Where?' and turned round, it'd vanished. That was the sum total of our sightseeing, though we were in for a feast when we crossed the River Tiber near the ground. A tall, white stone obelisk graced the entrance to the Olympic Way. Behind it was a tree-lined stone avenue that led to the stadium. The sun was still laughing, making the avenue glow ultra-white with veins of red as thousands of Kopites streamed towards the Roman arena. When I got out the cab, I felt like kissing the deck. I was eighteen, I was raw and I was buzzing. This place looked like heaven on earth.

On the avenue red and white chequered flags were changing hands faster than an Olympic baton, at five thousand lires each (about three pound fifty). I reckon the I-tie who sold them must've retired on the banks of Lake Como from the business he did that night, though I wouldn't begrudge him a single lire, because his flags were about to become a defining symbol of this whole amazing night, a visual jaw-dropper that'd soon be written into LFC history. A bit further on a couple more lads who I knew from town, Strodey and Ray Baccino, looked spaced out. At first I thought they were blitzed on vino, till Strodey managed to get his words out: 'Davey, me prayers in the Vatican have been answered. We've just met Shankly.' It was true. Shanks had walked up to the ground, mingling with all the Reds. 'We're gonna win this tonight, boys' were the great man's exact words. Strodey was totally gone. 'Even the Roman statues were bowing as he walked past,' he said.

Outside the stadium bizzies were frisking everyone for ale. It had been banned inside. I got past them and unravelled me battered match ticket. After three days' worth of dossing, it looked like one of the Dead Sea Scrolls. The final stage of the pilgrimage was passing through those turnstiles. I closed me eyes for a sec, clenched me fists. I was in.

If there's one sight I wanna see on me deathbed, it's the scene that greeted me when I walked onto the Curva Nord terrace: a red and white panoramic rush of waving chequered flags, home-made banners, epaulettes, scarves, hats and streamers stretching three-quarters of the way around the ground. As far as breath-taking colour and beauty goes, it was right up there with the Swiss Alps – a vision that'll never fade. Some of the raised banners I saw in our end are now legendary:

> When in Rome, do as the Scousers do
> Here we go gathering cups in May

. . . and the mother, daddy and now grandad of them all, a twenty-four foot by eight-foot banner that became the story of Rome, the Scouse version of the Bayeux Tapestry that will be talked about and revered by Reds until the Liverbirds take flight: 'Joey ate the frogs' legs, made the Swiss roll, now he's munching Gladbach'.

It was an honour to be in its presence. To Phil Downey, Jimmy and Phil Cummings, all's I can say is well in boys – your banner will wave and echo in eternity.

Down at the front I was looking at the half-deserted Gladbach end when there was a tap on me shoulder. I turned around and, fuck me, I couldn't believe what I was seeing. It was Vinnie, standing there grinning like Wardy. His white clobber was absolutely rotten. First thing out of his mouth was, 'I hope yer haven't ate me sarnies.' We laughed for ages. He'd managed to bunk a special via the platform nine fire-escape ladder. Lime Street was the only ticket checkpoint on the entire trip. I asked him about getting home. 'Who cares?' he said. Seeing him just added to the buzz. Everything was going right.

The racket from our end was non-stop and loud – not bad considering we were in an open-air stadium. Horns added to the din. You could see that the players were shell-shocked when they walked out and saw us all.

Tommy Smith: 'I couldn't believe it . . . and it did hit you.'

Emlyn Hughes: 'Jesus Christ, we're back in Liverpool.'

Terry McDermott: 'Christ, how can we get beat for these lot?'

Terry Mac's quote said it all. They couldn't get beat, and the result we all know (you know the score). Every one of them dug deep and gave everything and more that night. They were just young lads, but under the genius of Bob Paisley they understood the historical importance and massive responsibility of it all. They represented who we were – our city, hopes, dreams and fantasies. They were how most of us got through a working week, our escape route from the dole queues, building sites, factories, mundane offices, domestic shit, wedge troubles or family grief. We needed them, and they needed us. We existed for each other, and together on one beautiful spring night we made history. If I had to choose a phrase to describe the moment, I'd put a footy slant on that famous old Churchill quote: 'Never in the field of football memories has so much been owed by so many to so few.'

When the final whistle went, me, Jimmy and Wardy had a two-minute game of ring-a-ring o' roses, which didn't look out of place amongst the wreckage of the emotional bomb that hit the

Curva Nord. It was a scene of total ecstasy, with quite a few tears thrown in. A lad near me was sobbing and being consoled. 'He's thinking of someone,' his mate said. It'd be quite a few years till I'd understand where that lad went to that night, though he wasn't in the zone for long. Minutes later he was buzzing alongside me on the front fence, watching the Reds parading on the running track. In between us a line of paranoid-looking bizzies ring-fenced our end. It was my first-ever glimpse of Big Ears. It looked massive, and it dazzled under the floodlights, shining brighter than Emlyn Hughes's teeth. We all milked the glory till the boys disappeared down the tunnel through a posse of photographers and flashing cameras. Everyone was emotionally punch-drunk. The moment felt surreal, like something from a movie. But it was no illusion. We weren't dreaming. Rome had just been conquered.

Arrivederci, Roma

To keep the rail hordes away from the city centre after the match, the I-ties diverted us all to Tibertina station, north of the city. They'd announced it in the stadium, though we never heard Jack shit. I don't know what happened to Vinnie. The last I saw of him was when Phil Neal's pen went in. He took off into the crowd like a rip-rap, screaming like a fella on fire. I was half looking out for our kid after seeing a lad called Gerry Cornett in the Curva Nord, who told me, 'Your Mick said if I see yer, to tell yer they'll meet yer at the station.'

Jimmy's gravel throat needed oiling, but he got a few songs going in a cafe near the station. 'We all agree, the FA Cup is an ashtray' was one. Then a classic: 'We all hate bambinos', which came about after some tithead told him that bambino was the Italian word for a dipper.

By 1.30 a.m. the queues outside the station were all over the place. No one asked to see our tickets. We squeezed through the gates into a commotion on the platform over packed-lunch buffets that some Reds had paid extra for – they'd all been snaffled or blagged. The train we boarded was all compartments. Most were chocka, apart from one that a fat, pissed-up fella was inside. He was shouting abuse at some harmless arl fella and his middle-aged son, keeping them out of the compartment by jamming the door. It ended up a tug of war with him and Wardy. Thirty seconds later we were all sitting down in the compartment looking at the fat beaut staring at us through the door. He kept coming back in and giving the arl fella stick. After the second time Wardy jumped up and launched him down the corridor, then sat back down . . . grinning, with his hat in his hand. After that it was all boot-room talk. We kicked every ball of the match before finally crashing out. Jimmy and the arl fella's son took first shift in the luggage racks.

The worst part of any footy trip is coming home. You just wanna get back. The buzz levels are back down, party horns have faded, corks have popped, fizz gone, adrenalin gone, laughter gone, conversation gone and wedge gone. The overnighters I'd had at Wembley were always quiet trips back, mainly involving popping Rennies while staring out the window of a train or van, eyes flickering, thinking of nothing apart from maybe me own bed. The joy of seeing us lift Big Ears for the first time definitely took the pain out of the first night's journey back, but waking up on the Thursday morning like a bag of shite knowing we had another day and a half to go was a killer. All's I had was four ciggies in a squashed Marlboro packet. They were that flat it was like smoking lolly-ice sticks. I badly needed a Rennie. I'd asked for some in a shop in Rome, but it was like talking to Manuel from *Fawlty Towers*. My heartburn was so severe that I could've lit a ciggy with me breath.

The arl fella in our compartment didn't exactly cheer us up. 'Most of the planes will be home by now,' he said, which was hard to take when you're still chugging through Italy. He was right. Plane loads of Reds had been arriving back at Speke from the early hours. A lot were applauded by airport staff as they came through. While all that was going on, we were over 1000 miles away, listening to the arl fella's son snoring in the luggage rack like a pig with sinusitis. If it got too loud, his arl fella would poke him with the stick end of a chequered flag. Jimmy woke up looking like something out of *Tales from the Crypt*. His sunburnt kite had bloated up, and his cheeks were full of criss-cross rope marks. He slid down from the rack groaning, saying, 'Where are we?' Then he looked out the window and shook his head: 'Them fuckin Alps again.' It captured everyone's mood. On the way over it was like going through paradise. Going home it was no different than going past the heights on Netherfield Road.

By midday the hunger was on top. A trip to the buffet car was a waste of time – it was as bare as Everton's trophy cabinet. The psychological side of it was the hardest – knowing you were trapped on a train for another day with no scoff or drinks. Most people were suffering. A few lads formed sarnie-raiding parties, mooching up and down the train hoping to swoop on a rare buttie bag while people slept. Others came round offering ciggies for food. The most offered was by some desperate fat fella who was opening compartments and pleading 'Twenty Embassy for any buttie'.

No one took a chance drinking the water in the bogs. The only time I went near it was to swill the dryness from me mouth, but it was like swigging a mouthful of lead filings. Adding to the torture was the hygiene grief. I don't care who you are, after roughing it on the piss for four days in searing hot temperatures wearing the same gear right down to your under-kecks, you're gonna start festering. BO was rampant. The worst part was passing someone in the narrow corridors. I had to hold me breath a few times. One fella I brushed past smelt like a YMCA mattress. The arl fella's son in our compartment was minging, and I mean badly minging. To be honest, if we'd dug up the body of a dead gladiator in Rome and brought it with us, it would have smelt better. At one point he took his suede boots off – fuck me, it was as if someone had just opened a mummy's tomb.

It was the same score when I opened the compartment of the Stewart brothers (the lads with the coal). The stench was pure, unadulterated sock-cyanide. Mick Stewart got the rancid socks and threw them out the window. What happened next was nuts.

By some fluke the socks blew into the window of the compartment behind. It had the same effect as a stun grenade. There was
a big commotion, groans of revulsion, cries of 'Dirty bastards',
then the sliding door burst open and about five lads bailed out
into the corridor, holding their mouths.

The Stewarts and Ged still had their pieces of coal, though
by now their white jeans looked like they'd just crawled out of
a coal bunker with them. Visual degeneration was everywhere.
Clumps of bum-fluff and stubble were on everyone's kite; some
were at the half-beard stage. Hairstyles were a mixture of mousey,
greasy strands or dry, frizzy straw. The women on board were
struggling. You know how birds are about appearances, being
organised, change of clobber and all that carry on. They can't
slum it or doss like fellas can. On a train full of lads it must've
been murder for them, with their perms fucked, no make-up,
minty underwear, couldn't eat, couldn't drink, couldn't fart. Most
of them ended up looking like fellas in drag. Even Jackie – the
one we were all perving on the way over – wasn't the same bird
going home. She walked past our compartment with a gaunt
white face full of spots and her perm in tatters. It looked like a
giant tarantula on her head. Jimmy took no prisoners: 'I'd rather
shag Tommy Smith.'

At every station the train would slow and crawl through
without stopping, but then, somewhere in Germany at around
6 p.m. on the Thursday, we slowed on approach to a station that
overlooked a small, picturesque village . . . then stopped. What
followed was like a scene from *The Vikings*. Every door on the
train burst open, and hundreds piled out and stampeded down a
steep hill towards the only shop in the tiny village. It wasn't
planned, it wasn't organised and it wasn't malicious – it was sheer
desperation. A few villagers froze. One woman ran. God knows
what they must've thought, seeing hundreds of unshaven fellas
steaming towards their secluded little town. The shop had bread
hanging on hooks and fruit baskets outside. Every loaf was ripped
down and eaten in the street. The fruit lasted about twenty
seconds. Inside was like a massive rugby scrum. Anything edible

was wolfed on the spot. Tinned stuff and drinks were slotted. Loads threw lire notes on the counter before emptying the shelves, though the Italian notes were no use to the Kraut shopkeeper, who was picking them up shouting, 'Nein, nein!' The whole thing was over in five minutes.

I was blowing for tugs eating peanut butter with me fingers on the way back up the hill. I don't know where that idyllic little place was, but to this day they must still talk about that incident. It's probably the biggest thing that's ever happened there. It was ironic that at the very same time as we were pillaging and scavenging in Germany, half of Liverpool was overindulging and partying, watching the team celebrate on the steps of the Picton Library back home.

That Thursday night was definitely the worst: dehydration, hunger, thirst, weariness, desolate expressions, dishevelled clobber, bouts of silence and basic self-survival. It was getting like the film King Rat. I didn't think anything could make me laugh that night, but some Scouser did. He opened our carriage door and stood there for a few seconds holding out his clenched fist. We all sat there baffled. Then he slowly opened his hand and said, 'Does anyone wanna buy a fly?' There was a dead fly in his palm. What's that old Scouse saying: 'If yer don't laugh, you'll cry.'

The only escape was sleep. It was mine and Wardy's turn in the luggage racks. Getting into them wasn't easy, like climbing into a narrow top bunk without a ladder. They were no more than two foot wide. The criss-cross rope was quite thick and sagged down between three metal support rails. The middle rail was the bastard. It was bang on line with your hip, your arse or your plums, depending on which way you turned. The only comfort was that you were lying down for a change, instead of trying to kip sitting upright. I psyched myself into thinking it was me own bed. After a while I couldn't feel the rail against my side or the rope on me cheek. It was a seriously rough doss, but it was the longest kip I had on the entire trip. Thursday passed into Friday.

As we got nearer the coast, the mood picked up. The buzz was similar to the feeling prisoners must get on the morning of their release. That's what the train felt like: a moving nick – restricted movement – confined cells – loss of freedom – claustrophobia. Though, as Wardy said, 'Even prisoners get food and drink.' We pulled into Ostend about half eight on the Friday morning. The sheer relief of disembarking was orgasmic. The Belgians in the station couldn't make us out. We looked like a train full of extras from *Planet of the Apes*. I remember inhaling the fresh sea air at the harbour. It was a boss feeling knowing we were only a gangplank away from an English brekkie.

The ship's cafe was always gonna struggle. Hundreds were skint and hadn't eaten for days, so any sense of conscience went right out the portholes . . . you know the score. Those cafe scenes are now known in Scouse circles as *The Invasion of the Brekkie Snatchers*. At least three pigs' worth of bacon went west. Some of the eating noises were primal. People were grunting and making sounds you'd only hear in a blue movie. In fact the breakfast afterglow was actually similar to post sex – sitting back smoking with a pervy, satisfied smirk on your gob. The rest of the crossing was spent on the top deck boozing in the sunshine. Jimmy sat in the shade due to his burnt, peeling kite. He wasn't the only victim of the Roman weather. A lad called Tony Burke from Walton was walking round like the tin man from *The Wizard of Oz*.

The ale did enough to prepare us for the final stint. I couldn't have faced getting on another bastard train without a few beers down me. We docked at Dover around half one, then right onto another rickety footy special. That last part was an absolute grueller. It seemed to take as long as the Europe trek. We read Friday's papers over and over. They were still paying tribute to the team and to the fans for the way we'd conducted ourselves in Italy. There wasn't one single incident or arrest. The Mayor of Rome was full of praise, stating that we were welcome back any time. It was the perfect scenario, the red ribbon on the cake. The match now seemed like a distant memory, like we'd been away for weeks. Then, after another five arse-torturing hours, at 7 p.m., Friday 27th, the train finally pulled into Lime Street, nearly forty hours after leaving Rome. We emerged like a cargo of refugees and shuffled slowly along the platform, round-shouldered, battered and exhausted.

Liverpool was as sunny as Rome that night. I stopped by the taxi rank with Jimmy and Wardy. They were amongst the many diehards who headed straight to Anfield for Tommy Smith's testimonial. I just don't know how any of them did it. I was like most Reds: a physical, mental and financial write-off. Before they jumped in a cab, we said our goodbyes, Jimmy half-cut and Wardy . . . grinning, with a can in his hand.

Going home on the bus, I stared through the window at nothing, thinking about Rome and the whole week. It was a strange feeling, a kind of hollow emptiness – I just didn't want it to end. The derelict, vandalised flats in Kirkby made me realise it was all over. I missed Jimmy and Wardy already. I suppose if we'd lost, the trip would have gone down as a five-day nightmare. But when you win Big Ears, even the worst nightmares can turn into epic adventures. I got off the bus and cut through the council estate to me ma's . . . and into LFC folklore.

*

Thirty years on and nearly fifty years of age, that trip means even more to me. If they ever invent a time machine, I swear I'd go back and relive it all again. We were the European Cup pioneers, the first Scousers out there, and Rome will always be our first love. It was the classic rags-to-riches fairy tale – a story of doggedness, devotion and a dream that came true.

I slid the match programme back in me footy box and climbed out the loft, me head too laden with memories to do a tap that morning. I poured another tea, dug out a CD then sat back and let Mario Lanza do the rest. There were mixed emotions as he waltzed me around the 'Seven Hills of Rome'. I thought about Emlyn Hughes, Bob Paisley, Shanks and all those Reds who made the trip in '77 who've now moved on. Then I pictured Jimmy's sunburnt, polluted kite, Wardy's grin, genie bottles, laughter, red chequered flags, Big Ears gleaming and the best night of me life. Oh yeah . . . and a dodgy diesel pump.

If the European Cup story had ended there, I'd still have been sitting here all these years later with a content smile. But something else happened in '77. In May a young Jock called Alan Hansen signed for a hundred grand from Partick. Then, on 10th August, another Scotsman arrived. His name: Kenneth Mathieson Dalglish.

London, 1978

NICKY ALLT

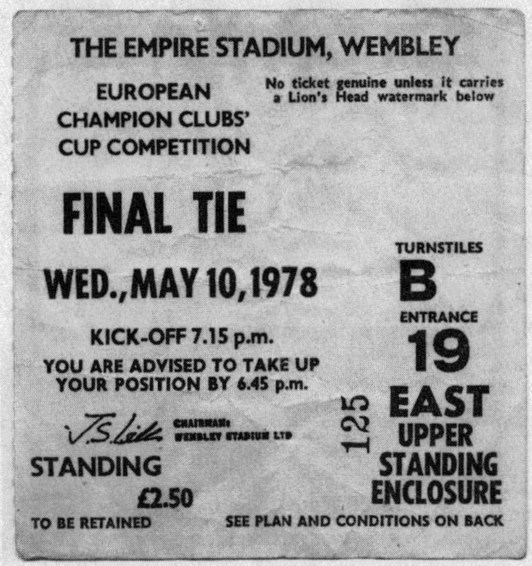

THE EMPIRE STADIUM, WEMBLEY

EUROPEAN
CHAMPION CLUBS'
CUP COMPETITION

No ticket genuine unless it carries
a Lion's Head watermark below

FINAL TIE

WED., MAY 10, 1978

KICK-OFF 7.15 p.m.
YOU ARE ADVISED TO TAKE UP
YOUR POSITION BY 6.45 p.m.

J.S. Leik CHAIRMAN:
WEMBLEY STADIUM LTD

STANDING
£2.50

TO BE RETAINED

TURNSTILES

B

ENTRANCE

19

125

EAST
UPPER
STANDING
ENCLOSURE

SEE PLAN AND CONDITIONS ON BACK

European Cup Final, 10th May 1978
Wembley Stadium, London
Attendance: 92,000

Liverpool FC   1–0   FC Bruges
Dalglish (65')

Substitutes: Steve Heighway, Steve Ogrizovic,
Joey Jones, Ian Callaghan, Colin Irwin

Manager: Bob Paisley

FC Bruges: Birger Jensen (1), Fons Bastijns (2, captain), Edi Krieger
(3), Georges Leekens (4), Gino Maes (5), Julien Cools (6), Dany
Decubber (7), René Vandereycken (8), Lajos Kü, Jan Simeon (10), Jan
Sørensen (11)

Substitutes used: Dirk Sanders, Jos Volders

Manager: Ernst Happel

Terrace Turning Point

Relaxed high on the Wembley steps, I felt I'd been running a marathon, and that that Belgian lard-fringe had chased me from Trafalgar Square to Clayton Square and back. Relieving the greasy tout of his match briefs was always the plan for a ticketless rag-arse like me, but, fucksake, how did I know he'd applied margarine to his fringe to help his barnet zip through London's streets faster than Joey O's todger in a German brass-gaff. Stretched out, with a glorious view over the crimson tide of Wembley Way, the Reds were coming up the hill boys. Our second Big-Eared final in a row, and, unbelievably, here was our little crew with tickets to ride. Felt good having a picture of those twin towers in pocket – you know, being the biggest club final of all. But having no kip the night before and the Belgian sprint had me rubbing my eyes like I was polishing a pair of AirWair. Feet crossed, sun on my face, I lay back to use the roll of final programmes I'd just relieved a Wembley vendor of as a pillow. Joey O', Fast Eddie and Little Whacker had shot off for hot dogs, buzzing about like miniature vibrators because they had precious entry passes on board. Drifting in and out, with the saxophone from Gerry Rafferty's 'Baker Street' swirling all over me, I thought of *Liverpool Echo* headlines about Wembley pledging the highest security in its history and, that it would be easier to break into Fort Knox – Ha to that! The turnstiles looked wider than the elastic on Bernard Manning's underpants.

Usually part of the wide-awake club, the ticket I held afforded me the luxury of a pre-match doze. Thanking me da and the Lord above I'd been born a son of Shanks, I looked skyward: another beautiful football day in the month of May. Down at the Bruges end of the stadium thousands of partying Scousers were making their way in. Their end had become our end, full of find-your-own-way Reds, ripped off by the allocation gangsters: UEFA's greasy-palmed officials. A few Belgians waved purple and white scarves. Being Europe's supreme team, I knew we were gonna win. Noticing purple, it wasn't for footy. I felt doubly assured. Looking odd among a sea of red and white, the three men and two women passed a friendly Scouser a camera, smiling for photographs. The tall, bubbly Liverpudlian encouraged a pose: 'Say cheese.' Checking each other, confused, they displayed their teeth. Belgian teeth and fringes full of lard . . . hmm. Stereotyping, they call it. Well, every Bruges fan I'd seen today had come straight off the turntables of a Belgian stereo. Even the women had been chewing Belgian breeze block. Entering the stadium, they were cheered all the way in. I drifted off again . . .

What a year it'd been: champions, yet again; hardly any goals conceded all season and a new king crowned with the golden hair, a man who freely scored as we adored. His name: Kenneth Mathieson Dalglish. With the king's arrival came a whole new scene for young terrace loons like me. Starting the campaign as European Champions elite, it seemed we'd also become the terrace-tearaways elite. Leaving nightclubs like the Night Owl, the Other Place, Michelle Claire's, the Swinging Apple and the Pez at six in the morning, we traipsed into Lime Street station like a crew of zombie bunkers; yet walking about away grounds of England and Europe, our little firm bounced around cocky as James Cagney with a hard-on. What a bunch of beauts we were. Funny, wise-arse, football-mad beauts, though! Our Cagney movie could have been called *Angels with Brand New Trainees*. Winning the big one last year had us walking about like god's gift to football grounds – like other team's supporters should be honoured that we and our glittering team had decided to visit their drab cities and enter their dreary, ramshackle stadiums every other Saturday. Reaching Limey, often with girls in tow, shoving them into crack-of-the-dawn-taxis, we'd been venturing down the hairy-scary station ladder to footy days out for a season or so. Simple penniless logic said: if you climbed down the never-ending metal ladder that took you to platform nine, you were with the Reds for the day; bottle out, and you were in a taxi for your bare tit, or back to beddy-boes at mother and father's humble drum on the banks of the Mersey.

From every home game and nine or ten away matches per season, I'd fast become a football gypsy. Not so much the ninety minutes – more the lifestyle and wanting to escape the claustrophobia of Coronation Street – my whole existence started revolving around the ladder, the crew, the clobber, music and clubs. But, more than all of that, the one thing that tipped me out of bed and got me energised in the morning was the perpetual travelling habit. My life map, timetable and diary were printed on a small cardboard fixture list that I waited for with crazed anticipation every boring summer.

The habitual gypsy lifestyle took over big time, here, last August, playing the Mancs in the season's opener, the Charity Shield. With a number of sceptic septics eyeing us warily, we upped the ante, walking by like Ziggy's original Spiders from Mars. Thinking they weren't going to say anything, the four foot two one in the long leather – always the narky midget, isn't it? – shouted, 'Don't forget, Scouse, we were't first ones in't UK to win it!' Presuming he meant the European Cup, Joey O' offered, 'Get yer facts right, Ronnie Corbett, it was Celtic in '67!'

There must've been twenty of them, probably ten of us – big fuckers the rest of them as well. Getting brave, another fella with that deadpan milltown accent, looking like he'd waltzed straight off a Slade LP, asked, 'What's wit' kecks yer bunch of queers?'

Suppose being the opening game, it was only proper the line he fed was the one we'd be hearing up and down the country all year. Laughing, I shouted back 'Get home to yer wife and kids yer German helmet!'

Looking embarrassed, the rest of his Slade roadies smirked. Clocking the kippers, though we were always game, I didn't fancy a battle with this bunch of Mighty Joe Youngs. Ronnie Corbett dusted his long leather down – a coat that would've been a leather bra on a normal sized person – as he tried to look big. Waiting for confrontation, and the next comment, the banter tailed off as we headed up Wembley Way. Glad, seeing as we wouldn't run, and did I as fuck fancy a headlock off one of Ronnie Corbett's crowd, I started to whistle the tune 'The Reds Are Coming Up the Hill, Boys'. Everyone joined in. Top of the flyover, where the stadium opens up, other young dressers waited at the spot we'd passed on after bumping into each other inside Liverpool's St John's Precinct a week prior. Standing out profoundly, the picture jammed itself in my memory box. The Huyton boys were there; some Scotty Road lads stood out, alongside a little firm of Kirkby dippers. Without signal, the thirty or so walked on together. A few ticket-take stories were passed around: who was carrying, who was bunking and who was tout snout.

A plan for entry was quickly passed along: meet at the top of the steps, rest up, wait for the nod, all march in. Easy-peasy! Everyone knew the 'getting into Wembley dance'. We were Liverpool – we'd been practising it longer than Jimmy Tarbuck had been practising being a Scouser. Gathered top of the steps, at the entrance gates, stood another crew: a few Halewood boys, cord grandad shoes an' all, some of Bootle's Fred Perry wearing bucks and the Norris Green, fringe benefits, laughing firm – named so, cos every one of them had a bigger quiff than Bryan Ferry, and those toothy, mad fuckers were forever greeting you with a serious Bugs Bunny.

Greetings and meetings over, morning tales swapped, the lads from different parts of Liverpool clocked the rig-outs on show. At first it was sly, admiring glances, till Joey O' put an end to the cool dude shit, asking Tony, a lad from Huyton, 'Where d'ya get those jeans, mate?'

'Some designer gaff on Kings Road this mornin'.'

'Was it a burn-off?' Joey enquired.

'Nosey aren't yer? Why, is it that obvious?'

Four lads in his crew stood stiff in the same brand-new jeans . . . yeah, it was obvious.

'Crackin' shirt that mate. Love those small collars.' One of the fringe benefits firm spoke through the usual ear-to-ear grin. 'Where's it from?'

'It's only from me arl fella's wardrobe. He's got loads of them.'

He'd been waiting for an abroad story; he knew I ventured. We'd met over the Channel before – Zurich – if I'm not wrong.

'Kiddin' aren't yer? My arl fella's a meff. How come yer da's got shirts like them?'

'Cos he thinks he's Billy Fury, still locked in the sixties.'

His mate spoke up. 'Think Billy Fury was the fifties lad. Anyway, no way could his arl fella be like him. More like Nobby Stiles in '66 but . . . if Nobby fell in a fire.'

We all laughed. Most kids had Adidas trainers, cord shoes or Jesus boots on, but this one kid, little cool-arse from Scotland Road, had these smart-looking training shoes that had me having a gander. 'Eh, mate, tasty slippers, them. Where are they from?'

'St Etienne, the quarter-final last year, lad. One-horse, shitty town, though!'

Being young, Scouse and football daft, it mattered. It all mattered: how you got from A to B on a Jaffa Cake crumb; how you wore the clobber of a GQ model with a week's worth of shite under your fingernails; and how you were gonna carry on travelling and dabbling with a ponce of a job, or, no job and the Sign-on Social bang on your case. Too right it fucking mattered! On the steps of Wembley Stadium the new kids in the togs asked various questions: where d'ya get those trainees mate? Eh, where d'ya get yer shirt lad? Where d'ya get those jeans kid? Some answered with a foreign French fable, others, West End shoplifting tales, while some told arl feller's wardrobe stories. Only one question remained the same on each set of ruby reds: what d'ya reckon this Dalglish fella's gonna be like?

The young Glaswegian, Celtic's Parkhead Prince, soon to be King of Anfield, answered the question early in the tight 0–0 draw. The ball played through looked a lost cause. We wanted a show of strength. From Old Firm TV clips, we knew he had guile. The situation read 60/40 in Alex Stepney's favour. It was only the Charity Shield . . . yeah, but it was Man U we were playing. Though Keegan had been idolised he'd have played the English gent and jumped the goalie. The Liverpool supporters held breath. The Glasgow boy went in with a solid steel Liverbird on his chest, crunching the ageing United idol. Scottish steel with a laser-beam eye, eh. And flair, boy did this fair-haired, Jock kid have flair. Kenny boy, Kenny boy; from the golden locks and golden vision, to the rump that could hold off a herd of slide-tackling elephants, it was love at first sight.

On the field of play – crunching tackle apart – the season's opener had shown nothing spectacular. Out on the sun-drenched streets of north-west London, meanwhile, something not so headline-grabbing but just as important to my little crew, and anybody else who held interest in footy culture, came the emergence of a new terrace style and attitude that would send the Bootboys back through their own centre parts to AirWair armchairs and Blow Wave Valley for good. Roughly a hundred boys sat atop those Wembley steps, as thousands of Mancs and Scousers walked the stadium concourse exhibiting their own piece of denim flair. Soon to become a young Scouser's match ID, if the new kids in the togs were northerners, like the rest of the Wembley masses then, they must have arrived in London via northern Mars, because, like Ziggy's Spiders, they were way off-kilter with the rest of the summery throng.

A week later we organised a meet on Lime Street's platform nine to catch a 'Special' for the season's opener. Usually jumping an 'ordinary' British Snail train, pulling the Boro first game – with the gaff being on-top central and us standing out . . . a bit – we concluded it would be good to meet up with all these young cool-arses on a more regular basis. Special it was. Queuing for the ancient, nit-seated choo-choo, Saturday morning, it seemed Liverpool had two different mobs: the hard-faced, Anny Road kids in the togs and the older Bootboy faithful in the flares. No one wore colours. Captain Crinkly Dick, on Lime Street plod patrol, squinted a watchful eye under his cap. He'd train-jailed me in the buffet cage a couple of times last season. He knew we were all bunkers. But Crinkly would let you breathe a bit, he wasn't like Sergeant Flatnose, or Blackbeard who'd have the leather gloves on the moment they smelled Jaffa Cake crumbs. Whatever, we were all buzzing. I mean, fucksake, we were English and European champions!

The King of the Jungle – now King of the Kop – made his full league debut at Ayresome Park, Middlesboro, or, as we called it, Ayresome fuckin' trouble! A week or so after that oh-so-comfy Charity Shield game against the Mancs, I got tailed and chased through Middlesboro's mad precinct after Kenny did the damage. Happy with a 1–1 draw, but unhappy to see a hundred of Boro's worst loons flapping their family tent kecks in our tailwind, they seemed over-eager to let us see the season in with a few souvenir bruises on board. It was a long chase from the ground, past the park, through the Loony Tunes precinct to the station. Try as they might to catch us, they had no chance with pants full of wind and shoes that had blocks of ice cream for soles. Thank fuck we were a European city and knew about Adidas. It was still a relief to enter the subway to the station, but with no snack bar and, no dough to pay if there was one, we took the Cadbury's Fruit and Nut machine for the ride home. You could only take the piss in short bursts at the Boro; linger too long in the locals' gaze and soon enough that shopping precinct could turn into a football Alamo.

Those *Jackanory* hoolie books, especially the 'cor blimey guv'nor' ones, try and make out they always took an SAS mob up north and chased and battered everyone who didn't have blond streaks and Goodyear earrings like they did. Thing is, come opening day and, on most other days at the Boro, our crew was in the real SAS. See, we were all part of the Serious Arse Shufflers contingent, as we made sure we got back to the station in one piece. I was a sixteen-year-old rag-arse from Liverpool, but already wise to the fact that Boro was like 'little Liverpool,' concerning hard-case faces. Fuck that Alamo lark for a game of soldiers; it was too early in the season for a lumpy barnet.

Our new number seven started stroking the ball home in front of thousands of delirious Kopites, while three to four hundred lads stood down at the Anfield Road end of the ground clocking the empty visitors' section, clocking each others' clobber and atti-tude, and, it seemed, only half of them being bothered to clock the pitch when our opponents scored a forlorn consolation goal, just to see if anybody cheered. Newcastle at home, midweek, and Kenny nearly burst the net as the Kop exploded. West Brom, days later, he was at it again. We were on the march. Me, I was one of the marching legions that loved the footy, the clobber and the two-fingers-up attitude. Like all the legions, I'd seen the King and craved more.

Clocking Kenny Instead of Clocking On

Landing an engineering apprenticeship at Kirkby Industrial Estate – a huge, Scouse overspill on the outskirts of Liverpool – me da, clocking my impassive glare, said I was supposed to be overjoyed. I wasn't; I was chokka! Starting as can lad on thirteen nicker a week was barely enough to keep my Cornflake, Vimto and Jaffa Cake addictions on the go. With clobber, footy trips and weekend benders on the Anny Road End on the agenda, making money in and around the game was an entrepreneurial must. The apprenticeship that would *supposedly* one day feed me and a mortgage had me steel-toecap-keen for the first two months. Once I could ride that big, fuck-off bike with thirty sausage dinners on board and had free chippy dinners and shop commission boxed off – seeing as I was giving these gaffs the newspaper, ciggy and lunchtime business of a hundred-strong workforce – my main apprenticeship: the how to get around Europe and into stadiums on a Jaffa Cake crumb, went into swerve-the-clippy overdrive.

Before Kenny had curled in twenty beauties, I had a full City and Guilds in stadium turnstile, players' entrance and train and boat manoeuvres. Before Chrimbo '77, I knew Lime Street station and Channel Port timetables better than the fed up clippies who worked for British Snail and the Sloppy Shipping lines. Dover, Folkstone and Felixstowe all had crossings, so, to avoid face recognition we regularly swapped ports. My one-year passport, folded to quarter size, started looking like a piece of used bog roll with a photo on. Mr Evans, the Coventry-supporting boss, dragged me into his office to discuss my attendance, meaning, my adversity in attending. First year in graft I took twenty-two weeks off for football-related illnesses. My GP, another Red loon-ball, made sure I received a detailed letter to get sick pay, providing he got every matchday programme and the ticket stubs he collected. Mad eh! All those sick notes were really double-click notes to make sure I was in attendance wherever the Redmen played. Good job the union (TGWU) had power, because once I'd learned to ride the huge factory bike and squeeze me some dinner, the little Irish underboss, Pat McCann, tried shipping me out pronto. And, all because I kept going on Transalpino walkabouts! Mind you, he was a bitter Blue, seeming to resent that while I was in Europe scratching a living with the Reds, he was on the shop floor scratching his ball sack with the Blues. Boro game onwards, for a load of rag-arse Reds from Bootle, Huyton, Kirkby, Kensington, Scotty, Breck, Noggsie, Crocky, Waterloo, Netherley, Speke and Halewood, boy, were we on one!

After our home wins we ended up in Birmingham, where the biggest rock fight since Freddie Flintstone tried to outdo Barney Rubble in the cave-conservatory stakes took place between opposing supporters throughout the game. If you wanted to watch King Kenny and the footy, there was a good chance you wouldn't notice the large piece of crumbling terrace heading straight for your eye socket. The young rag-arses of Liverpool threw everything they could get their hands on, including a demolished tea bar, at the punks and car mechanics of Brum. The spiky-haired petrol attendants returned the concrete compliment in full.

Few weeks later, Leeds away, and the bootboys and young smoothies were at it again. Leaving Elland Road after a fine victory, two hundred Liverpool bootboys attacked a two-hundred-strong mob of younger Road End smoothies, who they must've mistaken for a Leeds gay-rights march. How those mad fuckers hugged and laughed when the recognition switch got turned on. Leeds's fans had been singing Queer, Faggot and Arse-bandit songs all afternoon to the Red rag-arse contingent, but no way did we think our own people would attempt a mass ambush in the car park. With the great trouser divide getting wider, or narrower, whichever way you wore your strides, and homophobia still living in San

Francisco, their mob grew smaller by the week as our motley crew multiplied into the Sicilian match Mafia. This crew had no gangster Gambinos but a horde of football bambinos, with the average age being about seventeen. The Kopite–Road End confrontation in the Yorkshire hills was a defining, time-standing-still moment, alright.

With Europe fast approaching, dough fast departing and Scouse bootboys fast diminishing, I thought about how I could make a few quid extra – within the parameters of my job, of course. Believe me, as I entered the Road End for the League Cup game against Coventry, prior to Christmas, I knew I was lucky to be in collar. On a freezing cold, foggy night, Coventry brought one of the first big mobs to Anfield. They all seemed to be wearing sheepskin coats. Being a skint Red fanatic, I was up on the fence in nothing but a Fred Perry, trading the usual insults with the opposition support. Jumping up and down on the partition fence, singing my heart out to keep warm more than anything, 65 minutes in, among the mist and sheepies, I noticed Mr Evans, the boss of the firm, eyeing me square on across the fence. Leaping down into a mob of our lads, 'Fucksake,' I'm thinking, 'I'm bound to get sacked now!' Hoping he wouldn't have a cob on in work next day, I was almost glad the jammy bastards got a 2–2 draw.

First trip overseas, I tasted my first foreign jug. Getting collared with no ticket to ride, no passport and no dough aboard a Russia-bound rattler, I was cuffed and led through the streets like a kid caught stealing a loaf in Dublin a hundred years ago. On our way to Dresden, East Germany, I got as far as Antwerp in Belgium. With all the dark, gothic buildings of the Belgium port, and black-clothed people abounding, it seemed I'd been locked up in Transylvania with Desk-Sergeant Dracula keeping dixie. Fangs like golf tees, with no front railings, the Dracula version of a gummy Belgian held the keys to my near future. While he'd lost his front peggies, I lost almost a stone, as the Belgian sarnies they brought me for three days smelled like a pensioner's drawers on a tube train in summer. Unable to touch the bloody meat, never mind chew it, meant a diet of bruised apples, mouldy bread crust and serial weight loss. Being a twenty-eight-inch waist meant my Belgian version of a Slimfast diet – no milkshakes but loads of headaches – did me no good at all, as my kecks fell down all the way back to Liverpool.

Few weeks later and we were off to Keegan's Hamburg for the Super Cup final. Fast Eddie seemed keener than usual, waffling on and on about the red-lighted Reeperbahn while stood in the Road End at the home game before we hit the white cliffs. Mentioning the Beatles and how they all caught ball-ache in Hamburg almost twenty years ago, I asked Eddie could he warble and was he bringing his guitar? I further enquired, seeing as the Fab Four had at least twanged their way to some press-up practice, how was he gonna pay to get a pair of suspenders wrapped around his back?

We bunked it all the way there and back on a diet of strange, German white chocolate, Jaffa Cakes and whatever lager we could drink, wherever they'd let you run up a tab before burning off without paying. Hours before the game, bleary-eyed and blitzed, we escaped the booze bill by falling out of the pay-as-you-leave Bierkeller onto tandem bikes that the locals had parked outside. Dodging Volkswagens, Mercs and BMs for a mile or so, laughing, we crashed into a hot-dog stall and each other somewhere in the city centre. Losing Fast Eddie along the way, we never saw him again till Liverpool. Joey O' reckoned Eddie, who was even skinnier than me, kept falling down those wider European drains. In any town we got fed, whether it was Co-Op crumbs or restaurant runners, but once aboard the boat or train, it was bunk, bunk, bunk and concentration-camp meals. In other words: get in the bogs and forget about the scoff.

Arriving home starved after a 1–1 draw and a twenty-four hour travel, with a waistline like a candy-floss stick and a belly emptier than Tranmere's ground, I begged me ma and da for chippy money. Not too happy about my latest disappearing act they paid up in the end. Though they had a nark on, they didn't want their son, like Fast Eddie, to slither down a hole in the floor.

Soon it was Chrimbo, and me ma, thank god, fattened me up

like the turkey she bought off the woollyback farmer a mile or two the back of Kirkby. Katie, the Liverpool Lou I'd been seeing, told me she liked the meatier version much better, inviting me to her family's New Year's Eve bash up in sunny Speke. 'Fuck that!' I'm thinking, 'It's miles away'. So I went to Newcastle instead. With only a few hundred making the trip, and with loads of us dressed in Christmas togs, we looked like a Freemans-catalogue day out. The Geordies we spoke to through the trouser divide told us what great, differently dressed fans we were, then, steamed into us outside. It was one of those things a lot of Liverpool supporters – the ones who didn't go away every week – didn't understand. Football gypos, like me and me brethren, were getting more organised to save a hiding, but being New Year's Eve everyone got drunk 'n' disorganised and had to mingle all the way back to the station – yet again.

King Kenny doubled our winning scoreline in the 89th minute, meaning the local giants turned double-nasty. It was easy to walk unnoticed with the crowd outside St James' Park, as most Geordies seemed to be seven-foot-high-broccoli eaters and, with me not fully grown yet, skint and still on the Jaffa Cake diet, nobody could see me anyway. I had what you might call a quiet, mingling, early New Year's Eve, till we got to the train and a Scouse football party erupted into the night. Katie from Speke didn't speak to me no more. But, I didn't give a shite; that girl must've been bathing in exhaust fumes from the nearby Ford plant, as she had a better muzzy than our new signing, Graeme Souness.

The season, fast turning into the new clobber wearers on speed, bounced along. The attitude, the excitement, the clothes and music: it all felt different. And, as they say in the Liverpool French quarter of Bootle Le Strande, *Vive la difference*! Everywhere we went, the local football populace gawped, some in admiration, some with intent and some in awe – seriously. Joey O', making the most, had gotten himself a suzzy-wearing supporter in almost every town. Other footy studs followed suit. I didn't do too badly but most of the time couldn't be arsed spending a whole away-match morning with Rita from Sheffield just for the sake of a Thomas the Tank.

Chelsea in the Cup punk-rocked in; we got punk-rocked out. While the Chelsea punks tried to get at the Bowie freaks – that's what they were calling us – we were busy trying to get at the Kings Road shops. The Kicker shop got mass-raided as twenty pairs of tattered trainees got left behind. Stadium battles, laughs and street violence abounded all day. Bootboys onto young smoothies got replaced in London by Punks and highlighted blonds onto young smoothies. Fifteen minutes before kick-off we'd had to jib into the Shed End, but it was obvious after five minutes that among the Chelsea donkey jackets, chains and earrings, our little crew looked like a Mod band at a heavy-rock festival – time to bunk out!

Back in work, Monday, Mr Evans asked me if I'd been anywhere near the Stamford Bridge shenanigans, Saturday: 'Of course,' I replied, to his annoyance. Being contracted for a full four-year apprenticeship and a paid-up part of the union, I was past caring.

Arsenal in the semi-final of the League Cup had some of the worst match shenanigans ever seen at Anfield. Then, after the final replay against Forest, at Old Trafford, the streets lit up like bonfire night as hundreds went on a Manchester rampage when Forest were given a spot kick a mile and a half outside the box.

Good thing about the previous, drawn Wembley League Cup final against Forest: it allowed us a decent once-over of the stadium where the European Cup final was to be played a month or two later. Did I know we were gonna get there? Course I did. It seemed everybody was killing for Liverpool to lose, including the up-and-coming, anti-union milk-snatcher party, her political allies and success-starved woollybacks from Aberdeen to Plymouth. We didn't care. We were European and English champions and by far the greatest team in the land. It's an awesome feeling at the footy – truly awesome – you know, when you know you're the best. Funny thing was: dressing differently, with cockiness abounding, we felt the same on the streets and terraces; so, there you go . . .

Getting a bye – yeah, a bye – in the first round of Big Ears, we drew Dresden, where I reached that Antwerp jail somewhere near Transylvania. Benfica in the quarters came next and me and me snorkel were killing to get there. The convo went like this:

Mr Evans: 'You're not thinking of time off for Benfica are you Mr Allt?'

'Err, no Mr Evans. I've got a college exam for day release to revise for.'

'That's what I need to hear. You finally seeing sense?'

'Yeah, me da's been on me case about getting time-served.'

'Glad to hear it, boy!'

He was a decent fella, Mr Evans. Though past caring, he at least deserved a polite blag. But I'd have told him anything to keep me in collar and let me get to see the King. Slightly damaging a couple of college lathe machines, by acting the turner/miller, sounded like a good idea to get sent home from work so, blowing them up is what I did. I hated those coolant-spitting, toolmaking, acne-fabricating machines. They were to blame for half the zits on my forehead and neck. I wanted revenge. It didn't work. The engineering teacher said they were faulty anyway, insured, and I'd done the college a favour, as now they'd get new ones.

Our place, manufacturing forklift trucks, gave me a choice of engineering professions. I still hadn't made my mind up into which trade I'd wade. On day release I tried my hand at being an electrician. Useless with that fiddly, mathematical, wiring stuff, I almost committed hari-kari when I purposely electrocuted myself to get that precious little doctor's note. The lecturer found me leaning against a desk, shaking uncontrollably, like Elvis in *Jailhouse Rock*, with voltage surging through my Samba, Levi's and Fred Perry all the way up Rice Lane to Walton hospital. The hospital sent me to my own GP with an 'electric limp'. Jokingly he asked me to be more careful as he didn't want his programme and match-stub source to end.

Doing or saying anything to not get sacked and get the match, while secretly hating the whole, oily engineering game, I blamed Shankly, Paisley, even Billy Liddell, who'd jibbed it years before

I was born. But I'd blame anyone; fact was: I was a holes-in-me-undies football smackhead! Only Liverpool smack, though. I wouldn't cross the road for a needle jab of anything else. If I needed an LFC fix, I'd sell me ma's last two Lladros to take a trip to Limey or Dover. Any blag would do. Older lads returning from St Etienne the year before told tales of battlement, clobber shops and French brass gaffs. I'd missed Dresden and Benfica away and been to every other game. Once the Portuguese had been walloped and we drew Moenchengladbach in the semi, they'd have had to chain me to a bunk bed in Rhyl Castle with a waltzer-size lock to keep me away from Dusseldorf.

Plans got drawn to see how and when we'd go. They went like this: get a bag and I'll see you at Lime Street, nine o'clock, Monday. Reaching Limey, no one had a proper bag. I wore two pairs of undies, allowing me to throw one away after they'd gone Sunblest crusty. After lashing my singing socks through the train window somewhere in Europe, I'd stopped wearing them altogether. Joey O' sported a Marksy's carrier bag with eight tins of ale, a cushion from his ma's couch and a change of socks and underwear inside. Asking him about the cushion, he goes, 'It's so I can get me head down on the boat.' I told him, 'As if!' Little Whacker had a tiny, Christmas-cracker screwdriver set, for bunking matters – that was it. Fast Eddie had ale, socks and toothpaste, but no cushion. Two from four had passports. Mine had finally fallen to bits in the washing machine. It didn't matter. You could get a photo at a booth, fill in a form and get a five-day pass at Victoria station. Liverpool to Euston was a simple 'in the bog' bunk; the tube to Victoria, 'double-click', easier. Whacker, with his freckles, looked fourteen, but he still got a five-dayer.

Getting to Dover, we had an 'in' on the staff gangplank, as Billy Two Bob, a Toxteth Red, had a brother who worked aboard (everyone in Liverpool had a sailor/seafarer relation). Being ticketless, we'd kept our heads down reaching the boat. Aboard the good ship *Ragarse*, with the Reds-a-rocking, our profile went up and we openly buzzed. If there'd been four headworkers aboard the train, there were three hundred aboard the boat. Queuing for a nosebag, it seemed nobody wanted to pay. Chicken Kievs and Captain's fish pies, followed by apple crumbles and trifles, passed from queue to table, side-swerving the till. The cook was a Scouse Joey from Walton who turned a Stevie Wonder to the chips 'n' gravy train, but, soon as El Capitano showed face, he winked, pulled the shutter down and scarpered from view. Half an hour later the bar and duty free were also closed. Passenger complaints to the stewardess fell on deaf ears. The staff locked themselves away, writing the crossing off as a private football function. With a huge 'Walk On' taking place and party packs of ale and sarnies being passed about, we didn't need them open. An elderly couple, squashed into a sleeping bag like a wrinkly, double hot dog, tried to sleep, asking everybody to stop singing. Within minutes, can-in-hand, they were along with the throng. The party sailed into the night, and, as morning broke and Ostend station prepared for three hundred Dusseldorf-bound Scousers, age-old bunkers' questions got asked: 'Where do we get dough?' And 'Where do we get scoff?' Answered by me: 'Fucking nowhere in Ostend at five in the morning!'

Thinking on his feet, Joey O' came up with a bastard of a bunker's blag about migraine headaches and sleep you can't be woken from. Borrowing train tickets from some Liverpool lads, we searched for the guard. Traipsing the length of the quarter-of-a-mile-long European rattler, with the lights of Ostend dancing upon Channel breakers, we caught up with El Stricto Guardo. 'Hello, Monsieur, you speak English?'

Confused, he clocked us.

Little Whacker spoke up: 'Alright big balls. This is the right train to get to Dusseldorf, Germany, yeah? Well see, our mate suffers with severe, mental headaches and the lad needs to sleep without disturbance or, he could die! Thing is, we all look after him, so clip our tickets now so we can get our heads down, then you won't have to wake him, or us – understand-ay? You speak English-ay, yeah?'

El Stricto's answer was abrupt: 'Non!'

'What do you mean "non"? No can clip tickets or no can speak English?'

'*Non!*'

'Err . . . when's the train leaving then?'

'*Non!*'

'Err, alright, what time do we get to Dusseldorf?'

'*Non!*'

'Fucksake, is that the only word you know?'

Whacker and Joey O' walked off up the platform muttering something about how they should at least have an English-speaking guard where British people disembark for the rest of Europe. I interrupted them. 'Come 'ed, I'm goosed anyway. We'll kip under the seats.'

Most seats were mounted on wooden boxes. If you unscrewed the front or side panel, you could crawl inside and your mate could screw it back. Little Whacker's tiny screwdriver set made light work of the panels, with me being the only one not screwed back in. Unable to handle the claustrophobic train coffin and years of accumulated passenger dirt, I was happy to leave the front panel off, sticking a carrier bag across the front. Little Whacker had no such problems. Once screwed in he'd have slept all the way to Moscow if you didn't give him a shout.

Getting to 'the Dorf' without any real clippy swerving, we headed straight for the hospital to give blood. Getting paid at the door, we dashed back to town to rejoin the party and replace a pint of blood with a few pints of Dusseldorf Delight. Like most German cities the Dorf was a great place to spend your blood money. First night, we kipped in a hospital bed. Noticing an empty ward after giving blood, closed off by a sign printed in sausage language, we crept back in that night, with single bed mattresses still in place. If I've ever caught some unknown disease, it was that night. Next day, we copped for sleeping bags hanging up outside a camping shop, before drunkenly entering Dusseldorf library near closing time. Stashing the sleeping bags behind the biggest German history books on offer – probably the ones written about small muzzies and greasy quiffs – we left a window slightly open, bunked into the match, got bevvied on some strong Hoffenbrau honch and returned to the open window to snore and fart for England. Noting no alarm in the part of the library we aimed to sleep in, we made more noise than the Moenchengladbach fans earlier that evening.

Though we'd been beaten 2–1, David Johnson put Borussia on the back foot by scoring a vital away goal in the 88th minute. Staying on the back foot, Borussia got walloped 3–0 at Anfield two weeks later in the second leg, with the King on the score-sheet once again. We didn't take much notice of the Anfield game; our party had started two weeks before after the away defeat. We knew we were through. With the King, Jimbo Case, Mighty Emlyn, Souness and a bouncing Kop we felt invincible and that nobody could beat Liverpool at home in the European Cup.

Returning from the Dorf after the first leg, the German rattler to Ostend, naturally, was a party train, meaning bunking was can-in-the-hand easy. Reaching the boat, me and Joey O' took our usual walk right around the port terminal building – the part where trainees with good grips and decent climbing agility were required passports – and clambered onto the side of the white-cliffs-bound boat. It was rocking. It looked like we were in our second European Cup final on the bounce. Billy Two Bob's brother made sure the party swung by sorting himself an on-board, half-price, amber-nectar agreement. Twenty miles from Belgian breakers, half-price became too much, when the drinkers demanded free juice and the journey turned pirate. Firstly, the boat got part-hijacked. Secondly the duty-free shop got ravaged. Thirdly, the crew's wages, including Two Bob's brother's, went west from the captain's office. Fourthly, to rub salt in old seafarers' wounds, the Liverpool supporters took down the ship's flag and raised their own. Oh, and finally, reaching the English side of the Channel, it was all rocky white cliffs, drunken white faces and waiting white stripes. Looking a bit portside, bang on top, it seemed half the southern police force stood at Dover Docks waiting to haul everybody into their dark-blue fishing nets. Even though I hadn't stolen a Juicy Fruit wrapper, Two Bob's kidder, surpris-ingly bearing no grudges, steamed to the upper-deck, warning people they were about to be collared, cuffed and questioned.

And me, I listened. Leaving via the staff gangplank, with it raining perfume, cigarettes and alcohol, I dodged the downpour, white stripes and Port Authorities, catching a fast train home to get back for graft next day.

Following morning, riding the big bike to the shops, morning papers stated loads were arrested. My workmates knew where I'd been but, Mr Evans, and his second-in-command, Everton's Pat McCann, being busy with a huge forklift order, still hadn't twigged, till some fitter/turner grass let them know where their travelling apprentice had been the last few days. Even worse, this jealous fool on the tools was forever making out what a big, boss Red he was. He probably resented the fact that I would not let any nine-to-five or cash constraints hold me down, thereby stopping them from turning me into another lip-driven oil slick like him. I won't name and shame him, but he looked like a greasier version of Shaggy from *Scooby Doo*, with a pimple-ridden kipper of forty skinheads on a raft.

Medals, Gear And Laughs . . . Every Time

Few weeks later, with Notts Forest crowned champions and eight-nicker specials to the final advertised everywhere, my brother and I ventured to Upton Park, West Ham, where they had to beat us to stay up. It sounded like a nice, sunny day out, and along with our mates from Kensington (Stevie Metcalfe, Gary Ryan, Tony Cooper and Anthony Garragoss) we didn't want to ruin our hundred-per-cent league. Not wanting to get sussed and battered, Stevie and Gary wore flares and pollyvelt shoes (cheese pasties with laces) so they could mingle with the West Ham fans. They were all sixteen, and this was one naughty ground to openly wear your Samba and snorkel. Telling me and our kid we were brave wearing our normal Scouse rig-outs, they didn't realise it was the only clobber we had. My wardrobe contained two snorkels – one green, one blue – one black Harrington, three Fred Perrys and a pair of Mamba, Bamba, Samba and Kickers. You couldn't change your Scouse ID with that collection, but, turn a snorkel inside out, with the orange lining on show, you transformed into a match steward or a NASA spaceman. Meanwhile, the tartan-lined Harrington worn inside out made you look like a lunatic Jock or a tablecloth. Standing out so much, with violent grounds abounding, I'd used both to escape the football-hooligan squads. The snorkel-lined spaceman look got you a walkover always. No home fan suspected anybody of mingling among them with a coat looking like that.

One fella who'd struggle to mingle with a crowd was Liverpool's own fiery-haired super-sub, Davy Fairclough. When the flame-top was in the mood and spinning, he had the ability to walk past defenders as if they were scared of getting singed by his hair. Sadly, for West Ham, the flame-top was spinning. Cutting to Davy's sprint, we were runners-up and didn't have to win so, Ginger ran amok and we did, leaving the Hammers sunk.

Leaving Upton Park I wished I had Stevie's flares on. Thinking Liverpool would ease up with the European Cup final in view, they took it as serious shooting practice for the big one, sending West Ham fans mental to second-division doldrums. Outside the stadium it was bedlam and doldrums; into the doldrums – but bedlam – if you get me twang. Bunking to the front of the huge end-of-game queue that normally forms outside Upton Park tube station, Cockney voices yelled at me to get in line. Looking up, I could see more than a few Scousers grinning among them.

Locked outside, about a hundred and fifty Liverpool lads had been running around West Ham's ground for most of the first half. Giving up on a mass bunk-in, with nobody to terrorise due to close Bizzie attendance, they gave up and hit the West End shops. With the Hammers traipsing home to lower-division dreams, the first Liverpool rattler out of Euston was a House of Fraser on wheels – with a pre-European Cup final party in full swing. Oh well, fair dos: they had a glut of jobs and earrings, while we had a stack of cheap clobber and football glory. An economist or true capitalist would say jobs, money and earrings always, but I was a footballist and sentimentalist, so I'd choose medals, gear and laughs every time.

The city was alight for our second Big-Eared final on the bounce. Meanwhile, I was slightly down-hearted. After the glorious triumph of Rome every smiling Scouser who'd witnessed the thousands of chequered flags in Italy wanted a piece of the pasta. Tickets were as scarce as Queen Lizzie dipping into her purse to buy a pint of milk. Being a footy gypsy, I wanted over the seas and far away, not another trip to Lizzie's front garden. Good thing about a Wembley final, though: no doctor's note needed, just a one-day bunk out.

Out bevvying with the lads one night, just prior to the final, I noticed a huge queue forming outside an old building in town. Thinking the final tickets were on sale, I traipsed over. Up close people were lying in sleeping bags all over the paving stones. Frustrated, I shouted what the fuck was going on, and why didn't I know about the ticket sale? Startling me, a nailed-on hippy, looking like he hadn't had a scrub since Woodstock, with a sharp likeness to the Cookie Monster from *Sesame Street*, stuck his matted head out of a rainbow sleeping bag to complain about the noise. Asking him what tickets were on sale, he replied, 'Bob Dylan. Now fuck off and keep the noise down!'

His eyes opened a little further when I asked, 'Who the fuck's Bob Dylan?' With mates pressuring me to jump a taxi to the next boozer, I told them I'd follow on and took a concrete seat next to No Soap as he went into detail about the world's greatest songwriter. Telling him about Bob Marley, The Clash and The Jam, he told me he knew about Bob Marley, but the other two sounded like *Starsky and Hutch* episodes. Being funny, I liked him straight away. That week I listened to *Blonde on Blonde* and *Desire*, my first ever Dylan albums, borrowed from an older neighbour. I agreed with the Cookie Monster in full.

On European Cup final Wednesday I rose from the flock to the sound of chiming bottles and a whistling milkman. It was the earliest I'd ever got up for work. Clocking on early doors, I went all dizzy, catching Euro flu off me clocking-in card a minute later. Free from drab collar, we were roaring down the M6 at nine bells. Me da, his mates and half of Liverpool were going on the ale all day in London. Me and our kid were happy to cadge a lift. Relaxed in his tasty Dolomite Sprint, thinking, 'Yes, Wembley early, no bunking, get to Euston and meet the boys,' the engine blew up at Hilton Park. Leaving his wheels behind, we had to try and hitch to London. His mates, none-the-wiser to our plight, had batted on. Half-panicking, we told him we'd cry our eyes out and never forgive him if we never made the final. He told us to shut our moaning gobs and to get our thumbs out pronto. Being a hard-shouldered urchin of the motorways, it felt weird hitching with me da. Without too long a wait, a football-loving, London-bound lorry driver squeezed us in and dropped us bang in the middle of the West End . . . still early.

Forgetting the Euston meet, walking straight to Trafalgar Square for the Red congregation, I parked my arse outside the National Art Gallery. With a decent viewing range, I caught sight of Eddie, Joey O' and Little Whacker among hundreds of young Road Enders. Most didn't have tickets, scurrying about trying to find touts or tourists with briefs to bump. Being like-minded, I made my way over. Walking down the steps, I became conscious that my mohair jumper seemed too blue, cumbersome and out of place. Exchanging greetings with the boys, the whole of Trafalgar Square was decked in red. Huge flags and banners hung from lions, columns and the walls of the square. One showed the picture of a Liverbird chomping on trophies with the heading 'Here we go gathering cups in May'. Another read 'We are not English, we are Scouse'. Fast Eddie, looking half-asleep as usual, hardly looked up, giving the merest of nods. Joey O', openly buzzing and full of life, clambered all over me like a stun-gunned ray of sunshine. Joey O' was a fella who microwaved people. What a brilliant, in-your-face character he was. For us two, *football days out* had become our drug of choice. Meanwhile, Little Whacker gave his normal lopsided grin that always had me feeling sorry for him. He had the features of an urchin street child, relaying malnutrition stories about how the kid should still be at his mother's nipple, getting milk and vitamins to help him expand and maybe put some colour among his madly freckled face.

Early talk was of how hot it was, how Bruges had no mob and, hardly any fans at all. But, on a good note, touts were apparently among the throng. Our 23,000 allocation was nowhere near enough for the 70–80,000 who wanted in. With capacity set at 92,000 and Bruges fans hardly making the trip, the back-slapping UEFA officials had once again kicked our fans in the teeth, while making sure fair-weather, pinstriped friends and parasitic touts had a fine day. Far as we were concerned, touts were for the taking.

Strolling back to Soho, we found the Marquee and some other punk clubs among the stinking sex dens. An old Liverpool saying stated the streets of London were paved with gold but stank of rats' piss. If that was so, then the streets of Soho were paved with brass and smelled like sewers of sperm. With a fishy whiff abounding, a street fight had already erupted outside one of the neon-signed peep shows. About twenty Scousers, wearing colours, were having a ding-dong battle with some flesh-den doormen. Two suzzy-wearing prostitutes came up the stairs, chased by two Liverpool lads. All of them ran straight to the heart of the porn brawl. Grabbing the brass by the hair, one of the chasing lads violently swung her round, maypole-style. Showing such lack of restraint, he'd clearly been robbed blind. Taking his lead, after he yelled instruction, the rest of the crew upped their violent attack. The ten or so doormen backed off, eventually squeezing down the same grotty hole in the ground the brasses had just emerged from. The piss-stained door got pelted and rammed with flagpoles, chairs and tables till Officer Brass Patrol showed face and twenty lads disrobed colours, silently melting into the background.

Nearby, a new-wave record shop held a large display of twelve-inch, Day-Glo punk singles. Little Whacker, eyes lighting up like a tramp-child in a toy store, went in and got the fella to show him the most colourful Jam, Clash and Pistols singles. Minutes later the door clanged open, and urchin freckles bounced out and down the road with an armful of music on board. The hot afternoon sun was predictably getting under a few collars, as the tinted-red West End vibrated and pulsed to a northern football beat. We didn't see the record-robbing Speedy Gonzales again till sat outside Her Majesty's two-up, two-down (crowns to wear downstairs watching telly, and crowns for upstairs in bed so they need never feel normal). Crowns apart, record robbers indeed!

Under a dazzling London sun the West End crowds heaved and weaved as a procession of banner-carrying Liverpool supporters, headed by two fellas holding a half-street-wide banner proclaiming 'We are the European champions', sang and danced. Suddenly, as if the banner united the passing throng and illuminated the more disguised Liverpudlians among the West End swarms, a small carnival atmosphere erupted into Gerrard Street and Chinatown. Chinese-restaurant workers, nattering idly in doorways, witnessed the carnival. 'Let's all go to Wembley, let's all go to Wembley, la la la la, la la la la.' Performing the hokey-cokey, they dragged passers-by to the centre of the shindig. Some Chinese people, wearing cooks', waiters' and waitresses' outfits, were prised from doorways, linked and brought to the dance.

Stood gawping nearby, an ice cream dripping raspberry sauce appeared in my face from nowhere. A soft voice implored me to take a lick. Glancing sideways, a beautiful young black girl ran her tongue seductively across glossy, swollen lips. She sounded public-school posh. She was a hot 'n' tot alright. Her less attractive but still stunning white girlfriend urged me to 'try it, go on, take a lick' in more of a Bow Bells cockney accent. Dipping her tongue provocatively into raspberry sauce atop of the cone, her shimmering, long black hair, blown by a passing summer breeze, blew across and onto my face. She smelled coconut good. Within seconds my mind left the football carnival and wandered to some far-off exotic country, with me and these two inside Sheik Your Money's Caravan of Love. Fucksake, I mightn't have had a banner or flag for the carnival, but I was carrying the best flagpole. My face quickly turned redder than any final rosette of the day. For the briefest I'd died and gone to raspberry heaven. Clocking the black girl's eyes, she definitely wasn't in London. Her friend: likewise. The two of them looked like they were afternoon tripping. Still drug naïve, I knew the difference between someone who walked the cobbled streets of London and someone who walked the wild side of litmus paper. Out in the open, they openly teased me. 'No shame, these two,' I'm thinking, followed by thoughts of the Caravan of Love and, whether there was any place like it among the seedy streets of Soho. Urging me again to take a lick, they stuck their tongues simultaneously into the ice cream. Instantly I thought about renting a caravan somewhere nearby Flagpole City. Thing is, in the capital you don't get much of a caravan for one pound fifty.

With the Chinatown carnival gathering pace and people, I asked their names. Putting fingers to my lips, they hushed me, saying it was unimportant, asking again if I was having a lick or not. With my Levi's telling Everest flagpole stories and the sun melting all inhibitions into the London sewers, I motioned to lick the ice cream. The black girl pulled it away, stating it was normally twenty pounds a lick, but seeing as I looked such an innocent young boy, it would only cost ten. My immediate thought was that the ice cream must've been bought in Harrods and why was everything expensive in London? The white girl caressed my back-side and told me to hurry, as they, and it, were melting. I couldn't breathe as the lump in my Levi's rose to my throat. Weeks and months of European football dreams had turned into European porn-star dreams in seconds. About to take a one-pound-fifty gamble and put an end to flagpole hell, the Red carnival heaved into us. Men, women and kids, dressed to the tails in red and white, swept the three of us into their gathering and directly away from each other. The melted ice cream hit the deck and got trampled into the pavement. I felt the same.

Usually the life and soul of any Red party, the hundred or so taking part in this one had just poured a bucket of ice water over me and my undergarments. Battling to get back to the ice-cream girls, the harder I tried, the softer I got and the more they seemed out of reach. Two older Liverpool women started kissing the gob off me, their breath telling whisky stories, pouring more cold water onto any porn-star notions. No question – get me – I had to join the dance, one of those mad, sweep-you-off-your-feet efforts. Already attuned to the notion that the people from my home town had a ferocious appetite to party, I realised on the spot that they also had the strongest headlocks in the country. Thinking I'd ride out the knees-up till I could snatch the ice-cream girls from the street, I bided time.

Stuck in the heart of the jamboree, Eddie and Joey O', arms linked, were hokey-cokeying like two old ladies who'd just taken the bingo for every penny. Clocking the separated ice-cream girls, the black one cavorted divinely, her gorgeous Afro-style hair bouncing all over Gerrard Street. I viewed the white girl's backside sat astride some heavyweight Scouser's back. Riding him like Lester Piggott in a pair of Wranglers, she playfully whipped him with his beloved red scarf. I started to think of what me arl fella had always taught me: he who hesitates never becomes a porn star – well, misses out is what he really used to say, but that's how it rang in my scorched nugget. Catching sight of the white girl, I made a grab, asking her where her friend was. Loosening the man's grip, she struggled free from the piggyback as the fella looked puzzled at my interruption. Unable to find her stunning playmate, she said her name was Yvonne, asking if I wanted to go with her. With the lads out of sight, I told her no. It was the two of them that had stretched me Levi's, and, anyway, I'd heard the rumour about Paul McCartney in his early Beatle days enjoying being the meat in a black and white sandwich. Thinking 'If it's good enough for old Beatle balls, it's got to be triple A for me' made Little Miss Coconut seem like a watered-down way to lose me mates, especially with her and her coconuts starting to look a bit spotty with all the sweating she was doing.

Unable to find the beautiful Miss Hot 'n' Tot, I shouted the lads it was time to get back on the ticket trail. Swinging to the full, it was a difficult knees-up to slope from. Once I knew the ice-cream girls were out of reach, and, hand in pocket, a few flagpole readjustments had taken place – warning me I was ticketless again – it was time to join the wide-awake crew. Strolling from Chinatown, my eyes scanned restaurant doorways and off-street jiggers, and back to the Red riot heaving to and fro. Those ladies of the cone that had given me the bone had disappeared as quick as they'd appeared. Some other Scouse scally, one with a quicker tongue and more dough than me, was probably down one of those dirty stinking jiggers proving to be the press-up king of the north. Bastard!

Weaving through Leicester Square, where a thousand movie stars had strutted a West End wobble for adoring fans and photographers, I thought about the only star that mattered to me: the fella who wore the number seven on the back of his red jersey. Dreaming of him scoring a Cup-final hat-trick, I hoped I'd be returning to this yard tonight to perform my own West End wobble. A party of Bruges supporters walked by; we stopped them by singing our 'Allez, les Rouges' song. As they clapped us on our way, I noted their even greasier fringes, heavy overcoats and piano-key smiles. Fucksake, it was roasting. I logged them as the cold-shouldered, Belgian-hardcore crew. I couldn't help clocking everybody; it was my own compulsive dis-something.

Street traders, doing roaring business in Liverpool colours, got hounded by our little mob, as they often did. 'Cockney beauts, got no team of yer own to sell? Nah – and yer know why? Cos yiss are all shite!'

They laughed, till Joey O' picked up a box of scarves and fled down the street leading to Trafalgar Square, shouting, 'They're our team, so these are our scarves!'

Thinking he'd turn and hand them back, he kept sprinting. Walking slowly on, we caught up with the middle-aged cockney trader bent double, breathing heavily and sweating like Ken Dodd coming home to find his missus had let the council in to put in free loft insulation. He looked up. His face looked like a swollen Arctic Roll. 'He'll bring them back in a minute mate. He's only having a laugh,' I offered.

'I've got angina mate, and a wife and five fackin' kids to feed!'

Sixth sense told me to believe him. Though he had a head like an Arctic Roll, he looked like a true, working-class Arctic Roll. Stooping to ask if he was OK, his fellow trader caught up. Together they were a scruff-bag version of Abbot and Costello. With oily suit pants covered in this morning's fried-egg stains, wrinkly, non-matching suit jackets with betting-office pens in the top pockets and the same cheap, Union Jack T-shirts underneath, they were a comedy duo alright! With the dancing black devil on one shoulder and the tiptoeing white angel on the other, the angel of sixth sense spoke truth. Telling them to wait up, I sprinted to Trafalgar Square. Joey O', already shouting to the massed gathering of Liverpudlians 'Get yer scarves, come on, get yer colours!' had turned trader. Catching him up, I told him about the rag-arse duo in their doss-house suits. Still thinking like a salesman, it took ten seconds to sink in. About to make his first sale, he reluctantly closed the box. Walking back to where the fella was still doubled over, he asked if he was OK.

'Yeah, I'm OK, Scouse. I'd have caught you when I was younger, when I was on Arsenal's books. Anyway, even if me ticker was better, I couldn't run fast in me suit.'

Laughing, Joey O' asked him, 'Why, was you a footballer, mate?'

'Long before you were born, Scouse.'

'Serious? Fuck . . . Don't believe yer!'

His fellow trader piped up. 'Take no notice. He might have taken it up the Arsenal, but that's about it!'

Getting to his feet, cooling down and catching breath, we laughed as he offered us a rosette each. Feeling guilty we pinned the colours to our chests. Each one read 'Liverpool FC: European Champions 1978'. Fully recovered, Eddie asked the arl fella, 'Eh, mate, are you Nostradamus? These are bad luck. It already says champions here.'

'Well, so fackin' what? You're not playing the Arsenal, so you'll win it anyway!'

Smiling, I asked, 'What d'yer mean, not playing the Arsenal?'

'This is about your fourth or fifth bleedin' final in five years, an' we sell at all the big games. You beat Moenchengladbach in '73, Newcastle in '74, Bruges in '76, Moenchengladbach in '77 an' now the Belgians again in '78. In fact the only time youse lot lost was to the Arsenal in '71 . . . see.'

'Eh, he's only right, yer know. Knows his history this fella.' Past midday, Fast Eddie seemed to be waking up.

'Who the fuck rattled your cot, dopey bollocks?' Joey O' took the words from my mouth. The arl fella wasn't exactly right, but, being a character was more important than being right. As they playfully fought, I wished the Abbot and Costello scarf traders well before heading back to the square.

Twin Crowns, Twin Towers, to Win Cups

Once I got past the huge shadow cast by the National Art Gallery, Trafalgar Square opened up. Having left one Red jamboree, we viewed a vast Scouse carnival taking place before our eyes. Sweating, tying my jumper round my waist, I was tempted to join the hundreds of young lads, and a few girls, who'd decided it was cool-down time as they jigged in the fountain. A couple of lads, drunkenly forgetting to strip before bailing into the water, frantically waved match tickets in the air. Thinking they were for sale, Eddie shot over . . . returning seconds later, realising they were trying to dry, not sell. Laughing again, Joey O' slapped him. 'I thought you'd finally woken up!'

Most of the bathers were down to undergarments, with jeans, tops and shoes in bundles around the water's edge. Two or three danced naked, with London plod chasing about, shouting at them to get down. One held a Liverpool flag like a bullfighter, teasing the baying crowd as he exposed himself by pulling it to one side. Each time he did, there was a massive cheer. The cold water had not shrivelled his pink python – it's always the Johnny Big Knobs who wanna get it out for the crowd, isn't it? Another crew of lads, who must've made the same in-pocket mistake, placed money and tickets flat on the pavement to dry while a mate stood guard. Noting the twin towers printed upon those precious little pieces of paper, I knew it was time to get to it.

'Allez, les Rouges' and 'Arrivederci, Roma' rang out, bouncing off the historical buildings surrounding the famous square. Hundreds of tourists stood marvelling at the sight, took photos like football paparazzi. Coach drivers on a go-slow, their passengers' faces jammed to the windows, stared in disbelief as the party gained numbers, strength and noise. Liverpudlians jumped from taxis and buses and came from holes in the floor in swarms, adding ranks to the already heaving throng. Some coaches slowed to a stop, parking alongside. Noting purple and white scarves aboard, I moseyed on over.

Watching intently, The Rottweiler, one of the Breck Road boys, motioned to me as we passed. Walking back, he told me the Jean-Claude standing inside the doorway of number-one coach was an A1 tout. It made sense. Something of a Johan Cruyff lookalike, he seemed to be lapping up the scene, sniffing for opportunity, looking to offload. He'd have to view me as an opportunity, a cock-eyed, more-money-than-sense customer. Trying to look the Bertie Big Balls, impersonating a pound-signed punter, I moved in close. 'Alright, mate, have yer got any tickets to sell?' With me motioning, Jean-Claude stood motionless till more Bertie Big Balls blew his lard fringe aside, revealing the eyelids going ker-ching like a till draw as he scanned me as a sterling opportunity. He was struggling with my accent, so I slowed it down to add a spot of Prince Charles. Inviting me onto the coach to talk shop, it seemed Jean-Claude liked a bit of Charlie.

The rest of the Belgian passengers had stepped from the coach. Huddled together, uneasy about joining the football party in case they got gobbled up by Liverpool fans, they eyed me Adidas to fringe as I stepped aboard. Asking if I was German, he offered a handshake, telling me not to speak so slowly. Stating he had tickets, I began to dream as he wandered to the back of the coach. I followed. Ordering me to wait outside, I glanced over my shoulder, thinking, 'Bossy Belgian tout, this Jean-Claude fella.' Reaching into the overhead compartment, he pulled down a small black bag. With me standing in the doorway but already in twin towers country, he returned, muttering stuff about being a footballer, what tickets I wanted and how much extra I'd have to pay. Noting his shiny, tasselled loafers and my ragged Adidas Samba, I reflected that Liverpool were already 1–0 up. Clocking Jabba the Hutt stuck in the driver's seat, his teeth all mangled and black, with The Rottweiler nowhere to be seen and no Bizzies in attendance, maybe it was 2–0. Bullying me out of the way to sit on a doorway step, I trod backwards till my feet felt the concrete flags that paved all the way to Wembley. Showing me a seated ticket, I balked at the price. With the little black bag grasped in both hands, he stuffed it back inside. Glancing at Jabba the driver, Quality Control at the Belgian chocolate factory, I'd have been surprised if he'd had the energy to indicate, never mind leave his seat. Could be 3–0.

Up on toes, half of me already inside Wembley, I struggled to retain the Bertie Big Balls impersonation. Bringing the black bag to rest on seated legs, he smiled, swivelled, then completely turned his back on me to delve inside. Looking over his shoulder, I briefly smiled back. A treble take of Jabba's lodged frame, the tout's grease-bound barnet and the square . . . SNATCH! I was off . . . Well, I thought I was. Playing tug of war at the foot of the coach doorway, I held sway on the bag. Fighting to grab at the parcel, he screamed for help. Ripping at my clothing, the buttons popped on my Fred Perry as Jean-Claude landed a glancing blow to the side of my head. About to wallop him back, a moment's clarity shot down the tubes. No violence! Unhinging his grip, I kicked him severely below the knee. The moment of clarity had not yet reached my Adidas. Soon as he winced, and the bag was my rugby ball, I stepped a yard from the coach doorway and legged it like Barry John against the English!

Thinking Belgian slip-ons were no match for slippery Samba, I didn't bother with the turbo engines. Looking back, Jean-Claude gave chase. Across the road, The Rottweiler had returned, shouting for me to stop, with his pups clocking me like I was the juiciest bone in the butcher's bin. Dripping from their Trafalgar soak, most of them were still in boxer shorts. Soon they'd be boxing me for a share of the spoils. Turbo time!

With greasy fringe and The Rottweiler and Co. bang on tail, I sprinted towards Soho with one thing in mind: hide out in a manky peep show. Zigzagging through Chinatown, then Soho's dingy streets, hundreds of Liverpudlians stared as I zipped between them trying to lose the trailing pack. Distant voices of people who knew me called out as I passed. Baggy Fannies looking for business were ruthlessly brushed aside as I bobbed and weaved the crowd. Quick over-the-shoulder told me I'd made space. Fifth or sixth black curtain on the block, another beckoning, slutty hostess, another glance back and I entered like a deranged sex case. Choosing the scruffiest-looking sex hovel and hostess, I knew it would be the unlikeliest to check. The girl welcomed me to her world of breakfast-on-frock, while I wondered who on earth would be interested in shagging a brass who couldn't be bothered cleaning spaghetti hoops from her dress. Supposedly in the business of guiding fellas off the street, she needed to guide herself to the first man-sized washing machine – soon as. If robbing tickets from Jean-Claude had placed me on a middle rung of the sleaze-ball ladder, this hostess was not far from the top just by being alive. She stank, the gaff should've been named Little Miss Crab Cakes and the booth I entered was a wood-chipped sperm-bank with a mangy viewing hole.

Getting comfy as possible, I positioned myself and the bag so we didn't touch the walls. Dropping money into the slot, a gigantic omelette of an arse almost blacked out my spying hole. Being widescreen, letter-box size, her bum looked like a massive plate of mash – not massive nice, massive saggy, like she'd been on a charity strip-starve and lost fourteen stone. Her crease-piece could've taken Visa all day, but I wanted the light to shine on my bag of goods. It definitely wasn't shining from her pink rosette. A neon sign told the peepers it was Shirley's shift. Other pervy letter boxes opened up as Shirley took herself and her Fu Yung cheeks for a trudge across the bed. With light flooding in and hope in my heart, I reached inside the bag. Again, her spotty bum played havoc with the light, and I had to move the bag about without touching the infected walls. Bingo! A wad of European Cup-final tickets told me all I needed to know: fifteen in all. The hundred and odd pound, plus some Belgian francs worth about a nifty, were pure bonus. Two passports showed the faces of Jean-Claude Van Tout and some other greasy-fringed Euro dragon who'd ventured from the dentist-hating streets of Belgium. I was ecstatic. Stashing the empty bag under a pile of gluey tissues I used a foot and the roll of money to push and hide. No way could I touch any of that contaminated bollock mush; and I wasn't happy at all about it touching the toe of my beloved Adidas Samba.

Making my way back to the square, I'd been gone under an hour. Walking through Chinatown, stopping at a Willy Wong's wok block, I washed my hands more times than Howard Hughes doing voluntary in a New York soup queue. Using a wad of bog roll, I gave the trainee's white toe a good scrub. Removing my blitzed Fred Perry, I merged with thousands of Liverpool fans thronging the seedy streets. Edging into Trafalgar, I scanned Jean-Claude speaking to two interested London plod. Walking back around the art gallery, I took a new approach that brought Fast Eddie and Joey O' into view. Distancing myself from Plod Patrol, I called a young girl to assist me. Her two friends pushed her in my direction. Telling me her name was Angela, her ribbons, scarf and rosette told football stories, while everything else screamed top-drawer Castle Street queen.

Any lunch hour in Liverpool, the most beautiful girls in the world pour from those stuffy offices, stretching long, suntanned legs in front of the dome-roofed town hall. This one had given her legs the day off to cheer her team in red. If she'd held my hand and guided me back to the peep show, I'd have stuffed all the contents of the black bag into that slot to witness five minutes of her doing the naked bed jive. Explaining why, I asked politely if she'd get the attention of my mates. Walking down the steps to tell them where I stood, she noticed me ogling her gorgeous form. Giggling, she caught my eye, as I nervously muttered some daft joke about Eddie and Joey O'. Gaining their attention, she kept me from Old Bill's viewing range.

Walking back to where I stood, partly hidden, I watched as they stared at Angela's backside swaying a few steps ahead. For mesmerised moments football meant sweet fuck all, as Trafalgar's steps became the Castle Street catwalk. Swallowing hard, an introduction was in order. 'Angela, this is Eddie and Joey O'.'

Joey O' spoke first: 'Where've you been soft lad?'

Then Fast Eddie: 'You been the peep shows?'

Angela shouted her two mates over. Speaking about how we'd all travelled, she pointed out the fidgeting fathers, already giving us the beady eye. Telling me they were short on tickets, I stuffed two into her palm, along with the two foreign passports, which I told her to hand to the Bizzies once I'd left the square. Joey and Eddie stared in disbelief. She returned with the required fiver. At face value, I'd done her a big favour. A hungry tout would've taken her for at least a week's wages. Touts were football wolves in sheepskin clothing. I bang-on hated touts – in fact, almost as much as I hated the FA and football authorities for acting the corporate whore in general. These were the heartless bastards who ordered measly ticket allocations for fanatically loyal supporters, while handing out bundles of preferential treatment and tickets to *other* bloated ties, double-dealing suits and big-game glory-hunters. Well, they could stop me getting match tickets using nepotism, snobbery and power play, but they could never stop me getting in.

Before I'd given her the tickets, Angela had kissed me goodbye on the cheek, with her dad throwing me a look that told me I was a pimp trying to lure her daughter onto the game. Handing him two Cup-final passes, he threw me a second glance that told me, 'Marry my daughter, what a handsome kid you are!' Football fanatics, eh, there were a few of them in Liverpool. Smelling alcohol on Angela's breath, I felt like getting rid of the parentage and friend shackles and hitting a few Covent Garden bars with her hips opening the saloon doors. Stating we'd win, but good luck anyway, she gave a second goodbye and we bid her and her friends farewell. Even the fidgeting fathers offered an amicable wave.

Walking back toward Soho, The Rottweiler turned up like he'd been watching proceedings from the National Gallery roof. Giving him a ticket, I blagged him about how many I'd taken from Jean-Claude, otherwise he'd have yelled and begged for more. A man who looked under starters for violence, like the beady-eyed fathers of Trafalgar, he changed into a jubilant soul, traipsing off, ticket in hand into the distance.

Back among the seediness of Soho, Joey O' and Eddie had recharged batteries, buzzing about like two miniature vibrators left on in a nympho's bedside drawer. Headed for Willie Wong's restaurant, Fast Eddie became intrigued by a few dingy, labelled doorways showing bells that rang through to red-lighted brass houses above. Some of the names had us laughing: Madame Za Za's (Dominatrix in Studded Boots), Miss Candy (Sweet Teen Queen) and Bouncing Barbara, in waiting. One in particular took his eye: Beautiful Buxom Renee (dark chocolate). Itching to climb the stairs, every time he tiptoed onto them and they creaked like the bedroom floor in a haunted house, we burst out laughing. Telling him the curtains were worse than his ma's and it was a shitty place to lose your virginity, he stopped abruptly. Thinking he was about to call me a cheeky cunt for skitting his ma's curtains, he looked at the two of us and said, 'There's no way I'm a virgin. I lost it years ago.' Well, we were in tears.

Laughing ourselves to a standstill, my guts were in agony, especially when Joey O' added, 'Get up to Madame Za Za's, it'll be Phil Thompson in a basque, suzzies and a pair of footy boots!'

'Youse two are a pair of cheeky cunts. At least I'm honest about wanting to go up.'

'Yeah, well yer name's Fast Eddie, so get up there and fill yer boots with Renee then soft shite. You know what they say about dark chocolate?'

Joey O', in stitches, battled to pull himself together before quizzing me. 'Yeah, go on then, Mr Know the Dance, what d'they say?'

'Well, that Renee's probably about seventy-two, with big, black teabags tucked into her socks. See, they reckon dark chocolate is only milk chocolate gone off!'

The more Fast Eddie told us it was time to stop laughing and, that he was going up, the more we were in bulk. Each time I looked across at Joey O' curled up on the pavement crying in agony, I lost control. Finally gaining some stability, thinking Eddie would climb the stairs and we'd wait outside, he sent us back into bulk, stating he wasn't going to bother, as we'd only laugh. Finally punching Renee's doorbell, a voice that sounded like a female version of Lurch from *The Addams Family* answered – meaning we were creased and wriggling on the pavement again.

It took ages to gain composure, as Fast Eddie's gob betrayed feelings of annoyance. Asking why he looked uneasy, he stated each time he'd visited a brass gaff in London, Liverpool had won. Quizzing him about when he'd paid a visit in the past, we realised it was true. He'd disappeared abroad, and a number of times when down in the smoke for league games. His brother was some Bamber Gascoigne whizz-kid in the City, and Eddie had told us he was off to see their kid who owned a fancy pad somewhere at the back of Euston, near Camden Town. Confessing he'd been visiting the worn-out flanges of the West End was no surprise; the only surprise lay in the fact he'd kept it secret. None of us could have given a shite for what Eddie did in his spare time with his own dough.

Taking our seats inside Willie Wong's scran-house, we were dim-summing ourselves all the way to Wembley. Fast Eddie's slow way of telling us about the press-ups he'd been doing in secret became secondary to the feast at hand. Once the morning glory had poured out of me, tickets and money been passed around and scoff scoffed, we headed over to Queen Lizzie's drum, up Buckingham Palace Road. The scene of a thousand parades leading to the gates of her majesty's two-up, two-down was being soldiered and guarded by Liverpool supporters. Everywhere you looked splashes of red dotted the capital landscape.

Drawing up to the gates, talking about the pomp and grandeur of the place, Joey O' reckoned the fella who had the wrought-iron job had graft for life, and the housekeeper was one of the only people alive who knew what size knickers and bras the Queen wore. He loved a surreal take on things. I told him she didn't wear drawers, she wore diamond-encrusted knickers stolen years ago from the Queen of Sheba's vault. Eddie stared blankly into space. Scrutinizing the palace, offering opinions on where the Duke and Queen watched telly, Little Whacker turned up with a carrier bag full of punk singles. Telling him he had a match ticket, I thought I saw some colour enter his famine-faced cheeks. The lad looked drastically undernourished. Passing him some loose change, we ordered him to go find a nosebag while we looked after his records. Me and Joey O' were laughing, shouting to Whacker he'd better stay away from any more music shops, otherwise he'd soon be listening to The Clash and the 'Jail Guitar Doors' for six months solid. Eddie still stared blankly at the palace.

Sitting on the rough ground, with the palace wall, structure and gates towering over us, we checked the guard with the black poodle on his head before emptying the rest of the tickets and francs onto the gravel. With Joey O' still shouting robber's abuse at Little Whacker, I told him to hush as we were in the presence of the greatest robbers of all time. Fast Eddie, as if finger-clicked from a trance, looked among the gathered tourists, footy fans and guards, asking who I meant. Pointing to the upstairs windows of Buckingham Palace, he looked mystified, then at me like I was losing the plot. Joey O' put him out of his misery, saying I meant the Royal Family moving behind the curtains. 'There's no way the Queen's a shoplifter,' he spluttered. Laughing out loud, fighting back belly waves, I tried to define the Empire and how the British Army had ransacked different countries' coffers all over the world, in the name of God, the Royal family and England. He said his great-grandfather and grandfather had fought in wars, before looking bewildered again when I told him I now knew where he'd learned to climb through windows.

Asking him what he'd been staring at for so long, he said he was wondering if the Queen ever watched the telly. While laughing, a large shadow momentarily blocked out the sun. Looking up, a man-mountain draped in a red scarf told us we should have more respect and stand when we were outside Her Majesty's palace. Waiting for a laugh or smile, it never came. Again, he asked us to rise. Ignoring him, he put a foot under Eddie's backside, trying to wedge him up. Finally standing to attention, I asked what he was on about and from which planet he'd landed. He told us this was Great Britain, and, as we were British subjects we should show more respect outside Buckingham Palace.

Telling him immediately to 'fuck right off', seeing as I had more respect for Hilda Ogden in *Coronation Street* than I did for the people who supposedly lived in that big house and that, given the chance, I'd be over the walls looking for a little bit of wealth redistribution, I thought that was that and he'd walk away. Looking us up and down, like he was Sergeant Depth Charge, who'd single-handedly won the last two world wars himself, he started up again. 'Well let me ask you, do you all carry British passports?'

'Err, chewed up ones, yeah.' I offered.

'Well, you should respect the people who died in wars for you, so you could be free to carry that passport abroad. The family who live in there are the symbol of the people who died, and of that freedom, so show some respect by standing when you're in the presence of greatness.'

I'm thinking, 'Fucksake, it's European Cup-final day. Where did we find this weirdo?'

'Listen, mate, I'd stand if it was Shankly or Paisley, or any of those pensioners who fought in the war and live in shitty old flats in places like Bootle, Dingle and East fuckin' London, but if you want us to salute these land-snatchin', money-grabbin' parasites then you're fuckin' seriously deluded!'

'But these are our leaders, and you should know your history.'

He was off again. Joey O' spoke up. 'Listen mate, I know my history, and these are not my fuckin' leaders, so just fuck off you boring prick!'

Seeing as we were not about to bow down to size, he nodded in the direction of his mates, who all looked as tall as him. Knowing we were in the presence of an immovable brick shithouse, and maybe more shithouses, I motioned for the boys to walk in the direction of where we'd sent Little Whacker. Sometimes it felt like I was a divvy magnet. How else do you explain meeting up with the Scouse Ian Paisley on European Cup-final day? Walking away, I came to the conclusion that he'd been camping outside all morning, waiting to tell young lads like us all about the Great British Empire and how lucky we were just to be born here. Well concerning our football team, city, music and culture, I did, but when it came to kings, queens, lords and ladies and bejewelled palaces, it was a bit like that noise you hear when someone hangs up the phone . . .

Whistling Bill Withers's 'Lovely Day' reminded me it was time we were Wembley-bound. Still early, Joey O' disagreed, saying we should go back to the square. Telling him I felt uneasy about Jean-Claude's whereabouts and I'd be unable to party in comfort, we agreed on finding Little Whacker and the nearest tube to take us to the stadium. Fast Eddie, butting in as usual, said it was too early and we should go back to Soho, seeing as we had cash in hand. He started going on about Busty Renee and how a nice pair of chocolate muffins would make his Cup-final day complete. Asking him how it could be complete, being nowhere near kick-off time, it dawned we had a sex case in our crew. I mean, most young lads will do anything for the sake of a bunk-up, but this fella was disappearing most trips, even at the sake of the footy. Now we knew where. Giving in to his lordship's sweaty palms, we shouted the approaching Little Whacker and headed over to Soho. Never one for early match entrance, I knew we were in for a buzz the minute Eddie's knob ruled his brain. Passing Trafalgar Square again, I viewed Angela, her mates and the beady-eyed fathers among the vast football crowd. Jean-Claude was nowhere in sight. Finding the doorbell of Renee's, Eddie stopped as though he had changed his mind. Joey O' asked, 'What's up Eddie lad, don't fancy it now?'

'No, it's not that. It's just I've already been in this morning, and I don't know if I want it twice.'

'Fuckin' hell, and which one did yer visit?' I asked.

'Renee of course, why did yer think I was so keen to go back?'

Turning to Joey O', I asked was it true.

'Well, he disappeared this morning for half an hour. He told me we should fan out, as we had a better chance of finding a tout. I wondered why I couldn't get him in vision when I looked around the square.'

Little Whacker scowled. 'You're a cheeky cunt, you, Eddie! Here's me an' Joey O' searchin' everywhere for tickets an' touts, and you're over in Soho actin' the Rod Stewart!'

'Ah, shut the fuck up cryin' arse and get in yerself. It might bring some colour to yer cheeks!'

'Kiddin' aren't yer? I wouldn't waste me money on any of those Scabby Fannies!'

'No, cos yer only interested in snatchin' records, not snatch, yer bender!'

'Snatch? Yer call that snatch? I call that a large hole where a million sweaty fellas have been that swallows up yer dough!'

'Yeah, I agree – probably large enough for you to get yer whole body in.'

While Eddie and Little Whacker wound each other up, Joey O' punched the bell as the two of us giggled, then stopped, then giggled again.

'Whole body or not, every race on earth, and you, have been in there today, and tell me, who the fuck would go after you?'

Whacker wouldn't let go. With the two of them still going at it, the Lurch voice intervened, asking would we like to come up and visit Miss Renee.

The moment Eddie trod the first stair, it creaked loudly. Impersonating the Addams-family butler, I said, 'You raaang?' Everyone fell about laughing. With Eddie marching up the stairs, each one gave a louder creak than the last. Our laughing increased accordingly. With the automatic door closed and him inside, we laughed our way to the fruit stall down the road. Sunlight bounced off the fruit display and through gaps in the cramped buildings. Seated at the kerb, munching on Granny Smiths, we waited for Fast Eddie, making conversation with the stall-owning barrow boy. Telling him where our mate was, we reckoned he'd been inside Renee's a few times. He said he'd never go in those places, especially when he'd seen first hand some of the sleazebags who entered.

Twenty minutes passed before Eddie came out fastening his shirt to the cry of 'Sleazebag! Sleazebag!' Calling him Eddie Empty Sack, he got leathered all the way to Leicester Square, where we jumped a tube before changing for Wembley. Hitting daylight with the stadium in view, we noticed a van offloading boxes of programmes. Reaching ground level, we offloaded a few ourselves, selling them along Wembley Way. Outside the stadium red flags unfurled everywhere. On main crossing points Scouse voices pleaded for tickets.

Reaching the grassy banks of the entrance gates we sat down to breathe it all in. The turnstiles looked Yankee-waistline wide. With twenty-eight-inch slender frames, it looked surefire for our little crew. Fifteen minutes later, tickets sold for face, the boys buzzing and the Reds in town, I breathed in some more. This was what it was all about. The European Cup final in May: the greatest Cup and Cup final in the world. The international World Cup – country football – Peru, Bolivia, France and England: it meant nothing to me. For me and my crew, and thousands of other Scousers, it didn't even come close. Lying on the grass, I witnessed the scene. The Reds were coming up the hill boys, and me, I was a football gypsy, a Liverpool football gypsy. Life didn't get any sweeter than hitting the road for Big Ears in May.

That night Kenny hit the onion with guile, precision and class. Our supporters and my season ticket from my Jaffa Cake wages helped pay Celtic for him. To us, and to people who really knew the game, he was undoubtedly the greatest footballer in the world. Chipping the goalie in slow-mo, I swear he did it on purpose to cause our rivals further agony. Every one of the 80,000 Redmen in a 92,000 crowd went delirious as we sang our hymns of praise and almost lifted the Wembley roof. Scanning about me, high on the huge Wembley steps, I clocked Sir Bob Paisley on the bench and his team on the park. Things looked rosy red for at least the next five years. For the briefest, I caught Little Whacker smiling, looking healthier with a Liverpool goal and a spot of sunburn on his face. Joey O', he was busy microwaving people with his infectious humour and grin, hardly watching the game, but laughing non-stop for ninety minutes. Fast Eddie, ball-drained and happy, opened his mouth wide to scream out the theme tune: 'Wo-oh-oh Ke-e-enny, oh-oh-oh Ke-e-enny, I'd walk a million miles for one of your goals, oh Ke-e-enny'. No legs-akimbo lady of the night could make him miss a show like this. Once Emlyn lifted that enormous silver trophy and an 80,000-strong roar hit the rafters, I realised, like the banner had said that, as we gathered cups I was about to amass more mileage than a war correspondent. The effect would cause untold conflict with present and future employers. Blame Shankly; blame Paisley; blame Dalglish . . . blame me!

Bunking the special home in the early hours, I found my speck high on the netted luggage rack. Drifting in and out, the party that swung all around was sweet, sweet music to my ears. Getting comfortable in my makeshift hammock, I wanted the effects of my drug of choice – football days out – to not wear off till August. When my eyes did close, I dreamt not of European Cup glory and that big, beautiful pot, but of the coming season, the tiny, cardboard fixture list and who we'd get in the first round, cross-channel, next year. With a Kop song repertoire steaming down the track, the train rocking and me drifting some more, I dreamed of a bike crash at the Super Cup final against Hamburg, and again, who we'd draw in that one next season; of Desk-Sergeant Dracula and weight loss in Antwerp; of Fast Eddie's naughty disappearance acts; of hospital beds and blood in Dusseldorf; of tasty clobber shops and boats full of pirates. It was brilliant having your dreams scattered all over Europe; brilliant being a Liverpudlian; and yeah, as Mrs Mac would say, brilliant gathering cups in May.

Paris, 1981

PETER HOOTON

European Cup Final, 27th May 1981
Parc des Princes, Paris
Attendance: 48,360

Liverpool FC   1–0   **Real Madrid**
Alan Kennedy (82')

Subsitutes: Jimmy Case, Steve Ogrizovic, Colin Irwin, Richard Money, Howard Gayle

Manager: Bob Paisley

Real Madrid: Agustín Rodríguez (1), Rafael García Cortés (2), Antonio García Navajas (3), Andrés Sabido (4), Vicente del Bosque (5), Angel de los Santos (6), José Camacho (7, captain), Uli Stielike (8), Juanito (9), Carlos Santillana (10), Laurie Cunningham (11)

Substitutes used: Francisco Pineda

Manager: Vujadin Boškov

Background

In 1981 things were different – very, very different. Liverpool regularly won the league title, the Kop was still a swaying mass and the preferred form of transport was the football special, the transit van or the coach. Mainland Europe still seemed a long way away – a mysterious place, in fact. Cheap air travel was unheard of, apart from Freddie Laker, whose airline lasted about five minutes; it was either pay top dollar or go with Transalpino, the student travel firm. We were only two years into Thatcher's reign, but Liverpool was beginning to feel the cold draught of her monetarist policies. The 'People's March for Jobs' from Liverpool to London to highlight the spiralling unemployment figures would take the whole of May '81 to descend on London. The war in Ireland was at its height, as Bobby Sands, the MP for Fermanagh and South Tyrone, had just died after a hunger strike. The second cold war showed no signs of thawing, and the Soviet Union was still very much intact.

No one in the country knew where the fuck the Falklands where, and if anyone had suggested riots would break out in the inner cities of our major conurbations that coming summer, they would have been laughed at. In fact, one lad speaking at a political meeting that me and a few of my mates went to suggested that Britain's inner cities would resemble Belfast sooner rather than later, and he was, err, laughed at! When his 'vision' had become reality later that year, we called him The Prophet and Nostradamus.

The Sony Walkman, which played tapes (remember them?), the iPod of its day, was taking the world by storm. As strange as it may seem now, Adam and the Ants had a stranglehold on the UK singles and album charts for much of 1981, and MTV went on the air for the first time. A new sensation had arrived on our shores in the form of the video cassette recorder, which the film industry thought would destroy Hollywood as we knew it. Pity it didn't destroy the British, Oscar-winning film *Chariots of Fire*, which took tinsel town by storm in 1981 with its quaint, nostalgic view of England.

Football-loving Bob Marley had just died of cancer at the tender age of 36, and Aids had just been recognised as a virus for the first time. Ronald Reagan, after being elected as the fortieth president of the USA, had been gunned down by a 'lone gunman' and survived to fight another day, like all good cowboys do! Pope John Paul II had been shot outside the Vatican, and the 'Yorkshire Ripper' had just been caught. And guess what? We only had three channels on the telly to watch all this mayhem. Never mind Channel 5; we didn't even have Channel 4, which wasn't on air until 1982. God, how we suffered. Try telling that to the kids of today, with their million channels of meaningless drivel. Ah, but we were happy then, because at the match you could just walk up to the turnstile and pay in, get a programme and still get change from two quid. Yes, two quid!

Some people, like my dad, did have season tickets, but they tended to be supporters in the Kemlyn Road and the Main Stand. Only the derby matches and the Manchester United fixtures tended to be all ticket, and who can forget the queues for those matches, sometimes stretching all around the ground and down Arkles Lane? As far as I can remember, tickets were always sold at the turnstiles; there were no ticket-office telephone numbers. In fact there was no ticket office as such, but a development office, and the souvenir shop had a couple of sun-faded scarves in the window. Oh, the days of innocence before sponsorship and replica kits were even heard of. In those days Liverpool didn't have thousands of fans travelling from all over the globe to go to home games and spend fortunes in the club shop; believe it or not it was mainly people from Liverpool who went the games.

The Early Rounds

After winning the European Cup in 1977 and 1978, Liverpool had two disappointing campaigns in 1979 and 1980, losing to Nottingham Forest and then the superb Dynamo Tbilisi in the first round of the competition. Remember, this was before the introduction of the group stages, when it was a straight knockout competition. The 1980–81 draw had been kinder to Liverpool, playing Oulun Palloseura of Finland and winning 11–2 on aggregate. Yes, 11–2. These were the days of early-round massacres – this being one of the biggest aggregate victories in our history.

The next round was more memorable for a number of reasons. Liverpool had been drawn against Aberdeen, who, under the leadership of Alex Ferguson, had become the dominant force north of the border. Another significant reason is that it was the fixture which Aberdeen fans point to as a turning point for their club. It was at these matches that they witnessed young Liverpool fans with no scarves, floppy hairstyles and a distinctive look.

When Liverpool fans arrived at Aberdeen station, the Aberdeen 'reception' committee just looked and stared. There was always a reception committee in those days. This particular welcoming party looked like a bunch of Billy Connollys. They had wild eyes, wild hair, beards and crazy clothing; they looked as if they should have still been fighting the Romans. They were the reason why Hadrian's Wall went up. This attack would go down in Liverpool folklore as the 'Attack of the Billy Connollys'. It didn't get any funnier than this! The Aberdonians were open-mouthed in amazement, taken aback by the Liverpool fans' 'clothes'. 'Ye Sassenach puffs,' they screamed, but soon their aggression evaporated, as confusion spread through their ranks. Whereas they all looked like Man United/Leeds fans circa 1974 – mad Birmos, sad jumpers, stack heels and tartan – Liverpool's crew looked like they were heading for a nightclub playing Talking Heads, Devo and Dillinger. Liverpool had been dressed in assorted training shoes, cagoules, lambswool crew necks and polo shirts since the summer of 1977, and Manchester's Perry boys had caught on pretty quick. Even Leeds had a little crew of 'dressers' by 1979, but Aberdeen was a classic case of the stereotypical footy hoolie as portrayed by the *Sun* newspaper, with baggy jeans, bovver boots and they were 100 per cent pure wool! After this match Aberdeen fans would never be the same again, and the infamous Aberdeen Casuals were born. From this point on Scottish terraces would be terrorised by the dreaded 'bloody casuals'. Jay Allan, in his book of the same name, remembers the return leg at Anfield:

> We were in the ground about 20 minutes before kick-off and Aberdeen were in full voice. Just next to us at the Anfield Road end there was about 500 or 600 young lads. None of them had scarves on and they all wore their hair in a side flick. I didn't know then who they were, but I now know they were the early dressers. Liverpool was the first city to start the soccer trendies' boom and these were the Liverpool Scallies.

For Liverpool fans, however, the most memorable thing about this fixture had nothing to do with terrace fashion but was the fact that egg and chips were served up on a Liverpool football special. Connoisseurs of this form of transport will be only too aware that the only thing that used to be served up from the 'cage' (an empty train carriage with, believe it or not, a cage in it) was stale sarnies, crisps and cups of tea and Oxo. Along with Jo-Jo from Dodge in Netherton (a notorious Liverpool fan and ever-present on the specials) asking for your odds, the appalling catering was the only constant.

One of the legendary Leather Bottle crowd from Halewood remembers the day well: 'It was a dead early start from Lime Street, then all of a sudden, a couple of hours into the journey, someone said that egg and chips were being served up. No one could believe it – it had never happened before, and I don't think it ever happened again – but it went down well with the lads. Egg and chips: it was the talk of the train. Maybe British Rail staff felt sorry for us, because it was such a long journey. I just don't know, but we were made up. It was a case of "go the match on an egg!".'

The crowd that went to Aberdeen that night were typical of Liverpool fans in those days. People didn't tend to wear colours, and a football special would hold up to about five hundred supporters. The trains were usually old wrecks that dated from the 1940s and 1950s and were taken out the sidings. They were basic, to say the least, and looked as if they had been vandalised before you'd even got on them. That was the whole idea, I suppose. The only real hazard on these hulks was when a train was pulling into or out of rival stations. It was always best to pull the dilapidated blinds down to take the full weight of the half-set brick and flying glass which would inevitably hit at least one window.

Sometimes these trains were open plan with tables, but more often than not they were carriages with compartments and sliding doors. If people moan about Virgin Trains, they have obviously never been near a footy special. The carriages smelt of cigarettes and alcohol, and if you banged the seats, years and years of dust would pollute the air.

Just like nowadays, we moaned about the way we were treated, the cattle trucks we were put into, week after week, but nobody ever did anything about it. Unlike nowadays, though, the transport was dirt cheap and totally unlike the travel 'options' we get now. In those days we expected to be treated like shite but put up with it because it was a) cheap, b) the quickest way to travel, and c) safety in numbers. Catering was an absolute joke, apart from the Aberdeen trip, and the cages where the usual delicacies were served up doubled up as holding areas for unruly fans.

The Aberdeen match was portrayed in the press as the Battle of Britain. How many of these battles can you have? The young manager of Aberdeen, a fresh-faced Alex Ferguson with no sign of a red nose just yet, had put Aberdeen on the map, and his loathing of Liverpool probably started during these fixtures, as Liverpool strolled through the tie, beating Aberdeen 1–0 at Pittodrie and 4–0 at Anfield.

In the next round CSKA Sofia of Bulgaria offered little resistance, as Liverpool progressed 6–1 on aggregate, with Graeme Souness scoring a hat-trick in the Anfield leg. The semi-final opponents, Bayern Munich, were an entirely different prospect. The very name struck fear into most teams, as Bayern had been a dominant force in the early 1970s, whereas Liverpool had dominated the late 70s. Nearly 78,000 attended the second leg at the Olympic Stadium, Munich, after the 0–0 stalemate at Anfield in the first leg. Liverpool fans had been in the news in the days before the match, as loads had been arrested in the bars and clubs of the red-light areas.

It was the usual script for a European away, even in those days, as fans descended on the red-light district in search of fun and games. These places were nothing like Soho in London, where the rip-off was a practised art form. Liverpool fans knew that places like Soho were a no-no, whereas the fleshpots of the European cities were much more open and liberal. To wide-eyed youngsters from Liverpool, their attraction was aided by a huge, invisible magnet. Most of us were just curious, I think, trying to exorcise our Catholic guilt, but it was undoubtedly the only place to be. The anonymity of a large European city did wonders for many a shy, self-conscious choirboy.

Nobody could really put their finger on why the trouble started, but it had nothing to do with Bayern Munich fans. As in most cases when Liverpool fans were abroad, it involved doormen and bar owners. The usual scenario was the unpaid bill or a perceived lack of respect, but the bouncers usually got more than they bargained for from the fresh-faced, boy-next-door look of the Road Enders.

On the night before the game disturbances at the Munich Hofbrauhaus and the station resulted in arrests. Some of the lads, including a well-known Evertonian from Halewood, ended up doing time for the chaos, but most viewed this as par for the course. Several of the thirty-odd who were arrested were completely innocent and just happened to be observing the melee, and many spent forty-eight hours in custody without being charged. They missed the match that would go down in history as the game when Howie Gayle, the lad from Toxteth, stole the show with a fantastic performance. A late equaliser by Karl-Heinz Rummenigge wasn't enough to cancel out Ray Kennedy's eighty-third-minute goal. Liverpool reached the final on the away-goal rule, totally stunning the huge German crowd.

Transalpino

As soon as the final whistle went in Munich, everyone's thoughts immediately turned to Paris. Remember these were pre-Internet days, so people weren't hovering over laptops planning exotic routes in order to boast to mates/associates about how cheap their particular trip was. No, all thoughts turned to Myrtle Parade, the home of Transalpino, so we could boast to our mates how cheap our excursion into Europe was!

We might have pretended to ourselves that we had a choice of coach or train, but to most experienced Reds there was only one way to travel, and that was by train, which meant Transalpino. Set up as a student travel company to transport swots across Europe, they unwittingly helped the young tearaways of the Anfield Road End sample the delights of the Continent. The dingy office that became a Mecca for young scallies across Merseyside was run by a couple of mature students who must have been pleasantly surprised and bemused by the sheer number of trendy, wedged-hair Scouse 'students' the university had enrolled. The return trip to Paris was unbelievably cheap: train to Newhaven, ferry to Dieppe and then train to Paris, all for under twenty-five quid. Let the great adventure begin!

Lime Street Getaway

We left Lime Street on the Saturday night before the match. There was nothing unusual about this, as I'd been to London on several occasions on both the midnight train and the bright and early – a favoured experience for many fans who didn't like the 'organisation' and restriction of the London football specials. Big Joe, Mad Arse, The Mod, the lad who shall be known as The Wedge and *moi* all left on that late-night train.

Although most of us had flirted with the wedge hairstyle, The Wedge's was immaculate. He had a Parisian look about him, which we thought would be helpful when we tried to chat up young Parisian *filles*. He had it down to a fine art. Fashionable and intelligent, he was working for a sportswear company selling training shoes. If they were sought after and rare, he had them. He was Wade Smith before Wade Smith. (Wade Smith was the entrepreneur who latched on to Scousers' obsession with trainers and built an empire out of it a couple of years later.) He went to school with me in Bootle, but now he worked in a sports shop in the Arndale Centre, Manchester, and also sold trainees to his mates and other independent sports shops. He was ahead of his time. I remember going out in his van a couple of times when he was delivering to sports shops in the north-west, but most of the shop owners would only take a few pairs, not realising what was going on with the youth of Liverpool and Manchester and their insatiable appetite for new footwear.

I bought a pair of very rare red-leather Puma Menotti off him. Most of the lads wore blue Puma Argentina, presumably named after the World Cup-winning side of 1978, but The Wedge had put his hands on two pairs of red Menotti, named after the manager of Argentina. When you had a pair of trainees like that, you felt like you were king of the world, and I got fed up of answering questions about their origin. It is important to point out to our younger readers that, unlike nowadays, training shoes were nowhere to be found. The markets didn't sell them, shoe shops didn't sell them and specialist sports shops like Jack Sharps in Whitechapel catered for a completely different market, so most were acquired from abroad or by chance, when a sports shop had a salesman like The Wedge, who convinced them that a revolution was going on at street level, even though they weren't aware of it.

The talk on the train was of a place The Mod had been told existed somewhere in Paris called the Adidas Centre. We sat open-mouthed, transfixed, as we listened to his convincing explanation of a distribution centre for the rest of Europe. It made sense; it was logical; we would find it! This was our goal; this was OUR DESTINY!

After our train journey to Euston, we made our way to Victoria to catch the early-morning train to Newhaven, from where the ferry sailed to Dieppe. Starving and cold we boarded the ferry mid-morning and asked if we could pay for a cabin. No chance! The ferry was rammed, mainly with Scousers, so we sat down to witness the expected shenanigans. If you travelled on a cross-Channel ferry in those days, it would be a nap that the duty-free would be 'ragged' and the bar would turn into the *Star Wars* bar by the halfway point. We would not be disappointed; in fact it was high-seas piracy by any other name. So much booty was robbed from the duty-free that people were just giving it away in the end.

The Invasion of France

> 'Cold water in the face brings you back to this awful place'
> The Clash, 'The Magnificent Seven'

We could see them lined up at the Dieppe terminal like an army waiting to repel an invading force – scores of them kitted out in riot gear, brandishing water cannon. The bursar had obviously told the captain to radio ahead about the mutiny on board. As soon as we were in range, they opened up. It was the funniest thing of the trip so far. Ten in the morning after four hours of seasickness, revelry and expectation and the Dieppe riot squad were indulging in some target practice.

They sprayed the decks, they sprayed the side of the ferry and they sprayed us, only to be met with the laughter of disbelief. To be truthful, the water cannon they used wasn't like the high-powered ones they have now, and the water hardly reached the deck with any force. This increased the laughter level. They tried to hit anyone who looked like a football fan. They were mad, very mad, but you could see they were enjoying it, like most riot police seem to. They like a good riot, those riot police. Funny that! It didn't concern them that ninety-five per cent of the boat's passengers were innocent of any Robin Hood gestures; they just wanted to teach all of us a lesson. Their message was loud and clear: 'Welcome to France. Don't fuck around with us.' Their overreaction was comical, and had the opposite effect from the one intended:

> You can stick your water cannon up your arse,
> You can stick your water cannon up your arse,
> You can stick your water cannon,
> Stick your water cannon,
> Stick your water cannon up your arse,
> SIDEWAYS!

> We don't carry bottles, we don't carry lead,
> We only carry hatchets, to bury in your head.
> We are loyal supporters, fanatics every one,
> We all hate Man City, Leeds and Everton.
> We're the cream of Europe, the pride of Merseyside,
> We'll fight for no surrender, we'll fight for Shankly's pride.
> We hate Tottenham Hotspur, we hate Chelsea too,
> We hate all the bastards who play in Royal Blue!

They herded us onto the gangplank, and they were met with a chorus of sheep noises, as always seemed to happen in situations like this. Tense? Nervous headache? Just go BAAA! They were getting even more agitated by the second, truncheons drawn and spitting insults. That's the problem with overreaction. It's like the referee who gives out an early yellow and then can't stop giving them out. If the use of water cannon is met with laughter and amusement, what's the next step? Live ammo?

One thing is for sure: they couldn't wait to get rid of us. They pushed us onto waiting trains in the sidings as if we were enemies of Vichy France on our way to our fate. Once aboard, the first thing we noticed about these trains was the fact that they were miles better than our football specials. They were wider, more comfortable and they had catering – things were certainly looking up! We all agreed that if these were the shit trains for football fans, the good ones must be brilliant! Ah, a few more hours and we would be unleashed on the unsuspecting damsels in distress.

Gay Paree!

Paris is a city of a thousand clichés: rich in historical symbolism, the birthplace of revolutionary fervour, alluring, sophisticated, fashionable and, er, quite smelly! When we arrived at St Lazare station on the Sunday afternoon in light drizzle, it looked anything but alluring. Most areas around stations, in any city in the world, are usually drab and seedy, but this place was as depressing as they come. In the weeks leading up to our trip we had conjured up images of young, sexy French girls who would be bowled over by our dress sense, haircuts and training shoes, but on the corner of the first street outside the station we were greeted by a middle-aged, toothless prostitute holding a bunch of flowers.

The mere mention of Paree had induced fevered anticipation for weeks. Paris in the spring: what more could you wish for? We had left Liverpool to sample the delights of Paris, determined to have a great time, and nothing was going to stop us now. In the weeks leading up to the match we must have been unbearable. We were smug, boastful and arrogant. We thought we were witty; we thought we were sharp; we thought we liked the best music and knew we supported the best team; we thought we would take the unsuspecting Parisians by storm – we were total smart-arses! Our conversation had been two-dimensional: how to get there, and what we were going to do when we arrived there. We were young, free and single and convinced of our own immortality and the certainty of dangerous liaisons with the impressionable maidens of Paree! We had perfected our chat-up lines on the overnight journey: 'Cinq bières et un paquet de Durex, s'il vous plait.' Surely our basic O-level French would come in handy? How could we fail?

St Lazare resembled Victoria station in London and was just as busy. Our sturdy band of intrepid travellers alighted from the train with growing expectation. We swaggered with self-confidence, only to be met with total indifference and blank stares from Parisians. This was deffo not Aberdeen; it would take more than a few fresh-faced, trendy football fans to catch the attention of the locals. The only people who gave us any attention were the deformed prostitutes in the adjacent street.

A small group of fellow Liverpudlians had been at the station to greet us with tales of mayhem and debauchery, but we were the first set of fans to arrive en masse. Loads headed for a hotel overlooking the station and next to a Wimpy, but we went left out of the station towards Pigalle, the notorious red-light district, which seemed to be beckoning us like Catholic priests to Lourdes. We had no free will, you see, and seemed to be drawn by forces beyond our control and comprehension. After a few minutes' walk we came across a hotel which seemed to fit all the criteria – i.e. it was walking distance to the Moulin Rouge and the peep shows of the red light! If the truth be known – according to my experience, anyway – it was a *Fawlty Towers*-type gaff run by the French equivalent of Basil and Sybil. It's still there, and it's called the Hotel D'Athenes. Here's a 2007 review of it that echoed my feelings, though others, of course, might have had a perfectly pleasant stay:

> This is a terrible hotel. I just came back from a three-day trip to Paris and unfortunately had to spend all of the three days in this hotel due to the advance paid. The staff and especially the owner are stunningly rude and arrogant. Nothing, including the power points in its rooms, works. The sheets were not changed in the morning, the breakfast was awful, the room was not even ready when I arrived at 1 p.m. and I had to wait. At best it is less than a two-star hotel.

Mad Arse was not impressed either, back in '81. 'It's a fuckin' shithole,' he barked. 'I'm not staying here. They don't even speak English.' Not unreasonable observations but we were tired and weary and our hearts had just skipped a beat. Anyway it was a case of location, location, location for the rest of us. As long as we could stagger back from main drag, we would be happy. Mad Arse went off looking for a better bunk, but we knew he would be back, unless he could meet someone he knew and doss in their place. He would easily tolerate hovels as long as he didn't have to pay for them. Within an hour he was back: 'They're all the same: poxy little, smelly, horrible shitholes.' We tried to point out to Mad Arse that American tourists paid top dollar for these quaint boudoirs with a certain 'je ne sais quoi', but he dismissed the idea. 'Knobhead Texans, you mean. They must have more money than sense, the PRICKS!'

We would all get used to the atmosphere of Paris over the coming days, but it was certainly a culture shock. As it was one of the closest capital cities to Blighty, we expected something different, but we did get used to the peculiar smells of Gay Paree! Maybe it was the sewer system, but the lingering stench was almost everywhere. Most bars and restaurants didn't have toilets as we know them but holes in the floor. Squat thrusts, we called them. If you were feeling a bit queasy from a hangover, these bogs were a complete no-no. They reeked!

One morning, after a particularly heavy session, I trawled the bars near our hotel in search of a toilet that didn't smell of Giant Haystacks's jockstrap, but I gave up in the end. I entered a said squat-thrust khazi and within seconds unleashed a perfect projectile. The squat thrust was OK, I suppose, if you weren't loose, but as most experienced travellers will confirm, a couple of days abroad plus enormous amounts of alcohol plays havoc with your digestive system. My piece of advice from this particular trip: always bring more boxees than you need. For example, if you are on a six-day trip, like we were, it should be one pair per day plus another couple in case of accidents and follow-throughs – an occupational hazard for football fans abroad!

Setting up HQ

After unpacking and a bit of personal grooming, we set off to be corrupted by models. First of all we headed for the shady street next to St Lazare station. Loads of lads had jumped in a hotel right opposite the station, a hotel which we would later name the Madhouse, for reasons which will become clearer soon, and most of them were already on the ale in this street. We sat down and ordered our *'cinq bières'*. Heads turned. We convinced ourselves that everybody thought we were fascinating, but I think it was more like, 'Oh, no, the English are here.' The fact that we didn't really consider ourselves as English was neither here nor there. As far as the locals were concerned, the English hooligans/Vikings had arrived.

This rat-hole was low-rent-brass central. Seedy was not in it. Most doorways had a past-her-best hooker stood outside with a bunch of flowers in her hand. Weird or what? The punters were the stereotyped white-overcoat brigade, middle-aged pervs who liked their fantasies fulfilled by ageing women with ulcers on their legs. They were even uglier than our Liverpool streetwalkers. Get the picture? They were biblically ugly.

The goings-on in this street were hilarious, and we probably would have stayed there had it not been for the crew of lads who got off without paying their bar bill. You see, over in Paris, as in a lot of places in Europe, you paid your bill at the end of the night. Young Scousers couldn't believe the naïvety of this system, and at every opportunity they either underpaid or just did a runner. The problem with refusing to pay your bill is that when you stay in the same street, you should at least attempt to change your appearance. You know, false moustache or beard, dress up like an Aberdeen fan circa '81 even, or at least take your jacket off. These soft cunts just went to a bar about four doors away, laughing as they went. We tried to warn them as we saw the bar owner who had been ripped mustering support on the phone and explaining to any bar owners who would listen that he had been screwed. These lads were just a little too overconfident, and they actually said to us, 'What are they gonna do? There's too many of us.' We didn't recognise them

The Red Rogues' Gallery (Tony È, Missing In Action)

Hats off to Joey Jones at the station, 1977.
Copyright © *Liverpool Daily Post and Echo*.

Return Ticket for the 'Special': one-way ticket to hell more like.

Stadio Olimpico, Rome, 25th May 1977, featuring the legendary 'Munching Gladbachs' banner.
Copyright © *Liverpool Daily Post and Echo*.

That banner in full, 1977. Copyright © *Liverpool Daily Post and Echo*.

Kenny Dalglish celebrates yet another goal on the way to winning the European Cup, 1978. Copyright © *Liverpool Daily Post and Echo.*

Taking a dip in Trafalgar Square on European Cup final day, 1978.
Copyright © *Liverpool Daily Post and Echo*.

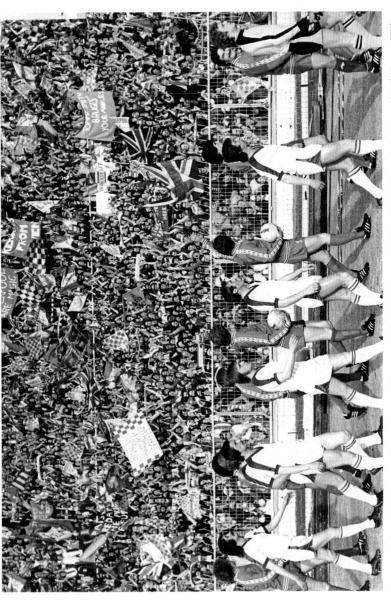

Liverpool FC and FC Bruges walk out in front of the ecstatic Wembley Redmen, 10th May 1978. Copyright © *Liverpool Daily Post and Echo*.

Parc des Princes, Paris, 27th May 1981: Adidas trainers out in full force
Copyright © Steve Hale.

The Reds suited, booted and bearded in Paris, 1981
Copyright © *Liverpool Daily Post and Echo*.

Alan Kennedy buries the winner to bring about Liverpool's third European Cup title, 1981. Copyright © *Liverpool Daily Post and Echo.*

from the Road End or the aways; they were just young lads who had a little too much Dutch courage. Half a brain cell would have told them that if you try to rip bars off in a seedy area, where all the bars will be connected to each other or will have backup on hand, you should vacate the area: EXIT STAGE LEFT!

We sensed what was coming. It was only early evening, but we knew how angry the bar staff were. We went to the end of the street to watch the world go by. Within half an hour they appeared all tooled up. Turkish looking (the Turks get blamed for everything) or maybe even Moroccan or Algerian, but they meant business. There is a theory that the red-light areas of the world are relatively safe, which, of course, is true, as long as you don't try to rip the rippers. They knew who they were looking for: anyone who was young and English! So, whether we liked it or not, we were caught up in it. It didn't last very long, but after it, with the small side street littered with glass and broken chairs, the bars shut as the riot police (CRS) arrived.

We were all at the top end of the street, and the CRS were at the bottom. Cue the *Pink Panther* theme, loud and clear from the fifty or so Liverpudlians. It was an honourable draw, but the bar owners had saved face, according to their twisted code of 'respect'. The lads they were after were not seriously hurt, and neither were we. The furniture came off worst, but they had fucked up our 'quiet' drink, and now the prostitutes had disappeared and the bars had shut. These bar owners are very dim. Say they lost about ten or twenty quid because of those lads; well, these pricks lost a whole night's takings because of the two minutes of 'ultra violence', as the police must've told them to close shop. That's just not good business. That is *very, very stupid*! A bit like that referee brandishing a yellow in the first minute of a game.

The Moulin Rouge

Our first attempt at HQ had been literally wrecked. We set off to find another. We went towards the famous Moulin Rouge and its exotic delights. A few hundred yards past the Moulin we found

a bar in a little square off the main road. Better still it had a fountain. It is always a good idea to set up camp next to a fountain,
as you usually don't have to wait that long before some knobhead
appears and jumps in fully clothed, singing the wrong words to
famous Liverpool songs. We didn't have to wait long, as even in
those days we had loads of beauts following us. Some things never
change.

Even at Wembley in the '78 final I remember thinking to myself,
'How do all these pricks get tickets?' We must have had 80,000
Liverpool fans at Wembley that night, and I distinctly remember
one of the diehards from Kirkby, Smigger, wearing a Bruges scarf on
Wembley Way. I think he must've been waiting for a reaction from
one of the divvies. Either that or he was on the mooch. Or maybe
he was just embarrassed by our support, like a lot of Scousers are
nowadays. But, as I say, that is nothing new. They wear replica shirts
now, so stand out more. Loads want to go to finals, but how about
Juve away? You should get final tickets for life if you went to that
one, never mind the shareholders!

Back at the new HQ on that Sunday night, within half an
hour we knew we had made the right choice. The streetwalkers
here were in a different league to the ones near St Lazare. No
sweet-smelling roses needed here! Around the bar about five or
six had their patch, and business was brisk. As more ale went
down, each punter was met with catcalls as they linked arms with
the girls and headed to the apartments just above. Most of the
clients seemed to resemble Gallic Woody Allens. The catcalls
turned to classic Liverpool chants:

> Na, na, na, na, na, goose, goose, goose, goose,
> Na, na, na, na, na, goose, goose.

And:

> We know where you're going,
> We know where you're going.

The working girls were getting upset with the noise and the fact that their takings were down, as punters were being scared away by all the attention. We were hampering their business, but what a laugh. The punters had that 'rabbit in the headlights' look about them! For years they had probably been doing the same sketch, and now, all of a sudden, they had a very vocal audience. They couldn't get away fast enough. The girls mustn't have had pimps, because they would have definitely been over to our bar to try to stop the singing.

Dirty, dirty bastards, na, na, na, na, na, nah . . .

The Adidas Centre

On the Monday we abandoned plans to visit places of interest like Notre-Dame, the Louvre or even the Eiffel Tower, because we were off in search of fashion and heading to the Boulevard St Germain in a desperate search for this Adidas Centre we had heard about, or rather The Mod had heard about.

He was called The Mod because, back in the days when some of the lads had flirted with the mod revival of 1979–80, he had been regular in the Scarlett's Bar in Hackins Hey in Liverpool city centre. The Scarlett's was just off Dale Street and was scally central. Loads of lads, both Liverpool and Everton, used to drink in there; it was like a Fagin's den. We always used to drink in the small pool room, where people used to admire each other's wedges and training shoes, amongst other things. Sounds a bit suspect that, but you know what I mean. On a Friday and Saturday the place used to be rammed, and I spent so much time in there I ended up going out with one of the barmaids. All sorts of characters used to go in there, and I remember that one enormous black fella called Gordon used to organise a load of young girl 'kiters' (credit-card fraudsters) from there. Anyway The Mod had met one of my mates at a Secret Affair concert (mod revivalist band) and he arranged to meet him in the Scarlett's pool room the following weekend. So this lad came into the pool room and remarked under his breath, 'How come your mates aren't real mods?' He meant that we didn't have Parkas on. Anyway, however he said it, it just didn't come out right, and basically his name stuck from that day onwards and he is still known as The Mod well into his 40s.

Our search for the Adidas Centre was leading us up blind alleys, and after a spectacularly unsuccessful day asking dumbfounded Parisians 'Please could you tell me, where is the Adidas Centre?' we gave up. We had repeated this mantra to everyone who would listen – shop assistants, traffic wardens, streetwalkers, policemen, waiters, nuns – but no one had the slightest idea what we were on about. Such was our desperation to find the place, we forgot all about the touristy things, but we did see most of Paris on foot, searching for this Holy Grail. The locals didn't seem to be impressed with being asked about this fictional centre by cocky, swaggering youths with wedge hairstyles when there was so much to see in their beloved city. Some uninitiated may view this as a criminal waste of time, but to us it made perfect sense. Everyone likes a good search, and it also enabled us to see much of the city.

Culture Vultures

Each afternoon our band of merry men would discuss at length the remote possibility of a cultural evening, but we would always find ourselves drawn back inexplicably to the Pigalle. On the Monday early evening, some of us did go to the Left Bank area on the other side of the Seine. This district is famous for its bohemian atmosphere, and it was quite good there, with buskers, poets and fire-eaters, but you just had no indication that we were two days away from a European Cup final. We just had an empty feeling there, like we were missing out on the goings-on near the Moulin Rouge. We hardly saw any Liverpool fans on the Left Bank and can't remember having come across one Real Madrid fan since we arrived in Paris, so we decided to head back to our HQ bar. 'We've had enough of culture for one night,' said Mad

Arse. We all agreed, thinking to ourselves, 'Let's get back to the fun. Let's get back to Pigalle and the sins of the flesh!'

When we arrived at about ten-ish, things were in full swing. The brasses were out, as were the punters, and loads more Liverpool fans were there than the night before. We weren't really big singing types, as most of the Road Enders weren't in those days. Back then it was no colours and no singing, believe it or not, except for a few ditties like:

Kopites are gobshites

The Road End United will never be defeated!

Oh, I went to Man United, with a shotgun on my knee,
We're gonna take the scoreboard, we're the boys from
    LFC.
We are the Road End, the pride of Merseyside,
We do all the fighting, while the Kopites run and hide.

Hit him on the head, hit him on the head with a base-
    ball bat, oh yeah, oh yeah.

We're not mad, we're not round the bend,
We're just the nutters from the Annie Road End.

We are EVIL! We are EVIL!

It was fairly tongue-in-cheek, piss-take stuff, but sometimes you could get carried away with Cup-final fervour and start singing, and this bar certainly induced singing en masse. Most of the time, rather than football songs, our lot liked to sing all the words to 'Down in the Tube Station at Midnight' and 'Smithers-Jones' by The Jam, and 'White Man in Hammersmith Palais', 'Stay Free' and 'English Civil War' by The Clash. We would travel long distances to see these groups, and going to a Jam concert in those days was like going to an away match. In fact two or three Jam concerts I went to at the Manchester Apollo and Deeside Leisure

Centre were like re-enactments of the Brighton beach scene in
Quadrophenia. Running battles, the lot!

Some hardcore types just wouldn't sing under any circumstances. I remember a Liverpool fan with a Union Jack wrapped
around his shoulders approach a group of about twenty or thirty
Road End lads I knew sitting outside a bar, trying to encourage
them to participate in the singing. 'Come on, lads,' he said. 'We
are in the European Cup final. Why don't you sing?' The scallies' blank expressions and shrug of the shoulders spoke a thousand words. He scurried off to laughter, and he must have realised
he had just met up with the Liverpool equivalent of the Mexican
Bandidos, sitting off, waiting for an opportunity or two.

Uncommon Kindness

HQ had changed its policy by the Monday to paying when you
ordered drinks, to stop the runners, and I always wondered to
myself whether or not they changed back when Liverpool left
town. Loads of fans came and went that night, but we liked it
there so much we stayed until the early hours. One of the denim-
clad pros opposite had worked a full shift, and in the hours we
were there I counted about ten punters. She was attractive, clad
in a denim outfit, with a very short skirt. She was tanned, with
black, straight hair and a noticeable gap in her front teeth that
was somehow strangely attractive. She was not much older than
us, probably in her early twenties, and as always I wanted to rescue
her from her life of hell. I went over to talk to her on a couple
of occasions, but she must've sensed I wasn't a punter. I tried to
engage her in conversation, but she didn't bite; she just told me
the rates.

I've always had this Catholic guilt thing which makes me
automatically want to save people like her – not because of any
religious conviction but because she was so attractive and was
stuck on the boulevard of broken dreams. I was curious. I wanted
to know her life story. How did she end up on that corner? I was
Travis Bickle from *Taxi Driver*; I was good against evil. I wanted

to help her, to change her, to give her money without the sex. She must have thought I was a right dickhead!

Many years later, in Prague, after a Liverpool game against Slovan Liberec, one of my mates, Mick P, and I spent the last couple of hours before our flight in the early hours giving money away to the homeless and the Bulgarian brasses around our hotel. This act of generosity was alcohol induced. It was five in the morning, and we probably only gave about the equivalent of twenty to thirty quid away in Czech money, but it was well worth it. Some of the homeless were too proud to take the money, probably thinking it was some sort of set-up, and some of the brasses got upset because they thought we didn't find them attractive enough to go with them, but we felt great after it, and most appreciated our stupidity. You should try it some time, but you've got to a) be bevvied, b) have money you don't think is easy to change back home, and c) have a captive audience of street people going nowhere who think you're minted.

Went Up the Eiffel Tower but Only for Half an Hour!

On the Tuesday morning we thought we should at least try to go up the Eiffel Tower. As we headed there, we continued to ask people, but this time in basic French, '*Ou est le centre d'Adidas?*' but still got quizzical looks, as if we weren't of this planet. You can't fail to be impressed by the Eiffel Tower, but to tell you the truth I wanted to get back to St Germain's clothes shops to find a bargain.

By this time most of the sports shops and clothes shops had cottoned on that they were being cleared out, especially near St Lazare station. Shops had introduced a two-at-a-time policy, like sweet shops do for schoolkids. Security had been so lapse that people just took the piss. Most couldn't believe that such a big city could be so easy to rob. It actually became surreal. They even put pairs of training shoes out! We had heard of the Parisian mob storming the Bastille, but now it was the Liverpool mob storming the boutiques! Bouncers were introduced, as word spread like wildfire that these hooligans were not really hooligans at all but an army of shoplifters.

It was on the Tuesday that I first heard the Paris song. I'm sure it was penned by one of our group, but I'm not certain if he claimed it. It was definitely Big Joe who I first heard singing it:

How would you like to be,
A Scouser in Gay Paree?
Walking along on the banks of the Seine,
Winning the European Cup once again?
We went up the Eiffel Tower,
But only for half an hour,
Cos we won't be late,
When we celebrate,
A victory in Gay Paree!

Most fans were going around all week singing the following little ditty, to the 'Here We Go' tune:

On the dole in Paree drinking wine,
On the dole in Paree drinking wine,
On the dole in Paree drinking wine,
On the dole, drinking wine!

That song became the theme of the trip, and in its own way it was quite funny at the time. Some adapted the lyric to 'On the rob in Paree drinking wine', but it must be remembered that the stereotype of the Scouser wasn't as extreme as it is nowadays. It was more lovable rogue than hardened criminal. This was pre-yuppie and pre-Harry Enfield. *The End* magazine wouldn't be out for another year, and *Boys from the Blackstuff* wouldn't be broadcast until 1982. The 'On the dole in Paree' song was viewed as a two-fingered salute to Thatcher and the Tory press, but, like a lot of 'easy' songs, it was sung too often, and it just became irritating and got adopted by other teams, just like the 'Ring of Fire' tune. Even though loads of people still have 'Ring of Fire' as their ringtone, it's finished, it's history, and so is the 'On the dole in Paree' song.

Some songs last the distance because they are harder to learn, and only a select few will ever really know them and their twenty or so verses. If anyone wants to get to know some of these more obscure songs, just go into The Albert pub in the shadow of the Kop a couple of hours after a match and you will hear a variety of songmeisters battling it out. They either get the nod of approval from the song-police or the shaking of heads, disapproving looks and then silence. With the Internet nowadays it's quite easy to find out the right words, but even then there are disputes about the correct words and verses.

The Evertonian

As with most European away trips you would always get an Evertonian turning up. I knew quite a few who would travel with Liverpool, and it is still happening to this day. You can't really blame them, can you? Starved of European excursions themselves some turned up with us on a regular basis. On the Tuesday afternoon as we sat in HQ back in Pigalle, our Evertonian, Pete T, turned up. 'I'm not interested in going the match,' he declared unconvincingly. 'I've just come for a laugh.'

Within an hour he was doubled up on the floor, pissing himself laughing. The Mod wanted to indulge in a bit of 'peeping'. We tried to warn him that he would be ripped off, but he wouldn't have it. He went into the peep show next to our bar. After about ten minutes he comes out all excited and in a state of arousal, flicking his not very mod-like wedge. 'I'm in love,' he exclaimed. 'You wanna see her. She's gorgeous, Hooto, and she's just given me the eye. I think she likes my hair. They can't resist these John Lennon heads.'

He had not been educated at our school of cynics in Bootle. We soon realised he was serious and smitten. 'She's not a prossie, you know, and she's just given me the nod. She's got these puppy-dog eyes, and she's asked me to come for a drink.'

Oh, how we laughed, but The Mod was determined. We knew there was no point in trying to convince him otherwise, so we adopted a policy of damage limitation. 'Look, give us most of your money and get in there, but she'll take you to the cleaners.'

The Mod was adamant. 'She's not like that. I've been talking to her. She genuinely likes me. No way is she a brass. You lot are too sarcastic.'

Half an hour later a glum-faced Mod emerged. 'What happened?' we asked in unison. We probably hoped he had gone in and given her a good seeing to, but it wasn't to be.

'I went into this bar, and we sat down. She said she wanted a Coke, then these two sumos turned up and charged me two weeks' fuckin' wages. [He was a brickie.] That was it. I didn't even get me tit.'

Getting your tit in those days was an obsession with schoolboys – well, it was in our school. Most people lied, of course, about their sexual exploits, and one of my mates told a great story about a girl he had been with. When he attempted to go for the penalty area, she screamed 'No!' He stopped immediately, thinking that she didn't want to know, that she was frigid or something. Then she came out with the immortal words, 'TITS FIRST!'

Now, even if this was a figment of his imagination or an apocryphal story handed down, it's still as funny as when I first heard it! This particular lad was a dirty bastard, so I believed him.

Anyway, back to the rip-off. We had warned The Mod, but he wouldn't listen. The Evertonian couldn't stop laughing; we all couldn't stop laughing – even The Mod was laughing. 'What did you talk about?' we asked. He had told her that he came from a long line of Celtic warriors, but she wasn't interested. As soon as she got her drink, she was off. He was absolutely and genuinely gutted, which made it even more amusing.

Many years later we would fall victim to a similar sting in Prague. About fifteen of us went into a lap-dancing-type club, but as we tried to leave a bouncer sprayed me and Mick P at the bottom of the stairs. I escaped, but Mick was held hostage inside the club. The other lads from the Leather Bottle were all outside (they have a habit of always being outside, on their way to a KFC), so I told them they still had Mick as a hostage. We shouted to them to let him go or we would call the police or kick the door in. 'The police are coming. They are on their way,' they shouted through the locked door.

We smelt a very large, bubonic-plague-carrying rat. They'd attacked us and sprayed us; how come they were calling the police? The police arrived, and some of them looked like schoolkids. 'No problem,' they said. 'You pay the fine, approx one hundred pounds, and no charges, no prison.' We couldn't believe it. It was a stitch-up, and they were in on it.

That's what happens sometimes in these shady places. We paid up, and later we saw the police having hot dogs with their 'take' from the fine. Mick P was chocka that we paid up, because he was an innocent man and he was quite looking forward to sampling a Prague nick.

Several months later five members of the Northern Ireland team would visit the same bar and would be involved in a similar sting. As soon as I saw the photo of the glum-looking bouncer on the back of a newspaper, I recognised him. He was moaning that one of the squad had assaulted him and given him fifteen stitches, and he was after compo. Their version of events was an exact replica of ours. They had attempted to leave, and the bouncer had demanded money over a disputed bar bill. The bouncer prob-ably thought they were on a stag night and he would tax them, as he had done to countless others with the backup of a corrupt police force. Unfortunately for him he couldn't get his pepper spray out in time, and the punters in question were really the Northern Ireland team who had just played the Czech Republic. This became a diplomatic incident, so the truth came out, and all charges were dropped against the players. I laughed my head off when I saw the bouncer with a big gash on his head. What goes around comes around! The moral of the story: don't go into dark, shady-looking gaffs with a neon light outside.

Margaret Thatcher and the Donkey

We should have known better in Prague, as we had warned The Mod a couple of decades before not to go into the dark, shady gaff with the neon light outside. Maybe we were wiser/more sensible back then, but that's the ironic thing about it: when you get older, you become overconfident, even blasé, in some of these places.

Back to Paris. As The Mod was so pissed off, we thought we would cheer him up by taking him to a porno cinema a few hundred yards away. We would never have dreamed of going to a place like this back home, but, after all, we were in Paris and on holiday, so anything went. We had noticed a few days ago the lead film, which, loosely translated, was entitled *Margaret Thatcher has Sex with a Donkey*. Curiosity got the better of us, and we nervously entered the empty cinema. It was the political symbolism which attracted us, your honour!

It would be churlish to say it wasn't a classic. Basically the scenario was a Maggie Thatcher lookalike having sex with a pantomime donkey. I was relieved it was a panto donkey, and let's get this straight, I do not approve of bestiality, but we did try to get our francs back because it wasn't a real donkey. The cashier laughed, we laughed, and he explained that 'real donkey against the law'. He thought we were sickos; we thought he was. It was another Travis Bickle moment. They were coming thick and fast. All the animals come out at night . . .

The Street-Corner Sketch

Big Joe looked like one of Tony Soprano's mob. He was sharp and ruthless. He could give stick out, and if he had an opinion, he stuck to it. He was full of ideas. He had always been full of ideas, and I had been going to the match with him for years. A veteran of many football specials, including the infamous Rome special, when he told you to do something, you usually did it. He was forceful and persuasive, let's say. He was one of the best Liverpool fans at our school and went everywhere with the Reds.

You could always rely on him if you were in a bad situation.

On that Tuesday night, though, he decided he wanted to be a street pimp and try to sell The Wedge to a gay punter – just for a laugh, of course, a big piss-take. You remember, The Wedge was the handsome one who was just out of his teens and quite French looking. Big Joe purchased a John Lennon cord cap and placed it on The Wedge's head, before pretending to be trying to sell him. He stopped terrified passers-by, who couldn't get away quick enough. Maybe they set up on the wrong street corner, but there were no takers. Let me point out that The Wedge had no gay tendencies at all and was a bit of a Warren Beatty type, if you get my drift, but he went along with the joke. Big Joe thought it was hilarious; I thought it was hilarious; the Evertonian thought it was hilarious; The Mod thought it was hilarious; so did The Wedge, and Mad Arse was off being mad somewhere else. Even the real hookers witnessed what was going on and smiled. After half an hour of stopping Parisians and pointing at The Wedge, saying 'You like boys?' as The Wedge stood there in an exaggerated hand-on-hips stance, he gave up. We were very drunk and very young. You had to be there!

After our miserable failure we all hatched another plan. The bar was filling up with the type of fan whose only away game all season is a Cup final. We would get our revenge! We decided to run a raffle in the bar, the star prize being the girl with a gap in her teeth. Excitement gripped the bar at the news that a raffle was being held for the girl in denim. I don't think any one of us would be very proud of it now, but let's just blame the ale, and, oh yes, we were caught up in the atmosphere of the place.

Everyone in the bar threw in. We would make a handsome profit. All sorts of happily married men went for it, probably dreading having the winning ticket. I saw the looks on people's faces – no one could refuse to throw-in due to peer-group pressure, but hardly anyone really wanted to win either. Excitement was reaching fever pitch, as people gathered nervously around the litre glass full of raffle tickets. Big Joe conducted the draw. He pulled out the winning ticket. Shit. The blood drained from my face. Oh no, it was my number. How was I going to get out of this without losing face? There was no way I was going with denim girl. I knew how many punters she'd had over the last two days, and I wanted to 'save' her anyway, not exploit her. I went into a cold sweat.

'Number nine. Who has got number nine? Come on, someone must have it,' shouted Big Joe. I kept quiet, and after a few anxious seconds I suggested that the winner must've 'got off'. Everyone agreed; I was off the hook.

'OK, let's draw another one,' suggested a voice from the crowd. The number was drawn, and someone shouted 'that's me' and yelped a cry of delight. He was immediately off to the toilets of the bar to knock one out, as he declared that he didn't want to suffer premature ejaculation with Miss Denim. He was obviously experienced in these matters and looked to be in his late 30s. He soon emerged from the squat-thrust bog with his winnings and was soon linking Miss Denim and heading for the apartment, egged on by a huge cheer. He returned about twenty minutes later with a broad smile lighting up his face. He was a deserving winner! Somehow, I don't think he was a talker.

We walked back to St Lazare, and the riot vans were outside the Madhouse hotel. It appeared to have gone off in shady street – loads were being arrested and the hotel raided. Furniture had been thrown out of windows, fire extinguishers had been let off and Liverpool slogans daubed all over the hotel. It had been a two-star hotel; now it was down to a no star, with a little help from the Scousers.

It transpired that some of the lads had been snatching flowers off the more mature prostitutes in the area, just for a laugh, and giving them to passers-by. The bar owners had taken offence again; they just loved getting themselves shut down. Glass and bottles littered the street, with sirens still wailing.

As we approached our hotel in a side street, we noticed a mob of about thirty walking towards us. From a distance we immediately thought they were Scousers, as they had training shoes and some had 'wolf leathers' on (a leather coat, elasticated at the waist, popular in Liverpool at the time). But as we got nearer, we could hear them talking in French. Shit, or *merde*, in this case. If we gave the wrong reaction, we were fucked. If we gave it toes, we were so pissed we were bound to stumble and fall. We walked silently towards them. I just thought to myself 'why me?', as I had just recovered from a severe beating in London several months before. They had chair legs and weapons in their hands, and it was obvious they had just been battling with Liverpool fans. Miraculously, they stared at us but didn't ask us '*Quelle heure est-il?*' (the old 'what time is it' suss). We passed them by without a whisper. I can't imagine that ever happening in England. We breathed a collective sigh of relief. We would have stood no chance: five of us and about thirty of them. Someone was watching over us.

The Day of the Match

Hangover from hell! We weren't privy to the horrors of a Stella hangover back then. In those days it was all brown bitter (half a bitter and a bottle of brown), golden (half a lager and half a bitter) and snake-bite (half a lager and half a cider), or pints of non-export, weaker lager. Stella was a relatively new drink, more alcoholic than our usual stuff, and we didn't know it was like giving whisky to the Injuns. No wonder we had been trying to sell our mates in the seediest area of the city. We had a perverse sense of humour at the best of times, but that Stella had brought out the worst in us.

We weren't proud of our behaviour, but we were young and inebriated. And what the hell, we were heading for the Park des Princes and our third European Cup final. Last night's 'donkey' was just a bad dream. Had we really organised a raffle for a brass? What the fuck were we thinking of? Just blame the Stella! Did we really go into a porno cinema? Just blame the Stella! Did one of our party really fall in love with a peep-show dancer? Stella again! This Stella thingy would be getting the blame for a lot of things in the years to come.

On the morning of the match I decided to go to Notre-Dame to light a candle for the Reds and also for relatives no longer with us. I always try to do this if we play abroad, and most of the big cities have magnificent cathedrals. Then we made our way to the ground.

We had been told by the *Liverpool Echo* and the Merseyside Police that there would be a ring of steel around the ground and not to travel without tickets. It was the same sketch as always in Cup finals: lack of tickets, demand and supply. Liverpool chairman John Smith objected to UEFA over the 12,000 allocation apiece to Liverpool and Real Madrid and asked them to stop nominating stadiums to be used for major European finals before the finalists were known. Charles Lambert, in the *Liverpool Echo*, reported that Mr Smith would be meeting top UEFA officials to try to avoid the problem for future finals. Mr Smith called the allocation a 'French farce', and Liverpool's general secretary, Peter Robinson, stressed the club's view, saying, 'UEFA will have to be more flexible in the future. Quite often the ground they choose for the final is perfectly adequate, like Madrid last year and Munich the year before. But this time they should have realised that there would be problems with Paris (capacity 48,000) as soon as the four semi-finalists were known.' He added, 'When some of Europe's best-supported clubs are in the semis, like this year with Liverpool, Real Madrid, Bayern and Milan, they should consider switching the final.'

Fans were forced to scramble for a pitiful allocation. It seemed that nothing had been learnt from previous years, and Liverpool would take over to Paris more than three times their official allocation. The more things change, the more they stay the same. As a result, thousands of Liverpool fans travelled to Paris ticketless, ignoring pleas from the club and the Parisian police to stay at home. It's as simple as this: if your team is in the European Cup final, you want to be there, full stop.

Our Evertonian thought he would come to the ground for something to do, as he was adamant he didn't want to get in. We spent most of the afternoon having a great time in a bar about a mile from the ground. By the third or fourth pint, we were even singing Beatles songs. Everyone talks about the French being arrogant and unfriendly, but our Parisians weren't like that at all. The bar staff were made up with us, and we spent so much in there they started giving us sandwiches and croissants gratis.

The Ring of Steel

It must be said that the 'ring of steel' promised by the French authorities was not much cop. People were waltzing through this so-called ring of steel with ice creams in their hands. I had a ticket but didn't have to show it to get in the ground. By the time we got there, you could see the riot police were in a state of panic. They may have battered the Paris students in 1968, but Liverpool fans determined to get in to see their heroes were a different prospect altogether.

Basically Liverpool fans were legging the CRS all over the place. Ticket touts were being attacked, and the French authorities had lost control. By the time we arrived at the ground, they seemed to have given up. Liverpool FC had feared this, due to the massive demand and lack of allocation, but UEFA had ignored their pleas. Whereas a dozen or so Anfield Road police, led by the notorious Blackbeard and Bent-Nose, could control the terraces at Anfield, hundreds of these Robocop riot police just turned and gave it toes. Hilarious! I heard that the same brave policemen took their revenge on ordinary, innocent Liverpool fans later on.

The Evertonian with us who didn't even want to get in . . . well, got in, without even trying. He just walked behind me all the way, expecting to be challenged at each inadequate checkpoint. When we got to the turnstile, he just walked in behind me. He honestly wanted to get knocked back, so he had an excuse not to watch us. He would now be subjected to our third European Cup triumph.

One thing we all seemed to be disappointed by was the lack of Real Madrid fans inside, outside and around the city itself.

Even the ones who were there weren't very vocal. We had grown up on them being one of the great clubs of the world, but their fans didn't live up to their team's reputation. I did see one fan with a big drum outside the ground, but he had that confiscated by the Liverpool noise police. We were told that they could have sold their allocation four or five times over, but the difference is they didn't travel without tickets, whereas Liverpool fans always did. This was inevitably going to happen. History had told us this. We must've outnumbered them by three to one, no problem.

This is the fundamental difference in football culture that UEFA didn't seem to be able to comprehend. You see, Continental teams just don't tend to travel to away games en masse, even in their own countries, whereas in the UK it is a tradition passed down through the generations. As reports of UEFA officials scoffing their lobster and drinking their free champagne got back to us on the tear-gas-filled streets, it reminded me of the French aristocracy before the revolution. They simply had no idea of what was going on outside their cocooned environment in the hospitality tents, and the fact that Liverpool won the match covered up the chaos and the woeful shambles.

The Immortals

Bob Paisley's team wrote themselves into the record books with a hard-earned victory to lift their third European Cup. Phil Thompson declared after the win that the team had joined 'the immortals'. The game, though, never really caught fire, with both teams playing a cautious game, but who cared about that? Many people said the final was boring, but any match in which your team lifts the European Cup isn't going to be too boring, is it?

The late Laurie Cunningham (the stylish ex-West Brom forward) provided the Real Madrid threat up front, and Kenny Dalglish, Liverpool's main danger man, was closely marked throughout and was the target of some harsh tackles. Alan Kennedy scored the only goal of the match, in the eighty-first minute as the game seemed to be heading for extra-time. He collected the ball from a throw-in and galloped into the Madrid penalty area to fire a superb shot from an acute angle. If the match was a bit of a let-down in terms of spectacle, the celebrations after were anything but.

We headed back to HQ in Pigalle for a night of wild revelry. Our fountain was like Southport open-air baths. Paris had never seen anything like it since VE day. Well, that's what one of the locals observed! The trouble of the previous nights was forgotten about, and the Paris police breathed a collective sigh of relief. The tense pre-match atmosphere evaporated as Liverpool fans hugged bemused French waiters and complete strangers in the carnival atmosphere. On the Champs-Elysées thousands of supporters sang their hearts out in bars and cafes, toasting their heroes with beer and champagne. Flags, scarves and banners adorned famous buildings, including the Arc de Triomphe, where thousands of motorists beeped their horns and waved to the fans. And in some shady corner, even the Mexican Bandido crew smiled. It was a long night, and fans only went back to their hotels when they were hoarse or when it became light.

The following night the Liverpool team were given a rapturous welcome home by over half a million fans on the sixteen-mile victory route. Back in Paris, nursing hangovers and nearing exhaustion, our Red Army made its way slowly back to Liverpool. As is nearly always the case, the fans who travel to see the matches hardly ever see the homecoming. But we couldn't complain. We had seen our heroes in the flesh, and that's what it is all about. As we left Paris for Dieppe, I promised myself that I would return as soon as I could, to visit all the places I had wanted to see but couldn't, due to our search for the Adidas Centre.

The journey home was pretty uneventful, apart from the ferry, which resembled Greatie Market, as there was so much gear being sold and bartered. We arrived home late on Friday evening worn out but euphoric. We had witnessed history in the making and survived.

Four months later, in September '81, I did indeed go back to Paris and spent a week in the same hotel. I was lucky enough to see The Clash, The Beat and Wah! Heat on the same bill for seven consecutive nights at the Mogador Theatre, just around the corner from the *Fawlty Towers* hotel. But even that couldn't compare with our third European Cup triumph at the Parc des Princes on Wednesday 27th May, 1981. We never did find the mythical Adidas Centre and never once spoke to any normal French girls, but who cares? We had witnessed The Immortals!

Rome, 1984

JEGSY DODD

European Cup Final, 30th May 1984
Stadio Olympico, Rome
Attendance: 69,693

Liverpool FC   1–1   **AS Roma**
Neal (13')   Pruzzo (42')

PENALTIES: Liverpool win 4–2

Nicol	x	✓	Di Bartolomi
Neal	✓	x	Conti
Souness	✓	✓	Righetti
Rush	✓	x	Graziani
Kennedy	✓		

Substitutes: Steve Nicol, Bob Bolder, Gary Gillespie, Michael Robinson, David Hodgson

Manager: Joe Fagan

AS Roma: Franco Tancredi (1), Michele Nappi (2), Dario Bonetti (3), Ubaldo Righetti (4), Sebastiano Nela (5), Agostino Di Bartolomei (6, captain), Roberto Falcão (7), Toninho Cerezo (8), Bruno Conti (9), Rooberto Pruzzo (10), Francesco Graziani (11)

Substitutes used: Marco Strukeli, Odoacre Chierico

Manager: Nils Liedholm

L iverpool Football Club have always been my drug of choice. They have been a lifelong addiction for which there is no known cure. Some observers will tell you that it's like a marriage, with all its ups and downs and its peaks and troughs, but in reality it's far worse. You can walk away from marriage and fall in love with someone new. In fact it's not unusual for some people to do this on a number of occasions. With Liverpool FC it is not an option to turn your back and walk out and support someone else – that would be classed as a hanging offence. You have to face facts. There are no divorce loopholes or trial separations. You are in it for the long run. From the hyper-active kid with the cow's lick and grazed knees out playing footy in the street, to the incontinent, grumpy old bastard pinching the nurse's arse in the home for the bewildered, you will be Red. It's a lifetime journey with no dropping-off points, and the only time you will cease being obsessed with this club of ours is when you cease to exist altogether. If that all sounds dramatic and a little bit over the top for our new, squeaky-clean, corporate-type fan, may I suggest that you just don't understand the deep-rooted passion that fuels this club of ours.

I've been on this roller-coaster ride now for longer than I care to remember. Been to all the finals from Rome back in 1977 to Athens in 2007, and, believe me, it's been a mad one. I've been in every situation imaginable following this glorious team. There have been tears of joy and tears of utter dejection, and every year has been a unique adventure. The year I'm going to tell you about is 1984 – the year we played Roma in the final in their backyard. Strap yourselves in; it's gonna be a bumpy old ride.

This was supposed to be the year when the world would finally end. George Orwell had written his famous book with *Nineteen Eighty-Four* as the title, and the scaremongers had been proph-esying for more than half a century that it was all going to go

BANG. We cashed in our chips and sat on our hands and waited. The world just kept spinning, and the Reds kept on winning. It was business as usual. There were loads of things in the news, like the famine in Africa, the Brighton bomb and the fire at York Minster cathedral caused by lightning. (Surely that's an act of God? Oooooh, spooky.) The thing that stood out and signified the year for me, though, was the Miners' Strike, which began on 12th March and lasted for just on a year.

Liverpool didn't have miners, but what it did have was an army of social and political activists who would fight for justice at the drop of a hat. It was an exciting time, putting on benefit gigs and doing fund-raisers for the miners' families. Everybody wore the 'Coal Not Dole' stickers at the match, and the buckets used to get passed around in the boozers outside the ground and in town.

The End magazine was our bible at the time. It was kind of a humorous, left-wing, scally, fashion, music type of thing that attracted the nutter with a social conscience. Also, it kept you up to date with what was happening at street level like no other publication since has ever come near to. It deserves its place in Liverpool folklore, and its writers, like Hooton, Jones, Potter, etc., still nod in agreement when fat, balding middle-aged ex-hooligans collar them in town and get all misty eyed. Yes, *The End*, imitated many times, never bettered, sadly missed.

All through the '80s it seemed as if it was the City of Liverpool v. the Government. I think most Scousers have always secretly buzzed off the idea that the rest of the country thinks they're mad. When you think back to some of the anti-Liverpool headlines of that era, when the papers described the city as a 'Catholic Calcutta dying on its knees, begging for forgiveness' or the 'self-pity city', it only created a stronger resolve and a deeper sense of identity. Sometimes it bordered on a bit of a siege mentality, which made us feel different from the rest of the United Kingdom. A bit sepa-ratist and a bit 'People's Republic of Liverpool', but whichever way you looked at it, it was never a dull decade.

Even if we played Nottingham Forest tomorrow, after all these years, there would still be shouts of 'Scab'. The Nottingham miners broke the strike, while all those families in the pit villages in Yorkshire, Wales and beyond suffered no income for a whole year. Half the woodentops on the Kop these days wouldn't understand, but Scousers never forget when there's been an injustice.

I'm coming over a bit on the militant side here, but it must be said that I was never into all that 'one out, all out' (for the slightest reason) caper. I remember me dad when he was on the docks and he'd come home and announce that he was on strike again, and even though I was only about ten, I'd think, 'What the fuck is it now? You only went back to work last week.'

When I started getting involved with the music scene in that mid-'80s era, I wrote a song about the Liverpool that we knew then. It's called 'Always the Bridesmaid', and pardon me for saying this but it's a fuckin classic. Everything that I predicted more than twenty years ago has finally come true. Call me a prophet; call me a visionary; call me anything you want. Evertonians seem to favour the more direct 'dirty, horrible, Rednosed twat'. But whatever you do, if you get a chance to listen to it, do so. And all will be revealed.

Along with the football, the fashion and the music came women. Ah, yes, women – those strange creatures who we pretend to understand but never really do; the single most-important factor in splitting up the 'firm', bar none. The moment you start looking at that new sofa in DFS's ongoing sale is the day that train leaves platform nine without you on it. Wave goodbye to all those away days, sonny boy, because you are about to take your first steps towards being a Sky guy. You can get all vocal down at your local, bouncing up and down, knocking everyone's ale over when we score. You can even have a roll around in the car park with that big fat Evertonian bastard who only goes in there when Liverpool are on just to wind everyone up. That's if she'll *allow* you to go to the pub at all, seeing as you did promise to do the bathroom this weekend. Then, horror of horrors, she suggests you get Sky installed because 'it doesn't seem right going all the way to the pub to see it when you can stay at home and watch it with me'.

Ouch! You have been warned, boys. Read all of the warning signs. At least when the lads phone you, on the way back, you'll be able to tell them that the ball crossed the line, and, yes, it was offside. But you know, and they know, that life will never be the same again.

Some of our finest fans over the years have fallen inexplicably into the honeytrap. You see them in Asda pushing a trolley next to some fuckin big bloater, the type of bird the sea wouldn't take out, and you think, 'Jesus. He jibbed the match for that? Strange world!' You get closer, and he says, 'All right, lad, you still goin'?' You say, 'Oh aye, yeah.' And he says, 'Obviously you went to Istanbul?' 'Of course. Did you?' And you can tell before he opens his mouth that he didn't. 'We watched it in the pub, didn't we, love?' says the Hattie Jacques lookalike. 'It was brilliant. You should've been there,' she says. 'I was there,' I reply. He looks down and says, 'Anyway, lad, you take care. Keep the faith.' 'Yeah, see you around some day.' And with that, off they go, her like a baby elephant in the tightest trackie bottoms ever seen and him a broken man.

In 1984 I was probably in my prime – out every night on the razz, pulling birds, breaking promises and doing all the types of things lads do at that age. Me and me mates had a helluva time, and if the truth be known, yes, I shagged some absolute corkers. One night stands, three in a bed, all kinds of weird and wonderful things went on.

It goes without saying that sometimes the quality control would slip a little more than it should have done, due to large quantities of alcohol passing through the body. Even those lads who thought they were fireproof have let their guard down on more than the odd occasion. You know the score. It's three in the morning, you're putting in an Olympic-style performance with a girl who could pass for Marilyn Monroe and you wake a few hours later to discover she looks more like Marilyn Manson. Its panic stations, but you must remain calm. The king-size hangover kicks in, and the aim is to get out as quick as possible, with the minimum of fuss. Be polite, avoid morning sex, hope to God no eggs have been fertilised and get through that door unscathed. As you're walking away up the road, gurning with guilt behind your false beard and dark glasses, you can almost hear that ridiculous matchday announcement in your ears: 'All clear, Operation Anfield. Operation Anfield, all clear.'

On the other hand if she's a bit of a fox, you feel as if you're nailed to the bed, with a smile as smug as the one you had when Rushie scored four against the Infidels at Castle Doom. You close your eyes and drift away, dreaming of her feeding you grapes, then running along through the surf hand in hand (probably in slow motion). Suddenly you're awoken from your slumber by Miss World when she says, 'Listen, mate, it's been really nice meeting you and that, but you're gonna have to go. I've got people calling round soon.' And you're like, 'Erm, well, give us your number and we'll maybe go out for a drink some time.' Looking completely unimpressed, she says, 'No, you're OK. I'll just see you around. You're gonna have to go.' It's then that it dawns on you that Mrs Hot Lips doesn't exactly share your enthusiasm. It is her who has let her standards drop this time. Last night, in her drunken world, I was Mr Brad Pitt. This morning, in the cold light of day, I am Mr Mosh Pit.

You do her a favour and vacate the premises as quietly and quickly as possible – out of the back door, of course, so as not to be seen by the neighbours. Her parting shot confirms her embarrassment. 'By the way, you promise you won't tell anyone?' 'Promise.' And you're off. You're thinking, 'Fuckin hell, she's actually ashamed that I slept with her, but on the other hand she is the fittest bird for miles around, and I've seen her naked.'

It's Sunday afternoon, about four hours later, and you're in the local pub. The promise you gave her was broken within the first twenty seconds. By now (as you top yourself up from last night) your tongue is getting looser. You may as well go the whole hog and hire a town-crier's outfit, ring a bell and shout, 'Hear ye, hear ye, oyez, oyez. Guess who I shagged last night?' You've had a result; you might as well milk it.

The era which I'm talking about was a bit of a crossroads for me personally. I'd been working away for the past five or six summers. Ibiza in 1978 was unchartered territory for a fresh-faced nineteen year old. The only compilations released then had blokes with big muzzies on twangin' their geetars. Then on to the Isle of Man to finish off the holiday season. Hey, don't laugh. The Isle of Man was the canine's testicles. We did more shagging in those two months on the island than nearly double that in Eye Fackin' Beefa. It was Jersey in 1979. In 1980/81 it was a town called Hania in Crete, followed by a Greek island called Ios in '82. A village called Elne, by Perpignan, in France for 1983 and then home as always for the footy season.

It was a real novelty to bum around Europe those days. A bit of work here and there – fruit picking, labouring, whatever – always with a large slice of ducking and diving thrown in. These days every student or slacker is off to Australia via South East Asia with their mobile at their side, armed with credit cards, cheap flights, email addresses and easy access to Mummy and Daddy if things get a little uncomfortable. In those days if you ran out of wonga or you'd been beheaded or robbed, you just got on with it.

Don't get me wrong, all parents worry, but back then they'd probably receive just the one gnarled postcard saying, 'A'right, Mum, hope everything is OK with you and me dad. Everything here is sound. I've got a nice bronzy and I've met a lovely girl from Sweden who's a gymnast. She keeps me out of trouble, so there's no need to worry about anything. I'll be back in time for the start of the season. Missing you both, take care, blah, blah, blah, xxx.' Or something along those lines. Nowadays if your shoelace breaks or you've got a bit of a chesty cough, your parents are informed within minutes and a cheque to comfort the blow is in cyberspace before you can say Borussia Moenchengladbach.

Spending my summers abroad finally came to an end in the year we played the final in Rome. Like I said, it was a bit of a crossroads for me personally. It was goodbye to all the shenanigans of getting leathered every night and trying to shag as many different nationalities as possible before your nob drops off. And yes, I know it sounds stupid and childish, but yep, me and my mate Andy Faith, travelling companion (and Milwall fan), did keep a bit of a list of our Continental conquests on the inside of our rucksacks – exotic names from far-off places, but still the behaviour of sniggering, puerile schoolboys.

I've seen players getting interviewed, and that old chestnut about whether scoring a goal is better than sex or the other way round has cropped up more than once. Now, as you know, I'm just a fan, but here's my take on it. There's shags and shags, and there's goals and goals. For instance if you've been married for years and it's all been done before, it's a bit like scoring against Middlesbrough when you're already two up. It's a nice feeling, you've got a smile on your face and there's a warm glow, but you're hardly gonna cartwheel down Walton Breck Road screaming 'Get in there!'

On the other hand if you finally interfere with the statuesque goddess that you have admired, fantasised and dreamed about, well, that is the equivalent to scoring in a derby or against the Mancs.

But a last-minute winner against either of these two bastions of bile and bitterness is a different kettle of fish altogether. To match the feeling of utter, deranged elation as the ball hits the back of the net against either of these shower of bastards is nigh on impossible. When you 'spontaneously human combust' with joy in the Upper Bullens Road at Castle Doom or in Compost Corner at the Theatre of Screams, you know it doesn't get any better – a bigger rush of excitement than crack, smack and the combined exports of Peru, Bolivia and Colombia put together.

And here's the big one, more satisfying than throwing a mix into Pamela Anderson! Now I know what you're thinking. You're probably sitting there thinking, 'He's lost it. He's lost the plot. He's turned into a shirt-lifter. In fact he's probably reading *Sausage Jockey Monthly* as we speak.' But hold your horses and bear with me. My reasoning is simple. If you have sex, it is supposed to be a shared moment between two people (although I believe United fans prefer to have sex on their own, hence the reason they are known as a bunch of wankers). But when priceless goals are scored, in the most important games, it is a euphoria which is shared not just by thousands in the ground but by people in bars all over the world. It's like a communal outpouring of joy and relief. The battle songs that follow are sung with a power and conviction you could never replicate in daily life. You're still talking about the goal on Monday, and on Tuesday and Wednesday. Don't get me wrong, if you and your bird want to invite all the neighbours round to bounce around the living room singing sex songs to celebrate your successful bout of intercourse, that's up to you. Basically, great moments in footy are like communal orgasms without the mess and the need to get your head down for an hour after.

Football now is, without doubt, the global game, and with that it becomes a magnet for tourism for all the top teams. Everybody wants to watch Liverpool v. Man U or Barca v. Real, the Milan derby, and yes, it can be a pain in the arse sitting next to some bird who's spent hours getting ready to sit there on the phone the whole match telling every fucker she's ever met how fantastic it is, when she hasn't got a clue what's going on.

The touts outside The Albert pub will tell you they're not gonna sell you a ticket for the game at face price when some nugget from Ireland is over for the weekend dressed like a scarlet Christmas tree willing to pay a couple of hundred quid for the pleasure. Even I've been on a blag season ticket for the last fifteen or so years, so, really, I don't exist in the eyes of the club. Luckily I've been going long enough to know the movers and shakers, and I always get in everywhere, but it's a bit cloak and dagger. I just wanna go straight. I'm getting on a bit to be ducking and diving every time we play someone half-decent.

September '83 the Mighty Reds took to the field against BK Odense about a hundred miles from Copenhagen in the beautiful country of Denmark. It was a tricky one to get to for the travelling army, but, as always, they made it. As I said before, there were no discount flights, so the majority went overland by boat and train, or boat and car. These were always the best games for a bit of an adventure. Susceptible to the 'anything can happen' scenario, a road trip is a far better way of seeing a country than just arriving en masse at the airport and getting a cab to your hotel.

That's why I've always secretly preferred the UEFA Cup to the Big One. I know there's more prestige winning the European, with all its bling and showbiz hype and that, but from a pure fan's point of view, the UEFA Cup is a better laugh. You get to go to mad, tinpot towns in the middle of nowhere: remote places in Eastern Europe where we, the working class of Liverpool, strut around like the boys who broke the bank at Monte Carlo. Give me three days on the lash in Romania over three in Barcelona any time, and there's a better quality of fan that makes the journey. There are too many whoppers in places like Barca or Rome. But Kosice in the Czech Republic? There's only one winner – two pounds twenty for ten pints of Czech beer.

Most teams from the Champions League are from the major Westernised cities that you've probably been to already in some way, shape or form. You wouldn't play a team like Odense nowadays in the Champions League format unless it was in a qualifier, which is a shame. To appreciate the big European nights on foreign soil, I feel blessed to have served my apprenticeship on the crumbling terraces of the less glamorous stadiums. They all have their tales to tell. Anyway, we beat Odense 1–0. Kenny scored the goal. A crowd of 30,000 watched the game – more than twice the number that watched the following home leg. I could give you the team, but I really can't be arsed.

Oh, go on then: Bruce in goal, Phil Neal, Alan Kennedy, Lawrenson, Johnston, Jockey Hansen, Kenny, Sammy Lee, Rushie, Michael Robinson and Souness. I don't have to name every team from every match right through, do I? You're all football mad. As expected, the home leg was a piece of piss, the Reds winning 5–0 without too much fuss. Kenny scored a couple of first-half goals to overtake Denis Law's British record in the European Cup. Robinson scored his first goal since joining the club and added another one later on. The other goal (the fourth) was an own goal scored by some bloke called Clausen.

I suppose Clausen's oggy would rate in the 'football versus sex' debate as one of those moments in a long, boring relationship when you come home from the pub after a few too many with best intentions and decide halfway through it's not happening. Your mind has wandered, and you've forgotten why you wanted to do it in the first place. You abort the exercise, roll over, fart and go to sleep, with no recollection in the morning of either Clausen's goal or your feeble attempt to satisfy your long-suffering, understanding partner. She could have a G-spot the size of a penalty spot and you'd still have missed it.

Athletic Bilbao arrived at Anfield for the first leg of round two on 19th October with a bit of a reputation for being cynical and tough in equal measure. They got the 0–0 draw that they came for by being supremely disciplined. There was the usual time-wasting and no shortage of niggly fouls, but Liverpool never really came close. The crowd for the home leg was up on the last game against Odense, but still only 33,000, and the team was the same, which in these days is almost retro.

The second leg over there seemed quite a formidable proposition, and, to be honest, a lot of people thought we'd blown it. I didn't go to the away leg, because at the time I was giving Social Security the best years of my life. Back then away fans were almost justified in singing 'Sign On, Sign On' to our firm, because probably more than half *were* scratching around trying to make a quick buck.

Now what does my head in is spotty little gel-headed dickheads from somewhere like Berkshire standing in the away end supporting whoever's doing well from down south, singing dole/poverty songs at equally spotty gel-headed dickheads from somewhere like Hertfordshire wearing Liverpool tops standing next to them. If you're signing on now, it's because you've got a disability, you're a smackhead or you're just a pure lazy cunt. There is no excuse, not like there was 'back in the day'. If you want to earn an honest wage nowadays, it's there. All those away fans who sing these tiresome songs – give them the stick that they deserve.

The worst offenders are the fuckin' Geordies – probably the most unfunny, unfashionable fans in the Western world. To think some people actually say that Geordies and Scousers are alike; well, let me just piss on that little bonfire right here, right now. Newcastle is like the Third World compared to Liverpool. Of course everybody on Tyneside lives in a mansion or a castle and has always earned fantastic wages. There has never been a pit closure or a shipyard laying people off, and on the pitch they're always the most successful team in Britain every year . . . I don't think. With a bit of luck one year they'll come down to support their team and they'll walk through the door marked 'Twenty-First Century'. We can only hope.

For Athletic Bilbao away we needed a big, big performance to stay in the competition. This is what European football is all about, and this is the type of game where Liverpool excelled. A roaring, partisan crowd in this fiercely independent Basque stronghold willed the Spaniards on. Liverpool's only change from the previous ties was Stevie Nicol coming in for Craig Johnston. After a nervy start, when the home side went close a couple of times, the Redmen began to dominate. Graeme Souness gave a Man of the Match performance, and the home side's resistance was finally broken in the sixty-sixth minute when the greatest striker of all time powered in a downward header to break the Spaniards' hearts. You could always rely on Rushie to do the business when it really mattered.

Just the mention of the name Ian Rush to a room full of Evertonians would be enough to see them scatter, hiding under the settee and diving through plate-glass windows. Any man who has single-handedly inflicted so much pain and misery on Everton deserves (in my eyes) the title of a true legend. I've been lucky enough to have had the pleasure of Rushie's company over the years for the odd drink or two, and he, like big Jan Molby, has that rare talent which is sadly missing amongst today's fly-by-night footballers: the ability to go to the bar and get the ale in without having to be asked. Rushie, I will raise my glass and toast you till the day I die.

Do you want to hear what my top-five songs of that year were? I'm gonna tell you anyway. Straight in at number five was 'Pearly-Dewdrops' Drops' by the Cocteau Twins. Liz Fraser, the singer, had an amazing voice. And at number four, pop-pickers, we had 'Between the Wars' by the incomparable Billy Bragg – a great song with great lyrics by England's finest protest singer. Coming up on the rails, a surprise entry at number three, the Men They Couldn't Hang's cover of 'The Green Fields of France' – an absolute classic about the futility of war. Hang on! That's two mentions of war in the last two songs. Anyway, folks, let's have a big roll on the drums, because the top two were almost inseparable, but they both can't be number one. At number two, iiittts 'The Killing Moon' by Echo and The Bunnymen. As soon as you hear the opening chords, you think, 'Oh, yes, let's have it.' A timeless masterpiece! But we can't all be winners, and there has to be a winner. Mr McCulloch and Mr Sergeant of the Bunnies sit bemused in the wings, wondering what on earth could have beaten them to that much-coveted top spot. They're not gonna like it when I announce that Jegsy Dodd's number-one song for 1984 is . . . wait for it, is . . . 'What Difference Does it Make?' by The Smiths. Oooh, it's controversial, right enough. I can almost hear you saying 'the bastard's picked a Manchester band over a Liverpool band, blah, blah'. *Echo* sellers with a billboard next to them reading 'Washed-up local poet signs his own death warrant'. Urchins shout 'traitor' as I walk down Church Street. I go to the match and there's empty seats all around me, an exclusion zone. I can hear the bloke three rows behind me saying, 'That's him, the one with the bald patch and no mates.'

Next up for the third round were Benfica, the Portuguese champions. Things were starting to get serious, and we knew that this wouldn't be easy. Benfica were no mugs and had a glorious European history, so the Redmen had to be totally focused. The first leg was at Anfield, and the Kop was well up for it. The team was basically the same as usual, with only one change: Robinson coming in for Dalglish, and Kenny on the bench.

After a first-half stalemate in which few chances were created,

Joe Fagan, the manager at the time, threw on Kenny at the start of the second forty-five. It was an inspired substitution, as Kenny found the time and space to penetrate the Portuguese defence. The breakthrough came in the 67th minute when Whelan put Kennedy through down the left. He crosses to the far post, and guess who's waiting to power in a far-post header? Ian Rush, of course. As I said before, if the going's getting tough and we need to dig a result out, give it to the 'Rush monster' and everything will be just fine. The Reds pushed on and had a few more chances and a good shout for a penno turned down, but they had to make do with a flimsy 1–0 lead to take to the intimidating Stadium of Light in Lisbon.

The teams were greeted by 70,000 mad Benfica fans as they walked onto the pitch in a cauldron of noise. The fans have this tradition at their stadium for the big matches where an eagle is released before the game and it circumnavigates the pitch then swoops back down to its handler by the halfway line. It has to be said that it is an awesome sight to behold, but it got me thinking. You know all these British clubs with birds as their emblem or nickname, surely we could do something like that here? We've got the Eagles, the Seagulls, the Magpies, the Bluebirds, Peacocks, etc. Sheffield Wednesday would release an owl, and he'd say, 'Sorry, mate, I'm nocturnal. I only do night games.' Swansea's swan would say, 'You can fuck off. I'll do it if the pitch is waterlogged, but there's no way I'm prancing around on a dry centre circle.' The robins of Swindon Town would only be able to do January and February – December is far too busy with photo shoots for Christmas cards and the like. The rest of the year they'll be out of the country, as it's just too bloody hot.

Our dear neighbours in blue from Castle Doom could also get in on the act. They could join the fun by adopting a bird as their club emblem. How's about a dodo or maybe a turkey for their club badge? Seems logical to me. Then, at five to three on matchday, they could release eleven headless chickens onto the pitch to entertain their wonderfully gracious, fair-minded fans. I suppose it's too difficult to release any type of bird into the sky above their crumbling stadium due to the airspace being full of circling vultures ready to swoop down and pick on the bones of another season of famine and misery. Everton FC: don't you just love 'em?

So, the eagle is in the sky; the teams are on the pitch; the bottles of Superbok have been quaffed – it's time to get this quarter-final under way. It may be officially called round three, second leg, but to you and I it's the quarter-final, second leg. The place is bouncing and Benfica really fancy their chances. This is their manor, these are their fans and all they have to do is pull back a slender 1–0 deficit. I remember not being too confident before the game, thinking maybe Rushie might sneak an away goal but being wary of the atmosphere and the feeling of dread if we conceded early on. Obviously I needn't have worried, because from the moment their goalie, Bento, fumbled Ronnie Whelan's header into his own net in the ninth minute, it was one-way traffic.

This had to be one of our best performances on foreign soil ever. Benfica were a hugely respected club and feared throughout Europe, but we absolutely battered them that night. It was a night of despair for the hosts, as Dalglish, in particular, dictated everything, setting Craig Johnston up for a twenty-yarder, then crossing for that man Rush to head home, and then putting Ronnie Whelan through to squeeze number four home from a tight angle. The Portugeezers scored a consolation header from Nené, but it scarcely mattered as the Reds marched on and left the whole of Lisbon traumatised.

After that you got the feeling that this could be our year. We also won the Milk Cup that month, after beating our local rivals from across the park in a replay at Maine Road, Manchester, with Graeme Souness scoring the only goal of the game. The final the previous weekend had been legendary, as it was the first time the two Merseyside clubs had met each other at Wembley. It seems mad looking back now, but in those days we genuinely did get on together. We were all good mates.

I think a lot of it goes back to the way the rest of the country viewed us in the '80s. We were probably the least-liked city in the UK, and the reputation of Scousers was at its lowest ebb. We were treated as a far-flung outpost of the British Empire, and the disparaging comments came thick and fast. From the politicians to the newspapers to the stand-up comedians, we were the butt of everyone's jokes and the source of much contempt. So I suppose, in those kinds of situations, it's almost natural to pull up the drawbridge and stick together. The city had a kind of 'us against the rest of the world' feel to it, and the thought of almost being a separatist state was welcomed more than it was discouraged.

This was also the golden age of football hooliganism (although that would all change a year later, after Heysel). There were probably more hoolies bouncing around the nation's towns and cities on a Saturday afternoon than the entire armed forces and police put together. One thing's for certain, though: if a big, notorious crew of away supporters were due to converge on the city, Liverpool and Everton would always join up – because it was *our* city that they were trying to take over. Sadly our unique bond of friendship is no more, as anyone who has been to a derby in the last fifteen to twenty years will testify.

There are many differing opinions as to why the relationship between our two clubs has been so poisonous over the recent past. Everyone has their own take on it, but I think it's quite simple. Evertonians are frustrated because they will always live in the shadow of their more illustrious neighbours. They hate the thought of Liverpool v. Man U as a bigger game than the derby. They feel left out. We have the name of the city. We have the badge of the city. We have the cups, the worldwide fan base, while they have mediocrity. And that is the crux. They are insignificant in modern-day football. Nobody actually cares about them any more, and they are wounded. They will try any desperate measure to score points over their vastly superior rivals – none more so than the ridiculous 'People's Club' logo that has appeared in recent years. I know it's bollocks; you know it's bollocks; they know it's bollocks. In fact everyone on Merseyside knows it's bollocks, but they will persist with it. Funny how the smaller clubs with less success and fewer supporters always claim to be the People's Club. Torino to Juventus, Espanyol to Barca, Athletico to Real: see the pattern emerging? I shouldn't let it get to me, but it does. It winds me up every time I see a car sticker, every advert begging for new fans, every time I drive past that godforsaken ground of theirs. I find myself muttering expletives.

You see, the thing is, since Liverpool appeared from the doldrums in 1962, our fan base has always been bigger. It was as far back as 1970 when Everton's last average season's attendance was bigger than ours – long before we attracted the influx of our modern-day worldwide support. So to say Everton are the 'People's Club' is like Lincoln City fans singing 'We're by far the greatest team the world has ever seen'. Still, no one can stop them doing it.

That Milk Cup final in '84, though, was absolutely brilliant. I'd sorted out this pub in Camberwell called The William. Told a couple of girls I knew to make sure they brought their mates along because there was gonna be about twenty to thirty Northern playboys coming down. It worked a treat. The licensee was a bit wary at first, seeing a mixture of red and blue ski hats barge into his pub, looking like they could have a go, but it was one of those nights when everything just clicked. It was like New Year's Eve – everybody dancing, piggyback fights with the local birds on your back – just a perfect day, because the match was 0–0, so no one was really down. We went to some party later on, and a couple of lads got a bit of a result, so it was happy days. Imagine that happening now. Some pissed Bluenose would start singing 'Merrrdererrrs', and all hell would break loose. Sad really, isn't it?

Before I leave the Everton v. Liverpool thing, I've got to mention a funny incident that happened at the 1989 Cup final. I've always loved it when people shout humorous, off-the-cuff comments out at the match, and my all-time favourite was by the turnstiles at Wembley that year. Because of the Hillsborough disaster in the semi-final, and with it being an all-Merseyside Cup final, the authorities had decided to bend the rules a bit and allowed Gerry Marsden and old Liverpool folk group The Spinners to do a bit of a show before the teams came on.

As usual all the 'one game a season' dignitaries had the tickets, and us, the great unwashed, are doing anything we can to blag our way inside. There used to be a basic scam when you were ticketless that consisted of you just squashing up behind your mate as if you were glued to him as he went through the turnstile. It was known in the trade as the 'double-click'. It was hardly the most sophisticated piece of con-artistry but one of the most effective.

Anyway this lad gets collared as he breaks through. The stewards and the bizzies are on to him like a shot. He's shouting, 'Let me go, you bastards. Please let me go. You don't understand.'

As they're dragging him away, the main copper pauses and says to the lad, 'And what makes you so special? Why should we let you go?'

The lad, as quick as a flash, says, 'Because I haven't missed a Spinners concert in twenty-five years.'

Priceless! Even the bizzies were laughing. Don't know if he got in or not, but a classic shout all the same.

So, with the Milk Cup in the bag and the league within grasp, our hopes and dreams began to focus on the remaining obstacle on our way to the Eternal City: Dinamo Bucharest. They were not a name to set your pulse racing and were probably lacking the evocative whiff of say a Milan or a Madrid, but it was a hurdle that had to be negotiated all the same if we were going to be crowned champions of Europe again.

Both matches were bad-tempered affairs, with the Romanians trying every trick in the book to put Liverpool out of their stride. The first match was played at Anfield on 11th April and was a bitter war of attrition. The Redmen were victorious, but it was a horrible, cynical match, won with a headed goal by the smallest man on the pitch, Sammy Lee. After a succession of calculated fouls we got a free-kick on the wing when Johnston was scythed down. Alan Kennedy whipped the free-kick into the box, and little Sammy appeared from nowhere to nod home. The Romanians were lucky not to have anyone sent off but still had four players booked, which was a lot back then. The Liverpool team showed amazing restraint in the face of sheer provocation. Only Souness looked like he might snap, as Dinamo basically kicked the fuck out of anyone in a red shirt.

When they came out of defence, they could actually play a bit and went close when Augustin got through and shot past Brucie, only to see it come back off the post. But it was hard to feel sympathy for them; you felt justice had been done. But would 1–0 be enough over there? We hoped, but we knew it would be tough, because if they played like that over here in front of the Kop, what would it be like in Bucharest in front of their own fans? The away leg would need Liverpool to be strong, both mentally and physically.

The team more or less picked itself in those days – same one that played the home leg and the Benfica away leg. The match took place in the Romanian capital in front of 60,000 fans baying for blood. Bucharest in those days (before the fall of communism) was a bit of a mad place. Very few tourists ventured there, and those that did were constantly under surveillance. Rooms in the few international-standard hotels were bugged and people tailed by shady-looking blokes in dark glasses. I'm not joking either; this was proper, full-on, black-and-white movie, cold-war-espionage-type carry-on. It was only in the '90s that the country opened up.

Very few of our renowned Red Army managed to negotiate the trip, with all its flight changes and visa checks, but as usual the hardy one hundred were there on the terraces, telling tales on their return about a stranger on the next table staring over his newspaper at them, an air of suspicion wherever they went. Even when you wanted your keys from reception, the girl would have to have a word with someone, who would nod to some bloke the other side of the room, and there would always be the same serious bloke in the lift. Pure Hitchcock, pure paranoia, and the team had to get in, get a result and get out.

This was real European football, not like now, where all the players are on first-name terms after probably doing a fuckin' Nike advert together the previous week. It used to be more about us and them, and the cultural divides. Nowadays the overpaid fuckers will happily kiss whatever club badge you stick in front of them. Oh, the joys of the corporate pantomime we call modern-day football.

Anyway, back to Bucharest. I went over there myself in September 2000 in the UEFA Cup against Rapid, and we had a ball. With the communist government toppled after years of oppression, the locals had the look of people just released from a life sentence. I expected all the women to have moustaches and big, purple cardigans, trying to sell you lucky heather, but oh no. It was as if we'd arrived at Babe Central, like a hidden, undiscovered make-believe land where all the women were beautiful but unaffected and humble, with not a fat, tattooed, sweaty slapper amongst them. Obviously there was still the poor, the gypsies, the street urchins, etc., and it did have a dodgy feel to it late at night. But when has that ever got in the way of following the Reds around Europe? I think it always adds a bit of spice, instead of sitting in overpriced bars in some antiseptic town with no character.

The night before the game we ended up in this bizarre nightclub in the middle of a forest outside Bucharest. Some shell-shocked Scousers (try saying that after a couple) recommended it to us, with quotes like, 'I've travelled the world, lad – LA, Rio, Bangkok, Berlin – but this club is *the* best club ever.' There was no choice; we had to go and have a butcher's. Two taxis were sorted, a price agreed and Kev, Danny, Dava and me followed the four intrepid Scouse pilgrims out of the city and into the darkened forest ahead. There was a degree of cynicism in our car and jokes about Transylvania's most famous son as we snaked through the pitch black, but just when we thought it was going to be a bit of a wind-up, we arrived. Slap bang in the middle of the woods, there it was. I haven't got a clue what it was called, but it was one of the most surreal moments following the Reds ever.

We walked in like *Reservoir Dogs* and were greeted with the sight of literally hundreds of the most gorgeous young women on earth dancing on seats, tables and speakers. Within less than a couple of minutes we were surrounded by about fifty girls, all wanting us to be with them. It was like every Lynx advert you've ever seen rolled into one, times ten. Un-fuckin'-believable! We had suddenly morphed from being four reasonably unattractive blokes having a beer in Bucharest into a cross between the Chippendales and Take That. What happened in that taxi, I'll never know.

Like a scene from *The Lion, the Witch and the Wardrobe*, we were transported into an alternative reality, a place that those who experienced it will never forget. The first question that had to be asked was, 'Are all these honeys on the game or what?' Because, let's face it, Scousers are the most cynical people in England, and we have to know the score. Unlike followers of the national team, who would just get lagered up then start abusing the locals, we like to take stock of the situation and then deal with it. But this was just madness.

Although we'd been assured that none of the fine young things were making a living from the sex trade and everyone seemed happy and smiley as they bopped away, it felt as if we had come to save them. They certainly looked keen, which is mad, because they seemed to be having a great time – even more of a good time than the girls back home. As it got more claustrophobic, our interpreter bloke told us that they just wanted us to take them out, or marry them, so they could escape Romania. Quite sad really, having to pin your hopes of a bright new future on a handful of pissed has-beens that have somehow stumbled into your world the night before a footy match. Their vision of the West, painted through music and TV, is of a great capitalist Utopia, the ultimate in freedom and liberation, but the truth is so, so different.

Oh, and by the way, I know what you're thinking. No, we didn't. We only stayed for about an hour and then got off. I know that sounds a bit strange, but it was just too much. When we got back to the centre of Bucharest, we just sat and had a bevvy and said, 'What the fuck was that all about?'

Anyway, back to '84 and the communist Bucharest of then: one of the most polluted cities I've ever been to. Every day is a bad-air day in the capital. The Redmen took to the field one wet, inhospitable evening and were targeted right from the off by a very physical Dinamo side. Souness was deemed enemy number one by the locals, after an incident which occurred back in the first leg at Anfield. After a lot of shirt pulling, spitting and stamping by the Romanians, their key midfielder, Lica Movila, suffered a double fracture of the jaw. In the two weeks that led to the return leg, the media over there were convinced that Souness was the culprit. Obviously Souey claimed he was innocent, and with there being no footage, film or otherwise, he was free to play. But anyone who knew the tough Scot would tell you that it was going to be a war and you'd want him next to you, on your side.

How he got out alive after the away leg is still a mystery. We badly needed an early goal to settle us down, and it was the man in question who created it. Sammy Lee's corner was headed out, and Souness volleyed it superbly back in, for the maestro Ian Rush to go past a defender before lifting a delicate little chip from a tight angle past the goalie into the net. Get in there, Rushie lad!

Dinamo equalised with a curling free-kick over the Liverpool wall, scored by some geezer called Orac. After that the Reds had to sit back and soak up a bit of pressure as the 60,000 crowd roared on the home side. Just when they thought they might be in with a shout, we broke away and some bloke called Ian Rush scored from eight yards in the eighty-forth minute to kill off the game. No, I've never heard of him either. Justice had been done. We'd been kicked all over the park, but we stayed strong and won away again. We'd won on foreign soil in every round. Even for Liverpool that was impressive. Our fourth European Cup final in eight years. God, we were good.

And so it came to pass: Roma v. Liverpool in Rome. We always knew it was going to be a bit tasty, and tasty it was. Even the most sensible of Liverpudlians had that feeling of impending doom. Not in a football sense, mind. On the pitch we feared nobody. Our team was the best in Europe, and we knew it.

No, the thing that bothered most travelling Reds was the thought of playing in the capital of one of the most volatile football nations in the world against Italian champions AS Roma, whose home just happened to be the Olympic Stadium. A potential volcano was just waiting to erupt. The thing about Scousers, though: whatever the odds, they have this supreme confidence, the kind of 'been there, seen it' attitude, where someone always knows a boozer which is boxed off, no matter where you are in the world. Even that tilted-head, talk-out-of-the-side-of-the-mouth thing that we do, as if we're sharing top-secret information, gives us an air of assurance. We knew we were the coolest fans around, always one step ahead of the rest. Whether it was the way we dressed or the manner in which we ducked and dived, we set the trends and laid a benchmark for the rest to follow.

Our obsession with terrace fashion was always at the forefront of what was going on in the '70s and '80s. Nowadays every tinpot team from Nowheresville has a well-dressed bunch of gargoyles that follow them around, thinking they're the bee's knees. Even though most teams' fans more or less dress the same way these days, I still think you can spot a Scouser's walk a mile away. It's a kind of suspicious-looking-penguin-type walk, if you know what I mean. Bit of a roll of the shoulders and a head that's alert to its surroundings.

As usual the city of Liverpool was buzzing, with everybody plotting and scheming about the most ingenious ways of getting there. Even Everton won the FA Cup. I know, yeah! Everton winning a trophy – mad, isn't it? But if you think about it, it really was mad. We'd won the league, the League Cup, the Bluenoses had won the FA Cup and we were on our way to Rome to try to win the biggest of all – a clean sweep for Merseyside, yet the city, politically and economically, was on the bones of its arse.

For some reason I didn't travel with the usual suspects. Normally I would have been in the company of some of the finest nut jobs ever to stand on a football terrace – people like Ally Atkins, Tony Gill, Dutch, Fat Eddie (cultural ambassador and moaner of the year fifteen years running), the Heron brothers, Doggo, Stevie Tomo, Terry Mac, Billy Shandley and many more. But, strangely, not this time. I went with a lad called John Brundell, who was a good laugh and came from round our way. A Kenny Everett lookalike who liked a giggle, he could also be a little too serious if the going got tough, and, believe me, this trip was going to get tougher than anyone imagined.

I was out of work when the final came round, but, like many in the same boat, I managed to get there. We decided to go for a week to Rimini in the north and get the train down for the game. God knows how I got the money. I mean, for Christ's sake, this is Liverpool FC in the European Cup final we're talking about. You have to be there – no excuses. It's always in the back of your mind that it may never happen again. I'm one of the lucky few who've been to every one. I know each one could be my last.

I always get dead excited before big games and still suffer terribly from PMT (pre-match tension), but this time I was even more delirious than usual. The reason for this extra, childlike anticipation was simple: we were going by *plane*! Yes, I know it sounds stupid getting all excited about flying, but in those days we always got the train to European aways. Transalpino ruled supreme. We'd hide in the toilets, under the seats, fake death, rub the destination out on our tickets and put the actual, more expensive, one in. Rome and back in 1977 had nearly killed me – seventy hours on a train. Halfway home, with no food and the loos not working, cabin fever set in. By the time the 5000 or so pulled into Lime Street on the football specials, many had lost the plot – wide-eyed, dribbling at the mouth, talking gibberish. No more. This time we were gonna do it properly – fly there, stay in a lovely beach resort, take our cozzies, get a bronzy, have a few bevvies, win the Cup, Bob's your uncle. Sorted!

We flew out of Manchester, checked in and did what everyone does. You flick a few switches, open a few drawers, have a quick swill, change yer 'bills' and you're out on the ale within half an hour. It was a strange kind of place, Rimini. I didn't know what to make of it. Some places, soon as you arrive, you think, 'Bingo! This will do nicely.' Rimini seemed like a massive seafront town, with hardly any people in it. We mooched around for a while, having a drink here and there, until we found the one English pub in the town: The Rose and Crown. Now, I'm not big on gargling in themed boozers – English or Irish, for that matter – but needs must. Walked in, happy days: there's fifteen Scousers in there having a sing-song. Don't mind if I do.

Extending the hand of friendship, we introduced ourselves. There were about eight younger ones from Walton who seemed to be more up our street, if you know what I mean. I can only remember four of their names. There was Big Mark, a sound bloke I've seen a million times since. Also, there was a lad called Kirky, who was a good laugh, and who crops up every so often. They looked like the organisers. There was a lad called Macca, the butt of everybody's jokes, which was unfair. Then there was Jimmy McGill. Jimmy looked like the type of guy who could eat three Shredded Wheat no bother. If you looked out of the pub window and saw Jimmy pulling a tram down the street by his teeth, you wouldn't bat an eyelid – a tough lad, make no mistake.

We drank until the early hours. We talked about our hopes and dreams for the match. There were yards-of-ale drinking competitions, a DJ playing Eurodisco chart shite and even members of the opposite sex, although nothing to get too excited about. We said our goodbyes and headed off in separate directions, promising to meet the following day. As we walked back to the hotel, the local Italian lads kept riding past on scooters shouting stuff, and it certainly wasn't 'Good luck in the final'. I had a bottle of vino ready to crack open back at the hotel for a nightcap, but I was seriously considering shoving it up someone's spaghetti hoop if they didn't fuck off and leave us alone.

We reached base camp glad that the night had passed without major incident. All that riding around on your scooter with no helmet on, locks flowing in the wind: what's that all about? The only cool people to have ridden scooters are '60s mods on their way to cause mayhem at English seaside resorts. Helmets, shades, Parka, mirrors, bubble screen, back-rest with big, whippy aerials, the full hit. I don't buy into all this 'Italians are cool' bollocks. Dropping your jumper over your shoulders and having a shiny shoe has never impressed anybody in our house.

The next day was spent chillin' – the usual stuff: writing post-cards, checkin' the beach out, nursing the hangover and making plans for the evening. I like days like that, when you just do nothing; it's good for the soul.

That night we met up back at the Rose and Crown, now our official HQ. A couple more Reds had trickled into town, but they were office types who probably wouldn't appreciate our jiggery-pokery. We decided to have a walk and see what hidden treasures this place had to offer. The tourist strip, full of bars and clubs, went for about a mile, but you had the feeling it was out of season. Nowhere was chock-a-block.

We hopped from bar to bar and genuinely had a good laugh, but it was obvious that there was gonna be a confrontation with these annoying little twats on scooters. Ten English lads walking down the main drag together was always going to draw attention, and it wasn't too long before the first bit of argy-bargy. Though none of the local youths seemed able to speak English, they still took great delight in riding alongside us and shouting 'Fuck you', raising the middle finger. It was only a matter of time. A bottle smashed on the pavement right next to us. Within seconds it had gone off. There was a scooter on its side with the wheel still spin-ning and the lad getting pummelled everywhere. We're in the middle of the road, bouncing round like lunatics, beckoning anybody and everybody on.

It's a basic human trait: when under threat, we always resort to the animal behaviour of our ancestors. Watch any wildlife documentary and you will see the apes and gorillas act in exactly the same way. If there's a confrontation, there's a lot of shouting, screaming, chests getting puffed out and maybe a brief bit of physical combat, then it's over within seconds. Humans are no different, especially the British, who seem to be the masters of the art of street fighting. There's gangs all over the world who use knives and guns and stuff, but if you want a good, honest tear-up, the British hooligan has no equal. Witness a big, hairy baboon about to kick off, bopping up and down on the spot, and then witness a nutter from the footy about to kick off. The only real difference is that the baboon doesn't wear training shoes and could probably have wiped his arse a bit better.

Anyway, it was over within seconds, with us victorious, but we knew we'd meet again. We got off back to our hotels, knowing they would think we'd go back to the Rose and Crown. Tactics, son, tactics.

Next day we went to the station to book our tickets for the train to Roma. We were getting a night train to the capital so we could have a bit of a kip and be fresh for all the madness. Taking it easy all day, we had a few bevvies off the beaten track and went back for a nap. We steered clear of the Rose and Crown and met at the station all excited at about 10 p.m. The journey seemed to last forever, and not long after dawn broke we clunked into the vast station. So, this was it. With no turning back, we were about to witness one of the maddest twenty-four hours of our lives. Some of the lads were wearing colours when they got off the train, and within an hour of arriving, it became apparent we were not welcome.

No sooner had we reached the street than it started. It seemed the whole city was staring or shouting at us. We kept on walking regardless, ending up by a kind of open-air market. At first they started chucking bits of fruit at us. We thought, 'Oh yeah, fuck off, will yer?' Then, next minute, they attacked us: *at 7.30 in the morning*! I could walk around Baghdad with a stars 'n' stripes top hat on at 7.30 in the morning saying, 'I'm a yankee doodle dandy' and I wouldn't get attacked. This was not a good sign. We had to give it toes. Five of us managed to stay together as we legged it fast as we could two hundred yards up the road. We'd lost the others but couldn't go back. Instead we squashed into a taxi and headed back to the station. We didn't have a hotel, because we were due to get the half-past-midnight train back to Rimini. There was nowhere we could lock the door and chill, take stock of the situation and make plans.

The sightseeing and sitting around al fresco with banners draped everywhere was immediately cancelled. Even our audience with the big fella in the Vatican was gonna have to be postponed.

The crowd in all its glory watching Liverpool take on Roma, Stadio Olimpico, Rome, 30th May 1984. Copyright © *Liverpool Daily Post and Echo*.

Flags aplenty during the 1984 final. Copyright © Press Association.

Got to love the sunnies, 1984.

The End: a legend in its lifetime, 1985.

Ferry across the Mersey? Try taking the channel by storm.

Memorabilia of the Juventus 'fighters' from 1985, when Italian Ultras chose English names that reflected their passion and devotion for their team, not for violence.

Heysel Stadium, 29th May 1985. Spectators walk by scattered debris, all that remains in the aftermath of a disastrous clash between Liverpool fans and supporters of Juventus at the European Cup final. A perimeter wall collapsed in the panic, crushing spectators to death. The final death toll was 39, with more than 400 injured. One lone pennant bears poignant testimony to what should have been the pinnacle of the European football season. Those who lost their lives will never be forgotten. Copyright © PA Photos.

Vladimír Šmicer and John Arne Riise hold the trophy aloft following the 'miracle of Istanbul', when Liverpool came back from going three goals down in the first half of the Champions League final to beat AC Milan 3–2 on penalties at the Atatürk Olympic Stadium, 25th May 2005. Copyright © PA Photos.

Jamie Carragher celebrates with the delirious fans, 2005.
Copyright © *Liverpool Daily Post and Echo*.

The city of Liverpool was out in force to celebrate with its returning heroes, 2005.
Copyright © Press Association.

Greek police stop Liverpool fans and check their tickets before allowing them into the Olympic Stadium in Athens ahead of the Champions League final between Liverpool and AC Milan, 23rd May 2007. Copyright © PA Photos.

The original banner makes its way to Athens, 2007. From left to right: John Macdonald (the banner's owner), Dave Kirby, Tony Barrett, John Maguire, Nicky Allt, Jegsy Dodd, Peter Hooton, Tom Hooton and Kevin Sampson. Photograph © Paul Rodgers.

He must've been absolutely gutted when we didn't show. We went for a coffee to have a crisis meeting about what to do next. Oh, for a mobile phone. If only we could call the others to see if they were OK, or call our mates to see where they were. There were 15,000 other Scousers somewhere in this city, but we couldn't find any, like we were behind enemy lines and they'd all gone underground.

We waited and waited for something to happen. By late morning I decided to go with John for a mooch around, leaving the others but arranging a time and a place to meet up. When Rushie famously said in 1986 that Italy was like a foreign country, he wasn't fuckin' joking. After walking around for an hour like those suspicious penguins I mentioned earlier, our luck changed. I spotted a group of Scousers over the road. It was like being on a desert island and the rescue ship has just come over the horizon. I said, 'A'right, boys, what's happening?'

They proceeded to tell us all kinds of horror stories from the night before. Scousers had been getting hopped on left, right and centre. The picture they painted was pretty grim, but at least they knew the word on the street. The word was: all meet at the station at five o'clock. They knew a bar that was boxed off, a safe house. Funnily enough it was called the American Bar – the same name as the pub on Lime Street where we used to meet before games.

We shot back to the meeting point to tell the others. It took a while to find the bar, but it was worth it when we got there. You had to walk down steps into a huge room, which was full of Redmen. It was just wall-to-wall 'head the balls' – a most welcome sight. All the old faces from town were here: the Kenny crew, the Huyton Baddies, some from Scottie; it was the first time I'd felt OK since I'd got off the train. I suppose it's that safety-in-numbers thing. Don't get me wrong, I knew this was gonna be a long, hard day which would probably get a little bit whooh and a little bit whey before it was finished, but at least we were all in it together.

There seemed to be a general consensus that the hundred or so lads who were in this basement bar would be enough to get us to the ground safely. Most hooligan firms will tell you that it's not the quantity, it's the quality, and a decent coachload of dependable lads can go anywhere and rule the roost (known in the trade as a Naughty Forty).

On this occasion I had grave doubts. I reckoned if we walked it we were gonna need three to four hundred lads who would have to be game for anything. That meant no runners. It may sound over the top, but it would have to be done with military precision. But if panic set in and people started to run, pandemonium would reign and people would get hurt. We could have always sneaked off and got a taxi, but the thought of sticking together and safety in numbers was far more appealing. And anyway, most fans who get beaten up and hospitalised seem to be in twos and threes. I didn't fancy being one of those statistics, so it was 'all for one and one for all'.

The alcohol flowed and the bravado grew, as the songs got louder and more passionate. Suddenly there was a buzz about the place, as the word went round that we were about to make a move. We piled out into the Roman sunshine, some a little worse for wear, and headed to a line of bus stops up the road. Someone from the American Bar had obviously been doing his homework. Within minutes we'd commandeered two single-deckers which were going direct to the ground. Result!

Immediately our bus is absolutely rocking. We're on our way to see the Mighty Reds in the greatest club competition in the world, and the excitement is at fever pitch. We slow down at the lights, and all of a sudden, THUD! Something hits the side of the bus. Then, another loud bang. We look out of the window and there's about twenty Ultras running up to the coach armed with broom handles, faces covered by scarves, doing all that bouncing-up-and-down-on-the-spot business. The shout goes up: 'Come on, everybody off. Let's fuckin' give it to the cheeky twats!'

In less than half a minute we've evacuated the bus, punched fuck out of half a dozen of them and ran the rest up the road. The adrenalin rush is amazing as we get back on the bus, and the driver just smiles, shakes his head and says, 'Crazy boys.'

Amazingly no police turn up, which saves a lot of messing about. You can hear lads buzzing as they boast to their mates. 'Did you see me, eh? Did yer? The way I put that big, fat cunt on his arse?' The mood is triumphant. There's one or two who've taken knocks, but, being the first ones off the bus, that was expected. We've still got to get to the ground, though, watch the match and somehow get away after the game. *And*, it's gonna be dark then, and even moodier. Shit!

As we neared the ground, the tension grew even more intense. There was no visible evidence of Liverpool fans whatsoever, just wave upon wave of excitable Italians taking more than a passing interest in the contents of our bus. When we stopped, all hell broke loose. There were grown men older than me dad screaming in our faces, people getting jostled everywhere. There was no other thing for it; we had to split up. You couldn't walk round with fifty Reds; all you're gonna do is draw attention to yourselves. It was time to do a body swerve and mingle. This wasn't a time for heroes; it was a time for damage limitation.

You felt a sense of relief when you finally arrived outside the Liverpool end. Hardly anyone was talking about the match; it was all about everybody's individual experiences and the role of the inhospitable Italians. Everyone had a tale to tell, some horrific, some amusing and some just plain daft. Bullshitters exaggerated even more than normal, with tales like, 'Oh aye, yeah, so I'm on me own, and there's six of 'em, so you know I'm a black belt, don't yer?' Err, no. 'Well, anyway, I knocked them all out cold, then bumped into Miss Italy 1983, shagged her, then who's at the bar? None other than the Pope and his mates, asking me what I'd like to drink.' And you're like, 'Yeah, all right, mate. I've gotta go. I'll see you around.' Phew. Close shave. There's always one, lying through his teeth, desperate to be loved, searching for respect.

Anyway, fuck him, it's game on. Let's get in the ground and sort this final out. The atmosphere is electric. The ground is shaking like an earthquake. Seven years ago in this same stadium the travelling Redmen became legendary with their fantastic support. But tonight it was the Roma fans who were deafening.

You couldn't hear yourself think. There was smoke, flares, drums banging, flags bigger than anything you'd seen before – a truly amazing sight. You're staring open-mouthed, giving it the full wow factor, thinking to yourself, 'If we pull this one off, if we can actually win this cup and return to England victorious and unscathed, it will be one of the greatest sporting achievements by an English team on foreign soil in history. All we've got to do now is win it.'

It's a bit strange recalling such a momentous day and only being able to recollect the poisonous anti-Liverpool hostility that took place. I should be waxing lyrical about free-flowing football and tactical nous, but no, I couldn't tell you what formation we played or how we went about it. Obviously I know the result and who scored, but if I'm brutally honest, all I can remember is being bombarded with missiles and having to dodge incoming flares throughout the whole match. We were well and truly under siege from the moment we arrived until the moment we left, or should I say escaped? They say all roads lead to Rome, but after our final penalty I'd have given anything to see just one that led out of this fuckin' hellhole. Most people refer to the '84 final as the Grobbelaar (wobbly legs) final, but to anyone who was there it was the 'smoke, tear gas and flare' final. Grobbelaar was too far away for any of our fans to see his antics anyway. It was only when we got home that we knew what he was up to. Self-preservation was the most important issue on people's minds.

Just in case you've been trapped down a pothole for the last twenty-five years, I'll run through the facts for you. We scored first through Neal after fifteen minutes. (Yahoo!) They equalised through Pruzzo on forty-three. (Boo! Hiss!) The match then became a stalemate, with very few chances. Extra-time came and went, which meant, for the first time in history, the European Cup was about to be settled by pennos. Stevie Nicol ballooned the first one over the bar. Then Di Bartolomei netted for them. Phil Neal scored for us, and Conti missed for them. Game on. Souness put us in front, but Righetti equalised. Rushie slotted home, and then, crucially, Graziani put his effort over the bar. It was left to Alan Kennedy to take the most nerve-wracking penalty of his life.

I remember saying, 'If this goes in, we are dead.' It was like a double-edged sword. The more joy we experienced, the more pain would follow. If it was Rushie, you'd put your house on it, but with Barney Rubble, anything could happen. He walks up to the ball. He puts it on the spot. He takes a run-up. He hits it. Oh my fuckin' God; he's scored! Our end erupts into scenes of delirium. I'm screaming, 'Yeeees!' But thinking, 'Oooooh, shit!' It's almost like I'm faking an orgasm. I'm doing all the right moves, making all the right noises, hugging anybody and everybody, but I know, and everyone else knows, that trouble with a capital T is waiting just around the corner.

It's a weird atmosphere watching our heroes lift that massive cup and doing a lap of honour in front of scores of little fires that the Roma fans have lit by burning their own colours – a surreal and haunting backdrop to a strange old night. The talk on the terraces begins to drift to the more obvious concern of how on earth we are all going to get back to the centre. It's time for everyone to leave the comfort zone and somehow find safety amongst the danger.

When we finally leave the ground, all hell breaks loose. It's utter mayhem. No one knows what to do or where to go and we're getting attacked from all sides. Some of the lads get mobbed up and have a decent attempt at a counter-attack, but it's chaos. And here's me, a bit of a scally in my twenties and I'm shitting myself. Imagine having your wife and kids with you. There's all kinds of things being hurled at us: bottles, stones, even a toilet seat flies past me head – nice touch. Me heart's palpitating, the legs have turned to jelly and me hair must've looked like Don King's. I bumped into a couple of lads I know who'd just got back from seeing their hire car with English plates getting burnt out.

As the scene descended into something out of the film *Zulu*, the police played their trump card. Seeing as the Liverpool fans had been beaten from pillar to post for the last half-hour and suffered some serious injuries, including stab wounds, the Italian police had a cunning plan. It was a stroke of pure genius. In their wisdom they decided that, although the English supporters had been the victims, it would be a great idea to draw their batons and charge into us. The twisted logic of the Italian police never ceases to amaze me. They must've thought, 'Hey, why don't we just steam in and club anything that moves? That's bound to ease the situation and take the blame away from our fans.'

After about two hours of madness, some semblance of order slowly took place. The Ultras were beginning to trickle away, and even the police looked bored now. They'd just enjoyed their best night's action for decades, and I was sure in the following years they'd be swapping stories and telling tales of the day Liverpool FC came to town, how they'd had official clearance to beat the shit out of those cocky, self-assured English hooligans. At last the buses finally appeared, and we were marched like prisoners of war, in single file. Everybody looked wiped out. You wouldn't think we'd just won the Big One. No one was in the mood for singing or celebrating. Everyone was emotionally drained. As the buses set off for the city centre, the atmosphere was pretty subdued. Everybody, I suppose, had just about had enough.

Just when we were thinking the worst was behind us, we approached the River Tiber. Suddenly the bus was under attack. Within seconds half the bus's windows had been smashed and everyone was screaming and trying to lie in the aisle. I've got glass in me hair and down me back, and there's someone on top of me who's cut. I'm thinking to myself, 'For fuck's sake. I really, really have had enough now.' If you'd given me an AK-47, I swear I would've got off that bus and blown those snivelling little I-tie bastards to kingdom come.

Somehow the bus managed to limp through the city centre and deposit us at the main station. The walking wounded and the terminally traumatised limped from our shell of a coach and tried making sense of it all. It was about to get worse for me and John, as it dawned on us that our last train to Rimini left twenty minutes ago. We'd no hotel, were low on money and were tired and hungry. We were facing a major crisis, as there were packs of marauding Roma fans everywhere looking for stragglers.

This was not good. We were like two newborn lambs, lost and confused with predators around every corner. We'd run out of ideas and were basically waiting for divine intervention. I was looking up to the heavens, saying, 'Come on, big fella, give us a sign.' Then, as if by magic, about fifteen lads appeared out of nowhere – some lads from Wallasey we had met in the ground. Oh, thank you, God. It was like everything had gone into slow motion, as if they had shining lights around them like the Ready Brek advert. We ran over, embraced them and said, 'Fucking hell, are we pleased to see you! Any chance of dossing on your floor?'

'Yeah, no problem.' Things were looking up. We asked them where they were going, and they casually said, 'We're going for a few bevvies,' as if it was a quiet Sunday afternoon in Liverpool.

I'm so relieved that I'm talking like I've swallowed a vat of Red Bull and snorted half of Colombia. My mind is in neutral, my mouth is on autopilot, but for the moment I'm happy. We get to this pub and all hands are in there; in fact half the Annie Road End are in there. I'm ecstatic. These are my people, the people I should have been with in the first place, the ones who I know and trust. When they tell me that they all marched out together and chased the Roma fans over the bridge by the River Tiber, I'm gutted. They've walked all the way to town, crushing anyone who dared get in their way. I feel a right div now, don't I? Here's me having the nightmare of nightmares, hemmed in outside the ground with bog seats getting thrown at me, getting clubbed by the bizzies, bus windows getting shattered all around me, and this lot are bouncing around Rome like they own the place. What a nugget!

Anyway, we're OK now. We have a decent bevvy and then everyone starts to filter away. There are still dodgy carloads of Italians honking their horns at us, but we get back to the hotel unscathed. It's a shitty room, and the floor is uncomfortable, but after what we've been through it feels like Sandy Lane in Bar-fuckin-bados.

Another day dawns and me and John thank the lads for giving

us sanctuary. We say goodbye to Clink, Joey, Dicko, Guv, Avo, Phil, Mickey and all the others and tell them they will be mentioned in dispatches. I could've sworn Richie Long, Traff and Robbie Mather were there also, but maybe that was another game, in another cup, in another city. Who knows?

We did the long journey back to Rimini, which at the time felt like the Trans-Siberian Express – that was probably due to the lack of sleep and the mental stress of the last two days. The Italian newspapers all ran stories of the violence which marred the match. The headline in *La Republica* was 'Manhunt against the English'. *Il Corriere dello Sport* said, 'The aftermath of the match brought a night of vile, blind violence that disappointment cannot justify.' *Il Tiempo*, Rome's equivalent of *The Times*, said, 'This could have been an occasion to demonstrate civility. Instead the usual group of fans with knives, bottles and sticks went on an odious manhunt.'

Even after all these years it still goes on. Our match in 2001, when Michael Owen scored a couple to win 2–0, there were fourteen Liverpool supporters stabbed. Imagine if it was the other way around – our feet wouldn't touch the ground. We'd be banned from European football, end of story.

Our train finally pulled into Rimini about 10 p.m. We had a quick mooch up to the Rose and Crown to see if the Waltons were there, but for some reason it was closed. After a couple of swift ones elsewhere we decided to call it a day. A clean, white pillowcase under me swede for the first time in three days – bliss. I drifted off, thinking what Alan Kennedy's winning penalty would be in the goals v. sex debate. Could it be the honeytrap, when the beautiful female spy lets you have your evil way then leads you into the hands of the enemy? Or is it when you find out that the sexy beast you shagged last night is also the wife/daughter (delete where applicable) of the local gangster? Or could it be the S&M scenario of pleasure and pain? Or maybe, maybe, yawn, ah! Zzzzz.

Arise and shine. The best sleep for ages, and it's going-home time, folks. Well, I suppose it's been an adventure, but fuck me, it's been a grueller, and, if I'm honest, I can't wait to get home. Own bed an' all that. We meet the Walton lads at the check-in. They tell us that the Rose and Crown was closed because the local scooter divs had smashed it up on match night. Apparently there were loads of English tourists in there supporting the Reds. Well, frankly, my dear, I don't give a fuck. I'm going home to rest my weary head.

Me mum says, 'Did you have a nice time?'

I say, 'Yeah, it was OK.'

She says, 'No trouble I hope?'

'No, Mum. In fact it was quite quiet. Oh, by the way, I got you some ciggies. I've left them on the kitchen table'.

'Oh, you're a good 'un.'

Phone goes. It's TC. 'All right, you Rednosed bastard. What was it like? I heard there was trouble.'

I say, 'I'll tell you what, lad, if we ever meet an Italian team in a final again and it's on neutral ground, there'll be absolute murder.'

Brussels, 1985

KEVIN SAMPSON

European Cup Final, 29th May 1985
Heysel Stadium, Brussels
Attendance: 59,000

Juventus   1–0   Liverpool FC
Michel Platini (56', pen.)

Substitutes: Gary Gillespie, Chris Pile,
Craig Johnston, Jan Mølby, Sammy Lee

Manager: Joe Fagan

Juventus: Stefano Tacconi (1), Luciano Favero (2), Antonio Cabrini
(3), Sergio Brio (4), Gaetano Scirea (5, captain), Massimo Bonini (6),
Michel Platini (7), Marco Tardelli (8), Massimo Briaschi (9), Paolo
Rossi (10), Zbigniew Boniek (11)

Substitutes used: Cesare Prandelli, Benimiano Vignola

Manager: Giovanni Trappatoni

Roll Call

Redmen

BIG BILLSY AND LITTLE BILLSY: The Billsborough brothers from Walton

THE DAVAS: John, Paul and Terry Davies from Kirkdale

KEITH FROM DONNY: Keith Johnson, Doncaster's number-one 'dresser'

DANNY GILES: The gargling brickie who provided the inspiration for Rab C. Nesbitt

HOBO: Ian Hodrien, devout hedonist

HOOTO: Peter Hooton, editor of *The End* magazine, singist in The Farm

MILLSY: A fat lad from Bootle, not to be confused with Billsy, or Billsy

MURPHY: Paul Murphy, hands the size of skittles

POTTER: Mick 'the Chin' Potter son of Scotland Road and drinking partner

ROBBIE THE MOD: Robbie Paton, not a mod at all, in fact

Bluenoses

MARK JONES: Mark Jones

LYTTLE: Chris Lyttle, Huyton Goodie

TOWNSEND THORESEN: A lad whose real name was Dave

Other

The End: A mag that was ahead of and behind its time – simultaneously. Humorous publication that embraced music, street fashion, slang, poetry and politics, which blazed a trail for fanzine culture

And by no means least . . .

MAURO GARINO: Juventus fan, lifelong friend, tipsy legend – more of him later

H eysel Stadium, 29th May, 1985, approaching kick-off time and all heads were craned to the right as we tried to get a sense – and a view – of how bad the fighting had become. This was a game myself and Mauro had been dreaming about since we met – but nothing about the day was going to plan at all. After the way tickets had been allocated, after the way the police had been outside the ground, and after the wholesale brutality in Rome last year, it was no surprise that things were descending into chaos. But this was bad. I'd seen fighting inside football grounds from Stamford Bridge to St Andrews, and this was starting to look as bad as any of it.

It had been going on for five minutes now – a lifetime in terms of football fighting – and the police seemed to have surrendered the big, curved terrace to fate. Fate had brought Liverpool and Juventus together in Brussels, but it was never meant to end this way. The weirdest thing about Belgium, 1985, is that until that fateful hour before kick-off it was one of the funniest, most memorable away trips I'd ever been on . . .

Back in 1981, Chris Lyttle and my brother Neil had got as far as Calais, following myself and the rest of us to France. They were never the most sophisticated bunkers in the world, and it's a miracle they got that far. Seeming to accept the very fact of being on foreign soil as a result in itself, they hobbled off to the hypermarket, bought a slab of Kronenborg and sat down in the sunshine to postpone their next move. A few cans in, a young Italian lad approached them and asked for a light. He'd been to Scotland to watch Juventus play Celtic in a pre-season friendly and was now hitching back to Turin. The last food he'd eaten had been twenty-four hours ago, when a Juve-supporting waiter in a Glasgow Italian restaurant filled his boots for the road. Neil and Chris fed him lager and stories of Liverpool. He fed them *spinello* – a bit of draw. Names and numbers were scrawled down before they went their separate ways. His name was Mauro Garino, and his abiding wish was to stand on the Spion Kop.

Mauro visited that Christmas, and every subsequent Christmas too. He became well known in our pre- and post-match watering holes along Scotland Road: The Cunard, The Crown, The Jester. They mapped out a route to the ground that always, always ended with a mad taxi dash to get inside the Kop for kick-off. Somehow, we always did. Mauro came on the ordinary with me to Villa away and was spellbound by the sheer numbers Liverpool would take to a regular away game. He thought the Juventus and Roma fans were fanatical, but this was something completely different – lads in bobble hats skinning up at ten in the morning. There was already a train-load waiting at New Street when we got in, and five hundred-odd decided to walk to the ground, stopping off at a pub called The Pot of Beer en route. It's here that young Garino patented his legendary, and wholly ill-advised, phrase: 'I buy one beer for all boy.'

Repeatedly, Mauro and myself would return to the same topic. Wouldn't it be great if Liverpool and Juventus met in Europe one day? What'd it be like if we played each other in the European Cup final, hey? What would that be like! In May 1984 he sent photos of Via Roma in central Turin, resprayed and re-Christened Via Liverpool by the delighted Juventus hordes after Liverpool's smash-and-grab European Cup win in Rome's own citadel. Liverpool were a much-loved team in Juve circles, so, when fate finally threw the two teams together, both cities were buzzing with it. In Liverpool, in spite of the barbaric reception from the Romans the year before, the excitement of another European Cup final – our fifth in eight years – overran any thoughts of revenge.

That was before news of the ticket allocation leaked out. Sound familiar, this? The final was to be held at an old, inadequate athletics stadium with checkpoints instead of turnstiles. It had been built for spectators, who observe and applaud, rather than fans, who are, well, *fanatical*. Fans bounce, roar, sway, jump and fall all over each other in the delirium of a winning goal. Could the Heysel Stadium be up to that? UEFA thought so.

UEFA also thought it would be only right and fair that a 'neutrals' pen should be established that year. Both the popular ends of Heysel Stadium featured large, crescent-shaped, though badly maintained, terracing. Each terrace was divided into three sections, and each section could accommodate 3000 fans. The Juventus fans were to be given 15,000 tickets, including one entire terrace (three sections, so 9000 fans). Though we didn't know it in advance, the Liverpool support in 'our' end was going to be pegged at 6000, keeping the third section free for neutrals.

Liverpool's actual allocation was kept secret, inducing furore among fans. There seemed to be little rhyme or reason when it came to who qualified for a ticket. Even if we got the same 15,000 allocation as Juve – and it felt as though the club were being sworn to secrecy on the numbers game – we had twice that many season-ticket holders. Eventually tickets were handed out on the basis of the last digit of your season ticket's serial number. Only one person among our regular twenty or thirty match-goers qualified, and Millsy only owned up to that an hour before kick-off. That's how bad it got – people felt embarrassed and ashamed at being among the lucky ones. Like I say, sound familiar?

None of this dampened the mood in the city. Myself and Mick Potter had been unemployed for three years by May 1985. We got by on the fortnightly giro (luckily his came in the alternate week to mine, meaning we could carry each other). I was entre-preneurial in a Robin Hood (or so I liked to tell myself) way. Where others were discovering the boutiques and jewellers' shops of mainland Europe, I'd perfected a reliable white-collar ruse that also involved brief sorties abroad. Even now I fear the sniffer hounds of the nation's insurance companies scouring these pages for evidence, so I'll leave the details to yourselves to work out. But those little forays, plus the pocket money we earned from *The End*, saw us through several winters of discontent.

The End summed up the mood of defiant optimism in Liverpool in 1985. By then Thatcher had made her infamous comment about wishing the old city could be disconnected from the rest of mainland Britain, towed out into the Irish Sea and cast adrift, left to its own devices. She'd already done that without the need for oxyacetylene cutters and tugboats – and we *hated* her. If you were in your teens and from the city when Thatcher came to power in 1979, there was little or nothing down for you. You certainly wouldn't view the occasional rip-off of an insurance company as criminality – this was *justice*. It was payback. The insurance companies were part of the system, *her* system. They were part of the Thatcherite monetarist machine that was creating bounty for the rich and the greedy, and leaving the rest of us high and dry. That's how it felt to be young and out of work in 1985 – Us Against the World.

The one thing that drew us together, gave us pride and made sure we walked tall wherever we went was football. This went for Everton just as much as it did for the Redmen. Between 1977 and 1985 the youth of Liverpool dictated the way football fans all over the country dressed. We were always a step ahead, our travels abroad giving us access to brands and styles unheard of back home. We'd cherry-pick the best and abandon the rest. In an era where your sense of self and your civic pride was vulnerable, your dress code and your football team gave you your identity. You were someone, and you were part of something powerful, something immense, something that *mattered*. In May 1985 Everton were champions, FA Cup finalists and they'd just given the performance of a lifetime to overturn the mighty Bayern Munich in the semi-final of the Cup-Winners' Cup. Liverpool and Everton were both about to contest major European finals, and *The End* magazine celebrated our mutual joy with a half-red, half-blue edition entitled 'Liverpool's Annual Bender'.

Twenty years on it's hard to accept the enmity that now exists between Liverpool and Everton fans. Without becoming blinded by nostalgia, I remember how the shared sense of Scouse solidarity used to overrule petty rivalries. In 1984 we played the first all-Scouse final at Wembley, the first-ever Sunday kick-off for a League Cup final. Saturday night in Piccadilly was awash with red and blue. Everyone was out, together. An Evertonian mate we were with, Townsend Thoresen, was emotional as three hundred swept along Shaftesbury Avenue singing. He turned to me, genuinely moved by the sight, and said, 'Imagine if there was only one team, hey? What a boss mob that'd be!'

After the tragedy of Hillsborough, Liverpool suspended all fixtures, indefinitely. Our first game back was at Goodison. The entire ground sang 'You'll Never Walk Alone'. The grief was shared. When the FA Cup final was, reluctantly, played, it was fitting that Liverpool played Everton, the one team whose fans, we knew, would respect the poignancy of the occasion. You can only speculate as to why a sizeable minority of Everton fans now spend the derby game with one hand smothering their face as they imitate a head crushed up against a fence. Football is a game that arouses intense passion, and their passion for the team in blue is often best expressed by a hatred of the team in red. I understand that – I think. But it wasn't half good in the '80s.

So good, in fact, that after a boozy night at The System club I let myself be talked into coming to Rotterdam with the Bluenoses to see them play Rapid Vienna in the Cup-Winners' Cup final. I didn't take much persuading. My pleas as to how broke I was, how I was keeping all and any dough for our own Big One and how I couldn't physically get there and back in time to turn back round again and leave for Belgium all fell on deaf ears. Townsend and Mark Jones were adamant that myself and Hobo, a fellow Red, were coming with them. We could bunk the trains and doss down in their hotel room. And it threw up the opportunity for a quick policy heist.

One last time it's worth emphasising our mentality at the time. No doubt it's convenient for me to wash my hands and plead extenuating circumstances for the sheer dishonesty of our way of working back then. But, truly, that's how it was. That's how it felt. It didn't feel as though you were doing anything wrong. These companies and institutions existed to exploit us and make money out of us. All we wanted to do was follow our team, every-where – and there was British Rail, or Ramada Hotels, or UEFA slapping an excise duty on your life's passion. It was almost a call of duty to stick your thumb on your nose and go, 'Not me, you don't, gobshite.' Needless to say I daily hang my head in shame now, and barely a First Friday goes by that doesn't see me on my knees begging absolution for all the free rides I took during Thatcher's first two terms. I'm sorry. It was great. But I'm not sorry it was great.

Some other time I'd love to go into detail about that trip to Rotterdam: the Mark Jones stomach pump; the Ostend broom cupboard; the subtle differences between half a dozen types of hot-dog sausage, lovingly explained by Bert the Wurst; the Conversation Stopper; rat's breath; and why, exactly, that cracking young fella Townsend Thoresen was called Townsend Thoresen. But the big story of Rotterdam is all about the police. If ever there was a tale of two cities in footballing terms, it's in the radically differing ways that two nations' law-enforcement officers set about policing a major, but potentially volatile, football final.

Let's be frank. Any big fixture in Europe that features an English team has the potential for disorder. Often, as in Rome in 1984, or in Rotterdam the following year, it is not all the fault of the English fans, whose reputation precedes them. There is always an element in the local hardcore who want to try themselves out, make a name for themselves against the English. More often than not, we just can't be arsed – and that's how it turned out in Rotterdam.

Could've been a different story, though, if not for the plod. In spite of there being a good 15,000 Everton supporters in central Rotterdam on 15th May, the police's big job was to encircle the five hundred Viennese skinheads who were intent on a suicide mission. As the hot, hot afternoon baked on towards teatime, rumours grew about the size and nastiness of this legendary firm of meatheads. The more drink was consumed, the more determined the Blues became to break through the cordon and find the Vienna fans – even though no one knew exactly where they were. This is where the Dutch police were so brilliant at defusing the situation. What helps, clearly, is that they all speak perfect (if slightly American-twanged) English. But it seems they've all got a basic-level qualification in humour, too. One copper, for all the world like Harry Enfield's gay Dutch policeman, stood there, laughing, 'I've seen them. I promise you, they're nothing. You'd be wasting your time . . .'

His mate joined in. 'They're pansies, man . . .' It was the first time I'd ever heard a copper say 'man'. 'You'll waste all your time and energy marching over to the other side of the city, getting all hot and tired, and they'll just run away I promise you, they're homos. They'll take one look at you guys and run away . . .'

Amazingly, it worked. One by one, even the most up-for-a-row Everton fans were keeling over, laughing. A combination of the weed, the sunshine, the mood and the sheer weirdness of two coppers striking up this double act had everyone in bits. People were queuing up to get their photos taken with Van der Valk and Tintin (he had a flat-top). Warming to their task, they obligingly provided lights for spliffs, then dragooned their police pals into a football team to take on the Everton fans in the main square. I don't think I've seen anything quite like it before or since – a team of fully uniformed coppers playing football with a load of scals. All thoughts of the Rapid Vienna Nasty Crew were forgotten as the tired and emotional Blues tried to kick their way past the slick, sexy football of Cruyff's Cops.

If only Brussels had been like that. But we had to get there first. There were, as usual, no end of mad schemes for getting there. Hundreds were going Transalpino, to Blankenberge on the Belgian coast. We liked the idea of a coastal billet, but Blankenberge barely seemed to register on the map. What if it turned out to be a Belgian Prestatyn – without The Robin Hood Camp Social Club to keep us entertained?

In a pre-Internet era it was hard to gather much information on the various options, so Potter and myself spent an afternoon in Lewis's travel department, tucked away on a mad little mezzanine overlooking Central Station. We scoured the brochures, comparing pictures and coming to the conclusion that Ostend, of all the resorts, had the most going for it. Not that we were patrons of the venerable profession, but any mention of a red-light district tends to augur well. Red light means old town, and old towns are good things. Forget your gaudy discotheques and malls and leisure-complex monstrosities. The mug's guide to abroad can best be summarised thus: do what the locals do; it's good. And what ultimately made myself and Micky the Chin plump for Ostend was an airbrushed photo of a quaint little square with outdoor tables sheltered from the sun by red umbrellas bearing one word: Maes.

We booked for ourselves, Hobo, Robbie the Mod and Keith from Donny. Hooto, the Davas, the Singing Brickie and many, many more followed suit. The trip, through The Belgian Travel Service, was thirty-nine pounds for three nights in a two-star hotel in Ostend, travel from London Victoria included. Thirty-nine: the number was to take on even greater significance.

Over the Saturday and Sunday before the game I made plans with Mauro. We'd meet him and his mate Marco outside Brussels Central train station at exactly midday on the Wednesday. So the five of us set off for London on the Sunday night, using un-clipped tickets one of the guards from British Rail had recycled. Keith from Donny was almost uncontrollably excited. He and his Everton-supporting mate Ilo had first surfaced about a year before, writing letters to *The End* for advice on how to become Doncaster's top dressers. In spite of deliberately misleading tips to shop for galoshes at the Army and Navy and detailed advice on how to dye their moustaches blond, Keith and Ilo stuck it out, turned up at all The Farm's early gigs and *End* party nights and gradually became good and trusted mates.

There's a lot of drivel that gets talked about Scousers, wools and out-of-towners. From years back some of our best-known and most devout supporters were known mainly by the places they came from: Dover, Stokie, the Preston Lads, German Tommy, Jaffa from Bournemouth. Keith from Donny deserves his place in that canon of diehards who go everywhere, adding the stick they have to take for their accents to the general sacrifices you make as a football fan, and always come back for more. Keith and his two Everton-supporting mates, Ilo and Shaun from Huddersfield, were more clued-up, streetwise and better dressed than a lot of the dullards who knocked around Anfield and Goodison back then, trading off their postcode and resting on their laurels.

Keith had moved from Doncaster to Liverpool at the start of the season, so this was a brilliant bookend for an eighteen-year-old lad. Never a massive drinker, he was kale-eyed by the time we reached Euston and more than happy to take the floor of the Boro Brothers' flat on the Clissold Estate while the rest of us tussled for the couch and the one spare bed. Potter's Vesuvian snoring guaranteed the easy berth for himself.

Next morning it was up, quick swill and a short march to the greasy spoon on Stoke Newington's Church Street. We may as well have been in Brussels already for the cultural exchange that took place between Robbie the Mod and the cafe's chirpy madam.

'Full brekkie please, love.'

'Bubble?'

'Er, no. Just me own.'

'Yeah, but do you want bubble?'

'Babboo?'

And so it went on until the cultural attaché for Kirkdale, Mr Potter, strode over to tell his brother-in-law to stop being a beaut and just leave anything he didn't like. We lined our stomachs with cockerney fayre, ready for the ravages ahead.

Manor House to King's Cross, King's Cross to Victoria, Victoria to the justified and ancient port of Dover. Seagulls. Sea salt. The fair Channel winds whipping our ears and sharpening our thirst. Myself and Hobo both knew from our recent Rotterdam trip there'd be a half-hour hiatus before the duty-free opened (and if the Everton trip was any indicator, a full five minutes longer before it was closed again), so we skipped off to a pub with black and white mock-Tudor timbers to see what we could forage. Hallelujah! It was one of those relics from bygone times, a pub with an off-licence attached. We purchased as follows:

vodka, Smirnoff Black Label – one bottle of

Cinzano, white – one litre of

lemonade, Dr Whites – two bottles of

Colt 45 – twenty-four cans of

The aim was to get hog-whimpering drunk as quickly as possible – a prerequisite to fine times for any twenty-something football fan. Shuffling over the gangway onto the cross-Channel ferry, we had the makings of very fine times indeed. Task one was to empty two-thirds of the lemmo out of its bottle. (Potter was in bulk when Keith from Donny called it 'pop'.) The pop vessel would then be topped up with equal measures of Cinzano and vodka, shaken not stirred, and downed with gusto. The James Bond theme was purely coincidental, but, with Colt 45 chasers, we were ready to drive cars off the side of the boat before too long.

One big, long conga took us from the bowels of the ship up and out onto the top deck. Mick's banner, 'Liverpool's Annual Bender', was run up the mast, and a strange assortment of well-fuelled Liverpool fans ran through the hymn book again and again and again. About mid-Channel (this was a four-hour hop), the seas started getting choppy. This only added to our amusement, as we adopted Beach Boys-style surfing poses, trying to stay on our feet as the boat eddied this way and that. Concerned P&O staff (or whoever the shipping line was) coaxed us back downstairs with the promise of something called a 'deesco'. This turned out to be the highlight of the trip, as classic after classic ripped out of the tinny in-house system. The unforgettable spectacle of Millsy and Paul Murphy twisting – yes, *twisting* – to The Beat's 'Mirror in the Bathroom' was the stuff of legend. By the time we docked in Ostend, every table was rocking under the weight of pogoing, delirious Redmen singing 'Eton Rifles' and 'White Man in Hammersmith Palais'.

While the hoi polloi scrambled for taxis, searching for any clue as to which road led where, us Belgian Travel Service ponces were met by a fey little fellow holding up a cardboard sign: 'Pooter Party'.

Pooter! That one little juvenile gag was all it took to set us off again, giggling and bellowing with that infectious kind of laughter that, once it starts, is very hard to stop. Poor Keith, who'd been feeling a little unwell over the final hour of the crossing, was mastering the dark art of laughing and being sick at the same time. Myself, Hobo and Potter had tears of mirth rolling down our cheeks – over nothing. That was until the tour guide spoke. Again, I must apologise for the impetuosity and sheer stupidity of youth. The guide looked like a cross between Jean-Paul Gaultier and Kirk Brandon from Theatre of Hate. He was wearing a very tight, stripy top. His name was Fred.

"Allo, mah name ees Frrrrred!'

He gave a radiant grin – quickly to be extinguished by the hurricane of laughter that followed. Again, there was nothing in particular we were laughing at. It was like one of those skunk-fuelled moments where everything and anything can set you off. All it was ever going to take was just one of us to start guffawing and that was it – thunderous giggling, all the way. Poor Fred tried to tough it out. He led us to his minibus and went through the motions of pointing out landmarks and recommended bars and cafes. Pooter – as he remained for the next forty-eight hours – and Robbie the Mod were a lost cause, but Hobo started into the giggler's equivalent of sobering up.

'Come 'ed, this is tight. The lad's only trying to do his job. Give him a . . .'

Tragically, Hobo was unable to finish his sentence. You'll all have been there. You can all picture the scene. For no good reason on God's sacred earth he just caved in all over again, and this time it was fatal. His laughing fit turned into this savage, uncontrollable, near-hysterical laughter. He was red in the face, barely able to get his breath in: 'HAH-HAH-HAH-HAH-HAH!!!'

Poor Fred got us to the front door of the hotel, stood back with his arms tightly folded as we were made to carry our own bags out of the back, then threw his head back, refusing all handshakes and attempts at a tip as he flounced back into the driver's seat and drove off at high speed. We stood outside the hotel, gurning at each other: 'What did we say?'

Keith, of course, took the question at face value. Kirkdale's newest resident, and The Jester's answer to Geoff Boycott, chewed on this poser for a second and came back with words of true

Yorkshire wisdom: 'I think he were a gay.' Before anyone had a chance to react, he followed up with: 'They're that little bit sensitive, aren't they?'

For the next minute his slender head weaved and bobbed to avoid the knuckles coming its way.

We checked into Hotel Doom – for some, their first taste of the wondrous and arcane world of the two-star hotel. European two stars can be all things to all people. Possibly the greatest little hotel in the world is the Henry IV in Place Dauphine, Paris – no facilities, groaning pipes, one bathroom per floor, but what an absolute gem of a place. Anyone young enough to fall in love for the first time, try and do it there. The memories will sustain you a good few months beyond the traditional six-month watershed.

Back in Ostend the two-star lottery was not looking promising. We were greeted on the uppermost of two steps by what could only be described as a wizard. It was white haired, with a splendid beard, dressed from head to toe in flowing black and, perplexingly, had a cat on its shoulder. Yet it also had quite remarkably pendulous breasts – distending, at a conservative estimate, to the hip bone, if not beyond – and spoke with a smoky barroom drawl that would have been sensual coming from Sophia Lauren, or from anyone at all on the end of a phone. From Mama Cass here, though, it was – how, shall we say? – sobering.

The infantile, giggling crew of five minutes ago was replaced by a line of told-off schoolboys staring at their shoes, as Miss ran the rule over them. We all nodded tamely as the hotel regulations were drilled into us. Rooms and beds were bagged, and, to be fair, the place was scrupulously clean, if spartan. But knowing that she was drifting from floor to floor out there – at one stage Keith and I could see her spectral silhouette through the dimpled, bog-style door window – meant that any thoughts of a pre-bender catnap went right out of the window. This was to prove unwise.

We tottered along the prom in the vague direction of one continual drone of tuneless Liverpool singing. A long, diagonal side street gave onto a little square – Liverpool's entire history in Europe can be measured by escapades in little squares – where

Bobby Billsy, Brian Billsy, the Davas and Danny Giles were sat outside enjoying schooners of cold lager and a bite to eat. The less-enlightened element on our trip had been quick to disparage Belgian cuisine, with the obvious jibes about sprouts and mayonnaise. Here were some of Liverpool's finest, however, enjoying everything from pork chops and sauté potatoes to entire platters of *fruits de mer*. And one thing the Belgians do better than any nation, anywhere, is a fine-cut chipped potato. Zounds, but the Belgians love their chips! We sat at an adjoining table and tucked into mussels in white wine for starters, tender pork fillet and chips, hot, doughy bread and lashings of Alsace wine. For a balmy spell on that first afternoon, everything was calm and understated. We'd sung ourselves hoarse, we'd all been up with the sweet silver larks, and subconsciously we needed this downtime to recharge our batteries.

The genial cafe owner spoke animatedly of Trappist beers but to no avail. We stuck to the familiar Stella and Maes – at first. Unable to convert us through his passion and knowledge of the local brewers, he resorted to sheer bravado. This was a man who knew what we wanted and was determined to prove it to us. Singling out Danny Giles, for reasons that never made the public domain, he handed him an inch of cloudy beer in a small glass: 'Drink slow. Very strong.'

Somehow those two words, 'strong' and 'very', seemed to transform everybody into Lancastrians, ready to pat their stomachs contentedly and claim it was 'all paid for'. Danny smacked his lips and said, 'It's all right that, lad.'

Danny has been calling men three times his age 'lad' since he was fifteen. A full year before he was able to leave school and follow his dream profession of apprentice bricklayer, he was walking around Birkenhead with a toolbox, pretending to be a 'skilly'. The truth is that for as long as I have known Danny Giles he has wanted to be fifty-five years old. One day he will be, but out there in Ostend supping that vicious ale he was all of twenty-two. The seal of approval from such an august imbiber as Danny was not unlike Jeremy Clarkson saying your wheels go round or the Michelin Man himself wobbling into your cafe and giving it the old three stars. Triumphant at this virtual thumbs-up, the owner was out again with jugs of the stuff, smiling indulgently and licking his lips as each one of us took a sip. I couldn't help thinking of the Child Catcher in *Chitty Chitty Bang Bang*, reeling us all in, one by one. Whatever, I was in a minority of two who thought this chalky ale was, not to put too fine a point on it, last. Within an hour we were all talking broken biscuits again, and our comely host was having to hand back injudiciously large tips.

As we milled around in the square – more of an oblong, technically – a joyous sight occurred. It was Fred! Keen to make amends for his earlier trauma, keen to buy him cloudy ale and make sure he knew how loved he was, we legged it towards him, shouting, 'Fred!' A Monkees-style chase ensued, with Fred showing us a clean pair of heels as he weaved through Ostend's back passages. It was hopeless. Mistaking our pursuit for something altogether more sinister, he was hurdling tables in the end to get away from us.

Sad to have lost him, we at least found a little pot of joy at the end of the rainbow – quite liderally. The unmistakeable pong of grass hummed out from and hung above a box-like, glass-fronted, unprepossessing cafe. We poked our heads inside, sniffed the air like Irish Setters and traipsed in. A couple of surly bikers sat at the bar, and a borderline-pretty blonde girl gave an automated welcome grimace. The place was more or less empty, yet it had a heavy, oppressive atmosphere. We should have got up and left there and then – but hindsight is a wonderful thing.

The girl ushered us to a hemmed-in table at the furthest end of the cafe. It was a cul-de-sac with banquette seating and one livid orange Formica table. The walls were fully mirrored – probably to make the place look bigger – but whatever their purpose they quickly became instruments of my downfall. Boxed in and claustrophobic, the very last thing we should have done was to eat space cake. We ate some space cake. We drank some more Maes, small glasses this time.

Sounds of Liverpool fans singing started to filter in from the courtyard cafe opposite. The bikers grinned, rolled another joint. One of them got up, went to the door to have a look, went outside. He came back looking concerned and gabbled something to his mate in Flemish. They both got up, went to the door, stood on their tiptoes and pointed then returned to their bar stools. My general sense of impending doom became more and more pronounced. I kept glancing up to see where the Hell's Angels were. They were just sat at the bar, barely even alive to the fact we were there – but to me, the more stoned I got, the more it seemed obvious they were just sitting off, biding their time.

I'll come clean here – I'm rubbish at drugs. There isn't a narcotic, synthetic or natural that has ever 'worked' for me. On mushrooms I go mad. On acid I'm suicidal. Anything you need to snort or inject – forget it. Broken nose means nothing but snot and air gets through. Deep and dire needle phobia means I faint during a routine flu jab. If I was a smackhead, I'd have to go Wild Turkey. I can dab a bit of whizz, and I've had my moments on the Gary Abletts, but I think I was born to be straight. And of all the woozy substances that everyone else unwinds with, no form of cannabis has ever had any other effect on me than to make me paranoid, or nauseous, or both. For me to sit at the far end of a narrow bar smoking reefer cigarettes was only ever gonna have one outcome. I could feel my mouth drying up. I leaned over to Hobo: 'They keep looking over. Are you ready?'

Hobo has a fantastic grin. His eyes go dead narrow, and he's got gaps between his teeth. You can't help loving the lad when he grins at you – he exudes a good-time aura. 'Ready for what?'

'If they start. Are you ready?'

'Don't talk soft. They haven't even glanced at us.'

But when he grinned this time, I sensed it straight away. He was in on it. It was all starting to make sense. When he'd gone to the bar before and lingered behind, chatting with the two bikers, he'd been forging a plan. This was it, then. They were going to do me in and steal what little money I had. I fingered my paltry stack of notes out of my jeans pocket, folded them over and over into a chunky wrap and levered it into that little drug pocket by your right hip. I glanced past the bikers towards the exit. There were people at the table by the door now – of course there were – and the door was probably locked. I could feel my heart starting to crash in and out. I licked my lips, tried to stay calm, looked at myself in the mirror. What stared back at me, crazed, was a bug-eyed loon, blinking repeatedly, chewing his own mouth off.

From the bar across the street the singing had turned rowdy. You could hear the unmistakable furore of a fight breaking out, glasses smashing and, within seconds, the encroaching blare of police sirens. The two bikers got up, and I chose this moment, of all moments, to suck hard on the spliff and hold it deep down inside. I was already gone – maybe I just wanted to blot out whatever was coming. When I exhaled, my head was spinning. To be exact, I was seeing stars, trillions and trillions of tiny little pin-speck stars, and this trilling, zinging white noise was drilling in my ears. Everything was just shapes and shadows. I couldn't even make out Hobo, even though I was aware that he was on his feet, talking in this slowed-down Darth Vader voice: 'We better give it toes, you know. Coming on top out there . . .'

I tried to get to my feet, fell straight back down. Pathetic. I'd been up since six, I'd been drinking all day and I'd had a bit of space cake, but, compared to the others, who'd been hammering the Trappist ale and building up joint after joint, I'd had nothing. This made me feel even more unhinged. I held onto Keith from Donny's jacket as, lurching into tables, we made our way out of the bar.

'Hey! You pay! You pay!'

I was certain we'd paid already, but with two bearded monsters standing guard over the door, the last thing anyone wanted – or was capable of delivering – was trouble. We gave her a handful of coins – which, oddly, satisfied her – and staggered out into a maelstrom of barking hounds and the scintillating blue stroboscope of the police vans' revolving lights. While everyone else moved on, I stood there, transfixed. Heightened by the stimulants, and with that tingling note still zinging in my ear, I was mesmerised, as faces I knew were being led across the passage in cuffs. I went to shout, but nothing came. Then, the shame. A dog handler came up behind, urging his hound closer and closer, trying to chase me off. They wanted the area cleared so the meat wagons could move out, and there was me stood like a zombie right in the middle of the road.

Keith came running back, trying to drag me out of the line of fire. I felt the Alsatian's wet teeth snapping behind me, but as I turned to tell the handler it was fine, I was going, the dog got Keith by the wrist. No amount of reasoning, negotiation or barter would persuade them to let him go. Liverpool's most peaceable fan was manhandled into the back of a Black Maria and driven off to be charged with affray. When everyone got back together, it transpired a row had broken out in the other bar when the owners tried to charge a group of fans twice. Bouncers had been drafted in to make them pay, and things turned ugly.

I'm never going to stand here and claim that all our fans are innocent victims whenever things go wrong in Europe, but the trivial little things that spark the bigger incidents so rarely get reported. For every joyful tale of cold Cervezas in sun-kissed plazas, the seasoned traveller will have had his share of rip-offs, scams, corruption and naked collusion with the local police, too. We had a whip-round for Keith, bailed him out and called it a night.

Matchday. Everyone up and showered and down in the break-fast room, ready for the off. Mama Cass has perfected a way of gliding across the floor, almost hovering an inch or so above the bogging carpet so that she gets from table to table without seeming to move a limb. Quite some feat, for a fat bird. At this point I'd love to break from the stereotype of the inedible bilge that passes for breakfast in some of these places, but the hideous truth is that the grub in this one set a whole new standard for awfulness. Myself, Hobo and Potter had set ourselves a task of completing at least one meal every day we were there. That meal was onion soup.

Still, nothing was going to curb our enthusiasm, and we were all out and thronging the platform of Ostend station waiting for the rattler to the capital. Estimated time of arrival was eleven bells, giving us plenty of time to find a good bar near the station and await the arrival of Signore Mauro Garino. The journey up to Brussels was enhanced by our discovery of a previously undiscovered species: the wise-cracking Belgian lass. The train was overrun with promo girls from Marlborough cigarettes, patrolling the carriages with giveaway five-packs. Perfect. Hardly any of us smoked, but it was free, it was currency, and it gave us licence to talk to startlingly attractive women from a different country. And a different planet. They quickly made light of our puerile attempts at banter: 'Hey, girl, the last time I seen a pack like this it was 5 Park Drive.'

'Park Drive? What were you, a bell boy?'

They were dead, dead funny – perfectly at ease giving and taking stick, and more than capable of handling the lairy stuff. One strange young man who bore more than a passing resemblance to Napoleon Dynamite started with the predictable come-ons: 'Here y'are, love. You and me in the bogs, now.'

'Oh, you are too charming. But I must say no.'

'Come 'ed. I'll sort you, good style.'

She gives him a lovely, condescending, patronising smile. 'I think no.'

'Why? Scared, are you?'

'Scared only for you, sweetie. I think you have a tiny penis.'

There's very little anyone can say to come back from a sledge like this. The lad just went red, endured the volley of laughter in his face, muttered some none-too-pleasant at the girl and marched off. Marlborough Girl would have been feted all the way to Brussels had she and her cohorts not got off halfway there. To the tune of the 'On the dole in Paree' song she was serenaded off the train: 'Marlborough Girl, Marlborough Girl, Marlborough Girl!'

We never saw Napoleon Dynamite again.

Off the train, into the steaming heat of Brussels. Loads of African lads playing football in a gravel pit shaded by tall, dusty trees. Some of them had old footy tops on, Anderlecht and, weirdly, a Leeds United one, but most of them were wearing those kimono-type tops – lurid shades of gold and yellow and red and orange made out of some kind of fine, silky material. Dressed in tennis shirts and jeans, we were already feeling the stifling heat at eleven in the morning. Myself and Mick Potter attempted to join in the kick-around but were bamboozled for skill by baby-faced Kanus and Eto'os – and beaten by the high-noon sun.

Most of the crew were eager to get down to the Grand Place, the vast and majestic square that was the obvious venue for Scouse Central and the party that was sure to ensue. Myself and Mick sat off and waited for Mauro. The appointed time came and went. I couldn't believe he hadn't showed. As recently as Sunday we'd made fine-print plans to meet up for the game we'd always talked about. Maybe he'd been delayed. I shovelled a handful of coins into the payphone and got through to Mauro's sister, Silvia. The line was bad, and it sounded like she was saying he had lots of influence. My heart leapt at this – maybe he'd got us some tickets from Brussels-based Italians? I asked Silvia again which station Mauro's train would arrive at, but the pips went, and that was that. Potter and I made a half-hearted trawl of the other train stations, but somehow we knew we wouldn't be seeing old Garino after all.

We got down to the Grand Place, a crawling chaos of red and white. Juventus, we now knew, had 3000 more tickets than us, but there was precious little sign of any Italian presence whatsoever. The Liverpool contingent had completely taken over central Brussels, and the party was only just starting.

A ludicrous scenario unfolded. There have been many differing accounts of this tale over the decades, and perhaps there was more than one such incident, but this is what happened. A Maes delivery truck, stacked high with crate upon crate of the golden nectar, was attempting to make its way across the square to a couple of bar/restaurants in one corner. To envisage what took place, you have to bring to mind an area approximately the size of six football pitches. As European plazas go, the Grand Place in Brussels is a leviathan among pocket-handkerchief pretenders. But Liverpool fans, by two in the afternoon, were covering every visible square foot of it. Against this backdrop any attempt by any delivery truck to weave a peaceful passage through the massed ranks of Redmen was doomed. For such a truck, piled high with crates of ale, to come a-courting was pure folly. The only surprise is that it took as long as it did to be relieved of its load.

Our merry little firm was stood outside one of the two big cafe/bars in that corner of the Place, soaking up the sun and listening to tales of Blankenberge. I spotted the delivery truck a full five minutes before it got anywhere near our speck and gave it no further thought until there it was, right in front of us. I couldn't believe it. A couple of lads hopped up onto the back and began handing down crate after crate of Maes. Mick Potter was onto it quickly – as were about another 2000 Liverpool fans. I shouted Mick and Hobo to get round the blind side, and we held our arms out as they unloaded one, two, three crates of Maes to us before going back round the other side of the truck to let others have a crack. Bizarrely the delivery man continued his mission right up to the load-in point, and everyone just legged it when he switched off his engine. Either he didn't notice or didn't care about what was going on, but we had free drinks for the rest of the day.

The afternoon was another laugh-in. This seems hard to correlate in light of what was to come, but the atmosphere was absolutely swinging down there. Everyone was singing. A load of big daft lads from Wales were opening the Maes bottles for us with their teeth. Juve fans started to filter into the square, and everyone mingled just fine.

We were using the second-floor toilets of the big pizzeria, and the owners were OK with that, so long as we bought the occasional drink or slice of pizza. I was up there using the urinal, while a 50–50 mix of English and Italian fans queued up behind. There was a big, big picture window looking out onto the square, and down below the growing din of the Juve fans was drowned out by 'You'll Never Walk Alone' and 'Every Other Satdee'. Two

Juventus kids were waving down below to their dad. A sudden gust of wind slammed the main toilet door shut, and a clank from the other side told us the door handle had fallen off outside. One of the fellas in the queue tried the door, but it was fastened tight. We were stuck in there. We banged and banged, but no one came. The two kids shouted out of the window to their dad, but he couldn't hear a thing. Everyone started laughing self-consciously, the Liverpool fans asking if the toilets had a television set, the Italians hatching up a plan between themselves. One of the older Italian guys took off his scarf, went around all the other Juventus fans and borrowed their scarves too and started tying them together. He was a real pro, this guy, obviously an Italian Baden-Powell in the making, from the way he bound and secured his knots. These Juventus scarves were much wider and longer than the Liverpool version, and made of a woven cloth instead of wool. But six of them together was still nowhere near long enough to make the drop down from the second floor. Up until that point we'd been politely but awkwardly ignoring one another, but a Liverpool lad took off his scarf and handed it over. Then another one did the same, then another. Before long Akela had a big, long, half-Liverpool, half-Juventus scarf. He told the smaller of the two kids to grab tight hold, then lowered him slowly, but slowly, to the ground below. A minute later the grinning owner was outside to free the Grand Place sixteen. I doubt the kid's father was too thrilled about his son's flirtation with dangerous sports, either. But from the aftermath of Heysel itself to the right here and now, the symbolism of that simple act of human coop-eration has remained with me. In many respects it signalled the end of the fun, the end of innocence – and the start of the dark-ness ahead.

It was time to head up to the ground. Vanguards had been up to Heysel already to eye up the lie of the land, and what was coming back was sounding mixed. The stadium itself, everyone was saying, was 'easy'. But the police were horrible. They'd been knocking cans out of people's hands, emptying bottles of wine down the drains and clobbering anyone who complained. Having encountered only smiley, slightly bemused local police in the city centre, we were as yet unprepared for the riot squad waiting by the ground. I'd already had experience of these socially adept agents of tolerance in Europe before – in Italy, and on stepping off the boat in France in '81. I knew they took no prisoners, but still, it was hard to believe these stories of indiscriminate beatings that were getting back to us here in the Grand Place.

Nothing galvanises the common resolve of a group of Scousers like the threat of a common enemy. If there's a whiff of corruption or injustice about the way that enemy goes about its business – whether it's FC Basle fans steaming into a pub full of kids and shirt-wearers or a police force dishing out random hidings – there will be comeback. No big speeches or puffed-out chests, but if we're wronged, there'll be comeback. Yet as we boarded the metro up to the stadium, acts of violence seemed a million miles off the radar. Everyone was laughing; everyone was happy. A group of shift workers dressed in all-white, one-piece boiler suits and face masks got on, about thirty of them.

'Here y'are, make some room for these sprout miners,' someone shouted. 'You wouldn't be half the man you are today without these fellas.'

Not exactly side-splitting, but everyone seemed ready to laugh along with any daft shout. Yet as soon as we stepped out of the underground station and into the Heysel night, the atmosphere changed. I'll try to be as cold and as factual as I can about what happened next. It's obviously difficult for me to keep the emotion out of it – this was to be one of sporting history's worst human disasters, and one with direct personal impact for those of us who know Mauro. But there's a range of factors that all influenced what happened that night, and it's important to try to understand the chain of events as they unfolded.

Firstly, it's absolutely correct to say that even an hour before kick-off the police had lost control of the ground. Culpability for that lies in three areas – just as it did in Athens for the 2007 final. Liverpool fans have to shoulder some blame. We come from a city and a culture that is insanely passionate about football. We go to every game, home and away. At the 1985 European Cup final too many Liverpool fans loved their team so much that they were determined to get inside that stadium by fair means or foul.

It must be hard for the likes of William Gaillard and Michel Platini, coming from a country that prefers rugby, to begin to imagine the sort of devotion that compels somebody to get up at four in the morning and head off to the Riverside for a midday kick-off, let alone drive thousands of miles across Europe to be part of a footballing festival from which they've been excluded. But whatever UEFA and the Premier League and Sky television throw at us, we take it. We swallow it all, willingly, because at the end of it all we get to see our team. We provide the noise and the spectacle and the sheer carnival of sound and atmosphere that enhances UEFA's 'brand'. And when it all works for them – when they contrive to give us the tickets we crave, and need, and desire, and *deserve* – then they throw us the titbit of a UEFA prize for fair play. And let's make no mistake whatsoever: we are supporters the like of which UEFA will never comprehend, because our football club is our life. We are not spectators; we're fans. We are not English; we're Scouse. Where other fans desert the stadium in their droves the moment their team is beat, we stay behind to console our lads and salute the champions, whoever they are. Ask AC Milan, who were as bemused as they were delighted by the thunderous reception they received from the still-packed Liverpool end after they'd collected the Big Cup. In an ideal world our fans would not have to resort to rushing gates, paying ticket touts and gaining entry through forged tickets. But in an ideal world, UEFA would not treat us like halfwits, like product, like just another element in their marketing scheme. The day UEFA puts the fans before the product is the day the game wins back its soul.

As things transpired, getting in was a doddle. A few hefty kicks and huge holes appeared in the crumbling exterior walls. From there it was a game of tag, where nine out of every ten were managing to body-swerve the police inside the ground.

This is where UEFA must shoulder a hefty slice of blame, too. Why, oh why, play a major European sporting final in a small, derelict stadium unfit for greyhound racing? Why? Nobody has ever admitted to making or helping make that decision, let alone justified it. It was a shambles. It is a disgrace that Heysel Stadium was ever considered a worthy venue for such a huge occasion.

And as for the constabulary that policed the ground itself, in any event, and against any standard, they were ill-trained, reactionary and ultimately cowardly. But judged against those laughing policemen in Rotterdam, they were, quite simply, light years behind. There was neither rhyme nor reason for their selection of targets outside the ground. If you stood still for long enough, they'd hit you. When they thought they could get away with it, they'd hit you. For this, they have to take some blame for stoking up an atmosphere that turned from jubilant and celebratory to vengeful – as do the Liverpool fans who then took the law into their own hands.

Yet only minutes before entering the ground, Millsy and I stood there laughing. We were actually heads-back chortling at the spectacle of group after group of fans wandering up to the hole-riddled main exterior wall, ducking down and squeezing through. We thought it was funny, and valiant, and no mean payback for the shoddy way our fans had been treated across the board. The police were fully occupied trying to keep the bunk-in down to an acceptable minimum, so there was no security presence at all at the gateways into the seated areas. Only at this point did Millsy produce a ticket. 'Come on. We'll both get in with this. Doddle.'

And it was, too. There were no turnstiles, no checkpoints, nothing other than a couple of slightly bemused uniformed officials who stood back and smiled nervously as they waved you through. We found Millsy's seat and both stood there, eyes trained on 'our' end. It was obvious that the two nearest sections were already massively overpopulated. Whereas the heads in the Juve end were spaced apart, here they were packed tight, and any surge forward was sending whole columns of fans spilling down the terraces as one, unable to stem the force. Yet the third section – the one furthest away from us – was almost empty. This was to add insult to injury. Not only had UEFA handed us a woefully inadequate allocation of tickets for the final, they had actually cut into our take to accommodate the supposedly neutral section. Yet the only fans in that sparse section were wearing Juventus colours. It was a disgrace.

Nothing will ever justify what happened next. I'm not going to get into the folklore of fans taunting each other, or who or what set the mayhem in motion. I think it's as simple as this: 12,000 Liverpool fans were packed into a section designed for 6000 athletics fans. Next to them was an almost-empty pen, housing a few hundred Juventus fans. In the heat and the passion and the stoked-up atmosphere of indignation on the night, it boiled down to the fact that Juve fans were occupying 'our' end.

A sizeable minority of Liverpool fans began to storm that third enclosure. My impression was that they were intent on reclaiming that piece of terracing for the Liverpool support. The Italians would be escorted out and around the running track to Juve parts of the ground, while the crammed-tight Liverpool fans could spread out into an area that should, anyway, have been theirs. It's not as though huge amounts of planning go into such spur-of-the-moment actions, but I still believe that most of those involved with breaking through the barriers were mainly concerned with taking back the section, rather than clashing with the Juve fans. But of course there would have been those, too, who were thinking that if the Italians stayed and fought, well, there was still last year in Rome to be accounted for.

At first it was no more than a few dozen pulling at the flimsy dividing fences. More and more joined in, tearing at the wire-mesh barricades – woefully inadequate – and pulling them up. Fans flooded under and through and over the mesh fencing. The police resistance was brief, before they backed off, too. For a few minutes this was just a bad, prolonged football brawl. It seemed to go on and on – fans fighting and charging each other, back and forward. There were a fair few 'boys' among the neutral-section Italians – game-enough Juventus lads who were more than ready to have a go. But that only seemed to spur on more and more Liverpool fans to tear through no-man's-land and join in the melee. Eventually there was a completely fenceless stretch of about twenty yards in the centre, through which hundreds and hundreds of Liverpool fans poured. At this point most of the Italians turned and ran. Liverpool fans started hugging each other as though we'd scored a goal. Hardly any of them pursued the Italians. They'd won back their bit of terracing, and that was that. But the horror was only just starting. Millsy turned to me: 'Looks bad, you know.'

Down in the far corner of that third enclosure a funnel of people was building up. More and more fleeing bodies hurled themselves at the escape route, but nobody seemed to be getting out. We didn't know why at the time.

The first time we knew, for an absolute fact, that lives had been lost was in the taxi back to Ostend. There had been carefully worded tannoy announcements in three languages, yet the match had gone ahead. We could see that our teams' hearts were not in it as a disembodied game was played out.

The bare facts of the game are that Gary Gillespie, an early substitute for the injured Mark Lawrenson, brought Boniek down outside the box. The referee pointed to the spot. Current UEFA President Michael Platini stepped up, slotted the kick and Juventus won 1–0. From our point of view it looked like the Liverpool team lacked appetite for the game. Kick-off had been delayed by ninety minutes, and the Reds just seemed drained from the delays and misinformation and the fatal distraction of all the trouble behind the goal.

Rumours had started circulating that there had been a fatality – possibly more than one – but that was difficult to believe. Surely the match would not have been allowed to go ahead if people had lost their lives beforehand? Surely UEFA could not preside over such a decision? Yet, on the way out of the stadium, one of the uniformed stewards told us there was going to be trouble for all and any English fans if we ventured back into the city centre. 'Everybody is out to get you,' he said, face tense with fury. 'Italian, Belgian, African – everybody.'

Outside the ground was unreal. Hundreds of Juventus fans were flooding out, waving their flags. Passing cars tooted their horns at them. The Italians waved their flags back at them, faces alive with joy. The atmosphere was marginally better now than it had been directly before the game. We dealt with the practicalities. There was no way in the world we'd find any of the others. No meeting point had been arranged beforehand. One minute we were all outside the ground, the next it was just me and Millsy. We flagged a taxi, negotiated a rate back to Ostend and sat in utter silence most of the way. The driver put his radio on. I could see him darting looks at us through his rear-view mirror.

'Can you tell us what's happened, please?' I said.

You could see him weighing up the balance between the derision he wanted to pour on us and the not-insubstantial fare he'd be getting when we reached the coast. He swallowed his ire. 'Many dead,' he said. 'Many, many dead.'

Now my heart sank. Had Mauro's 'influence' got him tickets in that section? Was he one of the perished? We got back to the hotel. Mama Cass just stood there, looking down on us, shaking her head sadly. We waited in the bar for the others to arrive back, and, while I shall never know quite why, I asked her if there was any onion soup left.

Next day I braved it. I picked up the phone, dialled the number. The significance didn't dawn on me at the time, but the Italian code starts 39. I waited, and waited. The dialling tone is one long note – then silence. Another long note – then silence.

'Pronto?'

It was him. He was OK. Hearing my voice, his own dropped to a deathly hush. He was desperate to know, but desperate not to know, too, whether I'd been involved in the fighting. Only months later, when he brought a party of young Juve fans on a friendship trip to Liverpool, could I show him pictures of myself and Millsy in the seated area, the cursed curva way down to our right. We spoke a little. He explained to me that he hadn't been able to go to Brussels because he had a fever, influenza – 'influence'.

I said I'd phone him again when we got back to England.

The ferry back to Dover was in stark contrast to the love-boat that took us out. People were physically and emotionally drained. When we got back to Liverpool, Peter Hooton was straight on the phone: 'We've got to do something about this.'

'Agreed. But what *can* we do?'

'You get in touch with Mauro and tell him that anyone, any of his mates that want to come to Liverpool, the doors are open. We can't waste time. The rebuilding starts now.'

With sterling work from Peter's colleagues in Social Services, Brian Reynolds and Mark Fitzsimmons, a bespoke mini-trip to Liverpool was arranged for forty-five young Juventus fans. It was to include free entry to nightclubs, a meal with wine at Bucco di Bacco, the city's premier Italian cafe, a reception from Derek Hatton at the Town Hall and four nights' stay at the Holiday Inn. Local businesses contributed towards air fares, while Brian Reynolds was able to commandeer a fifty-two-seat coach for the duration of their stay.

We picked the Italians up from Gatwick and, assuming they'd be hungry, suggested we stop off at a country pub for a ploughman's or a nice roast dinner. After going into a huddle and beating around the bush for a few minutes they came out with it: 'Could we please go to McDonald's?' The fast-food phenomenon had hit Rome, but as yet Turin had not fallen prey to Ronald's wiles. Happily scoffing the very first Big Macs of their lives, the Sicilian lads on the trip – Mauro told us he'd had to invite them, as leaders of the Ultras, in order to give the whole thing credibility – eyed us unblinkingly. After a beat the hardest-looking lad said, 'Who is most crazy hooligan in England. West Ham or Chelsea?'

Our peacekeeping initiative was working a treat.

Did it do any good? Who can say? Mauro thinks so. There was one glorious night on the Royal Iris ferry where a farewell party was DJ'd by the late, lamented John Peel. The Farm played; Ted Chippington played; but it was a local covers band, Groundpig, who stole the show. As they played out their show-closer, a cover of Peter Gabriel's 'Solsbury Hill', a clutch of sweaty Scouse lads invaded the little stage. Seconds later the Italian boys were up there with them – Liverpool, Everton and Juventus, arms around each other, pogoing to Peter Gabriel. For a moment it was normal-service resumed – a whole slew of tipsy, young footy fans pogoing like loons on a ferry boat, without a care in the world. It was going to take more than bonhomie and a ferry across the Mersey to heal the wounds, but it was a promising start. And they left town owing the Holiday Inn a grand in bar bills – half of it champagne – so something was in the air.

Bit by bit Mauro and I restored our relationship. Uncannily he was there with me at Hillsborough. He's been to dozens and dozens of Liverpool matches. It was inevitable that, one day, his beloved Juventus would meet our Liverpool in serious competition once again, and it was almost fated that it should take place exactly twenty years after Heysel. It was only in these circumstances – a meeting that mattered between the two clubs – that any of us could, truly, get close to closure on that tragic night in Brussels.

Liverpool FC presented Mauro with a carved marble plaque on the pitch before the match. It read 'In Memory and Friendship'. Many of the Juve fans chose to turn their backs on a mosaic bearing the same message. That's understandable. We ourselves are nowhere near ready to forgive the *Sun* newspaper its lies about Hillsborough, so what the Juventus fans do is purely a matter for themselves. For our part, the match gave us a chance to say 'We are sorry'. For our part in the tragedy of Heysel, we are sorry.

Liverpool won the game in 2005 2–1, on our way to the glory of Istanbul. As we walked away from Anfield, Mauro tried to put Heysel into some kind of context: 'But I don't know, Kev. Why this game happen in this ground?'

It's a question that is still being asked today.

Istanbul, 2005

JOHN MAGUIRE

Champions League Final, 25th May 2005
Atatürk, Istanbul
Attendance: 65,000

AC Milan	3–3	Liverpool FC
Maldini (1')		Gerrard (54')
Crespo (39', 44')		Šmicer (56')
		Alonso (60')

PENALTIES: Liverpool win 3–2

Serginho	x	✓	Hamann
Pirlo	x	✓	Cissé
Tomasson	✓	x	Riise
Kaká	✓	✓	Šmicer
Schevchenko	x		

1
Jerzy Dudek

3 Steve Finnan **23** Jamie Carragher **4** Sami Hyypiä **21** Djimi Traoré

14
Xabi Alonso

10 Luis García **8** Steven Gerrard **6** John Arne Riise

5 Milan Baroš **7** Harry Kewell

Substitutes: Scott Carson, Josemi, Dietmar Hamann, Antonio Núñez, Igor Bišćan, Djibril Cissé, Vladimír Šmicer

Manager: Rafael Benítez

AC Milan: Dida (1), Cafu (2), Jaap Stam (31), Alessandro Nesta (13), Paolo Maldini (3,captain), Andrea Pirlo (21), Gennaro Gattuso (8), Clarence Seedorf (20), Kaká (22), Andriy Shevchenko (7), Hernán Crespo (11)

Substitutes used: Rui Costa, Serginho, Jon Dahl Tomasson

Manager: Carlo Ancelotti

'**B**astard! You bandy-legged twat.'

Rivaldo had just made it 1–0 to Olympiakos, which more or less made it mission impossible for us to get through to the knockout phase of the European Cup and have a decent crack at one of the big guns of European football. I thought that if we could just get an equaliser before half-time, we'd be in with a chance, but as that half-time whistle blew, I feared the worse.

I'd been quite optimistic before the game, as I made my way from my evening job to Anfield. A half-night shift that starts at 5 p.m. and ends at 7 p.m. – I mean, what's the point trekking into town and back for a two-hour shift? Thing is, though, I had to keep an eye on the amount of annual leave I had left, and I couldn't afford to take a full (four hours!) night off work, so, for the midweek home games, it was the half-night off.

My journey from Graeme House, Derby Square, to Anfield involved a quick walk along Castle Street, usually stopping at Sainsbury's to get a packet of McCoy's cheese crisps, cos I wouldn't be getting me tea down me neck till 11 p.m. that night. That was an ordeal itself; they're like a full meal them crisps, leaving me with an aching jaw.

Anyway, I walked along Castle Street that night, taking in the gloriously majestic sight of Liverpool Town Hall at 7 p.m. on a chilly December evening. The building looked amazing, with them ground-level lights shining up onto the brickwork, making me think of the glorious history that that big balcony has seen. You see, football and music are the two most important things in my life, and that ledge has seen the two greats in each respective area, the late, great Mr Bill Shankly and the Beatles.

I took a sharp right onto Dale Street, having a quick glance over me left shoulder to see the two Liverbirds overlooking a River Mersey that was absolutely beautiful under the grim sky. I crossed over and quickened me swagger as I walked past The

Saddle and Rigbys and took in a lungful of the stale-ale air; then it was a quick left and up the escalator into Moorfields train station. I lost me radio signal on me MP3 player so had to swerve Radio Merseyside's pre-match build-up and get into some decent Scouse tunes instead, bands like Shack, The Real People and The La's – songs sprinkled with salt from the River Mersey.

I was feeling confident that we'd go through, to be honest. These games where we need to win by a certain amount of goals are always belters – like a few years ago when we needed to beat Roma by two goals. We done it that night to the backdrop of one of the greatest atmospheres I'd ever been part of. Thing is, though, that Fabio Capello Roma team from 2002 were shit-hot; these Greeks were nowhere near as good. Nah, no problemo tonight, la. Three or four nil, a great atmosphere and a few post-match celebratory bevvies to round it off – is right.

Must admit, I hate getting that soccer bus, though. It wouldn't be as bad if they let you get off the thing by the Royal Oak or by the legendary Dixie Dean's statue, cos the thing just pure snails it from that point onwards and it'd be well quicker walking the rest of the way. Plus, you have to listen to blerts chattin' shit about your beloved Redmen. That's what the arl MP3 player's for. Drown them out with Radio Merseyside and listen to Gary Gillespie or someone chattin' shit instead.

Off the bus it's uphill towards the King Harry boozer, me arl pre- and post-match drinking den. Once I got to the King Harry, turned into the entry and saw the floodlights lighting up the L4 sky, I could tell it was gonna be a special night. You could smell it in the air.

A quick look at me mobile tells me its half seven and there's fifteen minutes till kick-off – well sorted for time. Not much of a queue outside entrance gate E, and I'm in me seat right in the middle of the Spion Kop with five minutes to spare before our anthem starts. That's another good thing about going the game straight from work: no piss paranoias. I'm usually obsessed around this time about whether I'm gonna need a Geoff Hurst at some point during the first half. Shall I run the toilet now for a quick safety slash or shall I risk it? Nothing worse than needing a piss twenty minutes into the game; it means that by half-time you're in agony and have to walk to the pisser almost bent over cos of the arl bladder being fuller than the Red Army's trophy cabinets. None of that malarky tonight, though. No bevvies before the game equals no pissing during the match – sound.

And now, here I am, standing here by the lifts in the upper Kop concourse area, going through our half-time ritual of Sayers sausage roll and orange Capri-Sun. Me, Johnny Jones, Jimmy and his lad Nathan are feeling gutted. 'Looks like it's the UEFA Cup, then, dunnit?' The UEFA Cup. I just can't be bothered with that thing anymore. I hate Thursday-night games, meaning all your Saturday games are switched to the Sunday. I hate the Channel Five coverage, and I hate the teams that you have to play. I mean, it'd be sound for all the diehard, Euro-trekking Reds who travel everywhere, going to the lesser-known cities and towns like Liberec as well as the major cities, but as I don't get the chance to go to many Euro away games for the time being, it's hard to get yourself up for a game against a team that you know you should really be beating 3–0 or 4–0.

It's a no-win situation, cos even if we hammer them, it's no big deal; we were expected to. Nah, once you've tasted the Champions League, you don't want to be playing in the UEFA Cup. It's like munching on Netto beans when you're used to Marks & Spencer's food. I'd rather drop out of Europe completely and have a good crack at the league and FA Cup with no distraction. Don't get me wrong, like: Dortmund 2001 was a fantastic experience. One of my greatest moments was in that stadium when all the players and staff were singing 'You'll Never Walk Alone' with arms around each other right in front of me. The UEFA Cup was right for us at that time. But that was symbolic of the empire striking back. Rafa was taking us to the next level. Our cockiness was restored. The Anfield arrogance was back with a vengeance, and we will not settle for anything less than the best.

Anyway, let's get back up there and try to roar our lads to victory. We needed to score three goals and couldn't concede any more. Sound. That'll do. We love a bit of pressure. It brings out the best in us, the players and the crowd. Three goals, like? It's not mission impossible. Get an early goal and just take it from there. As long as the Reds are up for it and the crowd does their bit, we're in with a chance.

It's always good to get an early goal just after the break when you're behind, and we did, straight away. Gerrard was playing like a man possessed; he was everywhere. He'd said he didn't want to wake up in the morning and be in the UEFA Cup. None of us do, Stevie lad. The second goal didn't look like it was gonna happen at one point, what with a load of chances going begging. Then, about two minutes after Rafa threw the Mellor fella on for Baros, the young lad smacked a headed-down ball into the back of the net. What a celebration! No coolness here. None of this Thierry Henry nonsense, being too cool for school, thinking you're above celebrating a goal cos you're that good. Nah. Jib that. Get in there, Mellor lad!

We needed that all-important third goal, though. We beat PSG and Strasbourg 2–0 in the Anfield second leg, but we still went out the competition cos we needed three to go through. Tonight's script was written for Stevie, though. The lad's standing there about thirty yards out, both arms in the air, screaming for the ball, but Riise loses it before he can pass it to him. Then the ball goes to Carra, and Stevie's arms go up in the air again. The lad's dying to get hold of this ball. Carra chooses to float one into the box, which Mellor heads down to Stevie. Mellor's probably thinking, 'Here's the ball you've been screaming for for the past thirty seconds. Don't waste it.'

Stevie runs towards the bouncing ball, positioning himself for the half-volley as he approaches it, and BOOM! Gerrard blasts the ball with his right peg and it swerves with power into the right-hand side of the net. And then he's off, both arms pumping, running towards the corner of the Kop, running right up to the advertising hoarding and grabbing and hugging the first Kopite he can get his Huytonian hands on. The whole team's right behind him. It's the type of goal that makes everything worthwhile. All the shite you have to put up with being a football fan, getting fleeced by the club you love, pouring every penny you earn into this business that, if you're really being honest about it, doesn't give a shit about you. None of that matters when you get moments like that happening in your life.

The next stage was easy. Bayer Leverkusen: two great results, a new song added to the repertoire (Status Quo's 'Rockin' All Over the World') and we're in the quarter-finals of the European Cup. I started to get stupid feelings in my stomach around this time. Could we actually win this cup? 'Nah, fuckin' 'ell, lad, ye getting carried away there.' But who could possibly beat us over two legs? 'Oh, shurrup, eh? Just enjoy the ride, and whatever happens, happens.' Who's next?

It just had to be, didn't it? The twentieth anniversary of Heysel coming up, and we hadn't played them since that fateful night. Juventus lay in wait.

I'd recently started a work placement as part of my Social Work degree with a team based in Waterloo. This was to last about three months and was a pain in the arse, due to the fact that I had to be in work at five every night. So I'd be leaving the house at 8 a.m. and not getting home till 9.30 p.m. Long days them, la. Me mate Brian only lived round the corner from the place where I was based for me placement, so I arranged to meet him at about 4 p.m. at Waterloo train station. I'd booked the full night off work for this one. This was a massive game, possibly the biggest Anfield occasion I'd ever been to, so I wanted to make the most of it and join in with the pre-match ritual of having tapas in La Tasca.

Anyway, I met Brian at the station. Christie was already on the train, having moved down from the South End to Crosby, and after getting off the train at Moorfields it was straight to La Tasca to meet the rest of the lads. Christie's older brother, Tony, was already in there with his brother-in-law, Kevin, and a load of Kevin's mates. Before we'd even sat down, there was a jug of San Miguel getting poured out for us and three menus lashed our way. This is more like it. None of that two-hour-shift malarkey tonight, sitting on that soccer bus listening to some blert giving the Redmen 'down the banks'.

The tapas went down a treat – spicy meatballs in tomato sauce, spicy Spanish sausage (felt daft asking the lad for that) and these little roast potatoes with a load more red sauce on (gorgeous, though). Well better than me usual pre-match meal of cheese McCoy's, and all washed down with loads of San Miguel. This is the life. I could definitely get used to this preparation. After we'd weighed the waiters in, we dived a taxi to Epstein's on Anfield Road. Stood outside on the back patio, we had our pre-match-nerve-settlers before doing a dusty into the ground. Same speck as always: Kop Area 105, right in the middle. Me season ticket's in the Main Stand, but I like to have a bit of a sing-song for the cup games, and you can't beat the Spion Kop on a European night – nothing comes close.

The 'Friendship' mosaic was done and looked boss on the telly when I saw it later. Quite a big section of their fans, the front four or five rows, turned their backs on us as we held out the message of friendship. To be honest, it was probably just a few Ultras trying to act hard, and other supporters joined in for fear of getting a dig, or their arses slashed, which is the way Italian Ultras like to do things. At the end of the day, though, we did our bit with dignity. I'd heard that some of their lot had Hillsborough banners confiscated from them as they were taken to the Albert Docks Pump House boozer. If that's true, then, quite simply, fuck them.

Now with all the pre-match olive-branch-offering stuff out the way, it's down to business – let's knock these bastards out. The atmosphere was unbelievable – got to be the best I've ever experienced at Anfield. It's great seeing the likes of Ibrahimovic, Nedved, Del Piero, etc. at Anfield. This is what I mean about playing the top dogs of Europe. If you can't get up for this type of game, then you're never going to. It took just ten minutes to show these Italians that the boys in red meant business. A boss corner by Gerrard found the bonce of our little European specialist, Luis Garcia, who flicked the ball over everyone waiting in the box; then there's Sami running towards the ball, slightly adjusting his run to follow its flight before drawing back his left foot and slotting the ball in the net.

Then he's running along the Annie Road, right in front of the Juve fans, before sliding on his knees in anticipation of his teammates mobbing him. Turn ye backs on that, nobheads. Haha! Bought for just a measly three-million nicker, this fella is, in my opinion, one of the most important players in the history of this great club. Everything we've achieved since he signed in 1999, he has played a major part in. For years we've had to put up with reading match reports in the media slating our defence, referring to them as the 'Keystone Kops' as if we were a comedy act. The best signing Houllier ever made and the rock upon which he built the team that won the Treble in 2001, he has been one of the key players ever since. I salute you, Sami Hyypia – a true Anfield hero.

Our second goal was to be something very, very special. Le Tallec spotted that Luis was making a bit of a run, and in his wisdom, knowing that Luis was capable of the mercurial, he lobbed the ball over to him. Seeing the ball was going to bounce perfect, Luis let it land, quickly adjusted his feet, while never taking his eyes off the ball, then caught it on the rise with the top of his left boot from thirty yards out. The ball flew sweetly over the keeper. He didn't stand a chance. It was one of Luis's specials – an absolute rasper of a goal! Remember, this Buffon lad in goal for Juve is thirty-two-million bullets' worth of player.

Speaking of keepers, due to an injury to Dudek and the fact that Kirkland is actually made of glass, Rafa was forced to play Scottie Carson, a teenager who cost only seven hundred and fifty thousand quid. What a game to make your debut in. Talk about being thrown in at the deep end. He had a good game up till the sixty-fourth minute, when Cannavaro got an away goal for Juve, beating our keeper with a header he should've saved. It totally deflated me. It felt like a defeat. I clapped the team at the end with a frown on me face.

Running past the petrol station into the Sandon pub big room, still shaking me head, I was thinking about what could've been. I joined the 'Knights of the Round Table', as christened by Warren from Huyton, cos him and his mates have their post-match bevvy at one of the huge round tables upstairs in the Sandon. 'Fuckin 'ell, la. Hard luck with that Juve goal. I'm fuckin' gutted,' I said to Tony.

'Ye what? We've just beaten Juventus, we had a kid in goal and loads of other injuries – it's a fuckin' great result.' He was right. It's not like me to take the red-tinted bins off and be all doom and gloom. I'm usually the most Koptimistic lad you'll ever meet. Must admit, though, Juve only needing to win 1–0 at their gaff? Not many would bet against them, put it that way.

It turned out to be a fantastic performance from the men in red in Italy. Goalless at the final whistle meant one thing. Bring on Chelsea.

'No, no no no. Please fuckin God, no.' I'm sitting there in a lecture room at John Moores University, just staring at me phone. I'd just got a text off me mate, Andy Dixon, saying, 'What time's our flight home from Cologne? It's on the same day as the Chelsea semi home leg.'

Fuckin' 'ell. I knew something was gonna happen to ruin this. Me and eight of the lads had booked to go to Cologne for two days for my thirtieth birthday. I'd never been away with just the lads before, apart from a European game, and that was either a one-night stay or a straight there, straight back job. This was gonna be a belter. Nine of us running around Germany having a scream: eight Reds and one Blue. That's about the correct ratio for most gangs of Scouse mates. I remember that, on the day before the 1986 FA Cup final, our headmaster allowed us all to come into school in our footy kits. There must've been about five Bluenoses in their Everton tops out of the whole school. St Winefride's Junior School, Bootle, was Red. Fact!

Me mate Cassie's going, 'What's up? What's the matter?' as I'm frantically texting me ma to find out the time of the return flight from Cologne. I'm not missing this game. I'll cancel the trip and risk being the most unpopular lad in Bootle, but there is no way I am missing any part of the second leg of the semi-final of the European Cup. I haven't missed a game at Anfield (all competitions) since the 1997–98 season – a statistic I'm extremely proud of, and one that no one I know can match. When you think of weddings, funerals, christenings, holidays, birthdays, etc. that get thrown at you for reasons to give the match a miss 'just this once', it takes some doing, I'll tell you.

Me arl girl texted me back, and it was sound. It was gonna be a mad dash from Speke airport but was very doable. Andy sorted it for his mate from work to pick us up at the airport, drop us off at our spiritual home and take our bags back to his for us. Sorted! I didn't even want to think about any flight delays until the day we were coming home.

When the final whistle blew at Stamford Bridge and it was 0–0, there was no doubt who was going through to the final of the European Cup. Ninety minutes away now. Ninety minutes at Anfield. They had no chance. Mourinho came out in the press saying that 99.9 per cent of Scousers think they are in the final already. Fuckin' right we did!

I woke up on the morning of 3rd May in Cologne, Germany. We threw our bags in the hotel lock-up and made our way to Jameson's: the Irish bar where a few weeks earlier Rafa had joined the Travelling Red Army for a bevvy and a gab. The brekkie was gorgeous, washed down with a nice cold glass of Kölsch. I thought we'd be drinking out of them big massive stein glasses, served by buxom wenches with massive bangers spilling out of frilly tops. Nah, none of that, la; these were little skinny glasses, like test tubes. You had to order three drinks just to get a decent taste of it. Proper lovely lager, though. The sun was cracking the flags. A glorious start to a day that could end in extraordinarily glorious circumstances.

I'm badly thinking about the match now, though. Trying to have a decent bevvy with the lads and a bit of a laugh, but it's just not happening. I'm parro'd up about this getting-home malarkey. Can't believe it. If we're delayed by anything over an hour and a half, I could be in danger of missing *the* biggest game of my life.

Just got to try and put it to the back of me mind for the time being. Enjoy the last hour or two in Germany before the panic of the airport commences. There's bound to be a delay of some kind. I know I'm going to miss the match; just get used to it. Fuck that, mate, the power of positive thinking will get you there in plenty of time. Think positive, Mags lad, just think positive.

We went back the hotel to get our bags and jump a taxi to the airport. After checking in, I made me way to the departures lounge and stared at the planes on the tarmac, willing one of them to be ours. The tannoy goes off: one hour delay. I'll take that. I just knew there'd be some form of delay, and if it's only an hour then we'll be home in plenty of time. I go over, sit at the bar and have a couple more glasses of Kölsch, making the most before I go back to England and our shitty lager.

Right, mobile phone off, seat belt on, sorted for take off. Let's get this bird off the ground and back to my spiritual home, Anfield. 'Three cans of Kronenborg please, girl.' Sorted. That's me laughing for this journey. Liverpool v. Chelsea. To the winner: a place in the European Cup final in Istanbul, of all places. Bring it on. I could've done with an *Echo*, a *Mirror* or Internet access, though. This was mad, this: the build-up to a massive game and no pre-match literature. I blame me parents, giving birth to me thirty years ago on 1st May. Didn't they know the hassle it was going to cause me for my thirtieth-birthday weekend away? Selfish bastards!

We touched down at Bill Shankly airport, got our bags, and Dixon's mate was there waiting for us. The lads who weren't going the game got off in taxis, and we piled in the motor. We gets halfway down some road, in the South End somewhere, when Paddy gives it the arl 'Stop the car. I'm gonna be sick'. Ah, fuckin 'ell, Paddy lad, of all times to get 'Pat and Mick', why now? Here we are, ambassadors for the North End, and Paddy's showing us up. After a good spewing session, Paddy gets back in, and we're on our way again.

The atmosphere is proper tense. My head's a bit fuzzy and light because of the bevvies I've had, but I don't feel drunk in the slightest. I just feel excited and proper shitting myself at the same time. We bail out the car at the Cabbage and walk along the road towards the ground. You can feel the expectation in the air. It is impossible to be more up for a game. Everyone's making their way to the ground, whereas usually there'd be time for another two pints. Not tonight, though, la. Those boys in red are everyone's priority. There is no other option.

Paddy and Dixon stop off at the chippie to get a scran, and me and Brian walk down, toying with the idea of popping in the Sandon for a quick bottle of Becks before going in. Nah, let's get in there and make ourselves heard.

I got to me seat, which wasn't our usual speck, about twenty minutes away from kick-off. The place was rocking, songs starting up before the last one had finished – just constant singing. I took me coat off and lashed it over the seat in front, because I was pure sweating cobs. There were colours everywhere. For the first time in years I wanted to have a scarf; I wanted to contribute to the visual side of things as well as the audio. Ah well, just have to settle for a black Lacoste jumper. I did have a small 'Liverpool FC: Scouse and Proud' badge on, so I did play a little part in the massive display of colour that is so breathtaking when I look back at the pictures and footage of the Kop for this particular game. I'm positive that there have never been that many scarves in the Kop in its history.

As kick-off was approaching, things got more intense: the heat, the noise. You always hear about this ground being a cauldron, but tonight, for the first time, I actually thought it a true description. It was like we were being boiled. I must sound like a stuck record going on about the atmospheres at Anfield for this season's European Cup games, but I'm not blagging heads at all. Olympiakos was mad, Juve was even madder, but this? This was Section 3 of the Mental Health Act 1983: proper fuckin' barking, Looney Tunes, off its tits, pure craziness. The 'You'll Never Walk Alone' at the start was one of them versions where you're trying to sing it but struggling to breathe at the same time. I was drenched in sweat. The jumper had to come off, leaving me in just my Bill

Shankly T-shirt that me dad had got for me. He was fitting a kitchen for some fella and saw a big pile of Shankly T-shirts, still in the wrappers, so he goes, 'Whose are these tops 'ere? Can I have one for me lad?' Turned out that the fella he was fitting the kitchen for was in an '80s band, 35 Summers, and these were their T-shirts.

I wonder what the Chelsea players thought when they walked out of the tunnel and saw the Kop? Our players have seen slightly diluted versions of it before, but those players in blue must've shrunk a bit when they saw what they were up against. It doesn't matter what Mourinho put on his blackboard during his pre-match team talk. When you find yourself facing the Kop like this, you are fucked. There is nothing down for you.

Every time a Chelsea player was on the ball, the ground booed and whistled. Every time the ball was at the feet of a Liverpool player: cheers and shouting of encouragement. The constant, intense shouting, singing, booing, cheering and screaming went on for the full duration of the match. The second-loudest roar of the night went up when Riise played a ball through to Gerrard, who scooped it up with his right boot, playing the perfect lobbed pass for Baros to run onto. As Baros tries to lob the on-rushing keeper, he brings him down. PENALTY! Hold it, as the ball's bouncing slowly towards the net, Luis Garcia runs in from the right and gets enough on the ball to send it over the goal-line before William Gallas has a chance to hoof it clear.

I remember jumping up and down, screaming, but in the back of my mind I'm thinking, 'Is it in or what? What's going on?' I'm looking at Luis, looking at the linesman, then there's the ref, jogging towards, and pointing at, the centre circle. GOAL! Fuckin' 'ell. Deafening is the only word to describe the roar that greeted the realisation that it was a goal.

From that moment on the energy level of the Kop was relent-less. I think I was even jumping up and down at half-time when Johnny Jones was passing me my sausage roll and orange Capri-Sun. At one moment in the second half, I had to try and get me head together. I was standing there, panting, bent over, hands on me knees, trying to get me breath back and stop me head from being frazzled. The only way I can describe what I felt was like when you're trying to stand dead straight on a trampoline, while there's loads of people bouncing around you. The Kop was bouncing. I was telling me mates about it after the game, and one of them said, 'Yeah, it was like that for Olympiakos.' Nah, I'm not having that. I've never felt nothing like that before. It was literally moving up and down. It was quite scary, in hindsight.

Six minutes added-on time? I knew it was gonna be a lengthy one. We've held on this long; we can do it for another six minutes. It dragged on, though. Then something happened that still sends shivers down my Spion spine to this day. That Gudjohnsen miss is up there with the most important moments of my life. That millisecond where he pulled the trigger and the ball narrowly missed that Kop goalpost is the difference between . . . well, not exactly life and death. But, if that had've gone in . . . there wouldn't have been an Istanbul 2005, and, maybe, just maybe, if Istanbul never happened, life would have taken a different path. What was to come in twenty-two days' time was fuckin' life-changing. I watch that miss a lot, and it scares me how close we came to going out. That was the final action of the game, and it would've meant Chelsea going through on the away goal. It doesn't bear thinking about, but I still do.

Now I said before how the sound that greeted the goal was the second-loudest roar of the night. That's cos the noise that emanated from Anfield when that ref put the whistle to his lips and blew for the end of the game was insane. Never heard anything louder in all me life.

It was a sight to behold, the whole of the ground bouncing up and down, twirling scarves and flags over their heads, giving it the 'Ring of Fire'. Not just the Kop; the Road Enders, Paddockites, Main Standers and Upper and Lower Kemlyn-heads wanted to get in on the act. The whole ground went berserk. Roman Abramovich must've just looked around him and thought to himself, 'I've got all the money in the world, I can buy any player I want, but how the fuck can I get myself a crowd like this?' The answer is, Roman lad, you can't. Scouse solidarity and

Kop camaraderie cannot be purchased. It is something evolved over time. We are unique, like no others. We innovate, never imitate. We inspire and intimidate. We were the man of the match. We are the famous, the famous Kopites!

We stayed in the ground for ages after the final whistle blew. All our players were group hugging, screaming at each other, then breaking away and running towards the Kop – the heart and soul of this club and ground. Our lads were in the final of the European Cup – the first time we'd got there since that dark day in May 1985. I made me way down to the front of the Kop and carried on the party. I thought the players were gonna come back out onto the pitch to warm down, so we could sing their praises a little while longer, but it came over the tannoy that the players would not be coming back out and could we start making our way out of the ground. That's fuckin' charming, that. We've just more or less got our team to Istanbul, and they're telling us to do one now. Cheeky bastards. Hahaha!

Now this is where the fun starts. Who's going? How are we getting there? How much dough will we need? The only way I can get to Istanbul is if I get in and out as quickly as possible. Two days off work should be all right. It done me head in, though, cos lads were going there for a week, going to holiday resorts and then getting to Istanbul for the match. What a scream that would be.

We decided that we were all going to go with one of them travel companies who specialise in fleecing football supporters. But seeing as most of us never had the time to have a week away, the only option left was this type of trip. Rather than wait around for everyone to sort out what they would be going on, me and Brian decided to book ours together. Everyone else did the same, pairing up with someone. We'd all meet up when we got there anyway, so it didn't matter who your travelling companion was.

Our chosen travel company had twenty-one options available. Me and Brian chose staying in a hotel the night of the game, due to land back in Liverpool at 10 p.m. on the 26th. Sound. Two days off me placement meant it had to be added to the end of it. It cost about seven hundred bullets, but I wasn't arsed about the cost at all. Me ma and da would lend me any dough that was needed to get me to Istanbul. They knew how much it'd mean to me to be there.

During a discussion about the financial implications of getting to Istanbul, someone mentioned that if he attempted to go, his girlfriend would leave him. This got me thinking, and the conclusion I came to is that throughout your life, birds will come and go. Only one bird remains with you throughout your whole life, the fucking Liverbird. She may do your head in sometimes, but a life without her isn't even an option. I'll leave me bird, me job, me mortgage, me uni course and walk to Istanbul in me knack over broken bottles to see the mighty Redmen bring that big-eared bastard of a trophy home.

I've been waiting for this all me life, after all that footage of you arl bastards with your muzzies and your tight-as-fuck LFC tops tucked into your even-tighter-as-fuck light-blue jeans and red and white sun hats, getting off the train, swaggering to the nearest bar in your brand-new Sambas in anticipation of a famous European Cup-final victory. Scruffy cunts with big beards who sold Ford Cortinas to fund their quest for glory, sleeping on luggage racks on the train taking them to their date with destiny. Arriving there, stinking of BO and having to get a swill in the Trevi Fountain or whatever was available. I was ten the last time the Reds got to the final of the European Cup.

Istanbul 2005. Is fucking right! Seize the moment. The regret of non-attendance will be like a ball and chain around your neck for the rest of your life.

Now that organising the trip was out of the way, it was time for clobber! Liverpool FC in the final of the European Cup means a new rig-out from head to toe. Brand spanker pair of dark denim, straight-leg 501s is taken as Red. There are no other jeans. What with all these light-blue, big, baggy efforts with pockets dotted all over the show – jib that!

These new ones are even worse than the jeans I used to wear back in 1988, second-year seniors, aged twelve, thinking I was boss in a pair of baggy jeans turned up at the bottom with big, brown suede patches on the back bins, or even worse, them ones with about five or six 'Pachino' patches randomly sewed onto the legs. I even had matching denim shirts to the above 'clobber catastrophes'. I never owned the ones with pictures of The Flintstones on, though. Rig-outs from the stalls of St Johns market: those were(n't) the days. Swaggering into the Don Bosco youth centre, based in Savio high school (Carra's school as well) on a Thursday night in your new clobber thinking you look boss. Ready for a night of trying to cop-off with the girl you've been tormenting in school all week. Buzzing off the Judies' dance routines to Tiffany's 'I Think We're Alone Now' and Belinda Carlisle's 'Heaven is a Place on Earth'. Running up behind them and twanging their bra-straps. Taking her to the bushes in Giro fields to neck her half to death. Then meeting back up with your mates before jumping on the 135 bus (The Wonnie) to take you home. Getting the Wonnie from the Donnie. Memories.

Right now: trainees. What trabs are gonna be the Chosen Ones? Which lucky wheels will be strapped to my plates of meat while I'm running round Turkey with the European Cup, Istanbul 2005? A special event requires special trabs. Just like 501s are taken as Red, so is the brand of trainees I'd be getting: Adidas. No contest. The only choice required is what type of Adidas.

I moseyed into Ath Leisure. Nothing doing in there – all Lacoste trabs, K-Swiss and various white ones. Nah, I wanted navy ones. There is nothing smarter in this world than dark denim resting on a pair of navy Adidas trabs. The back of the jeans should sit nicely on the top of the sole – none of that dragging-along-the-floor malarkey, making them wear out and eventually having strands of denim dragging behind you like rats' tails. Fuck that student, bell-end shite right off!

Wade Smith would have a good selection of Adidas. I remember one of me first pair of proper trabs were bought from Wades – a pair of Adidas Jim, I think – from when it was a small shop on Bold Street. I had to save them for Chrimbo Day, but I went into school the next day with my Wade Smith carrier bag.

It was a rasper: white, light blue and dark blue, Adidas written down the bag about four times, with the trefoil symbol on it as well. Mad, that – I can't remember the exact trainees I bought, but I can still see that carrier bag vividly. I was the envy of St Winnie's when I walked into school with me PE kit in that bag.

In Wades the lucky trainees were found: Adidas Indoor Super. A navy suede trab, the first and third stripes were Liverpool red and the middle stripe was white. The sole of them was the same colour as a 'lazzie band'. Boss! It was all starting to fall into place now. I weren't gonna wear them until the morning of 25th May. I even felt like I was cheating when I had to try them on in the shop. New 'bills' and new 'mint rocks' and I'm sorted.

I'd spotted the top I was gonna wear in the LFC shop in Williamson Square: red T-shirt, 'Istanbul' written in white at the top of the shirt in the official logo that was starting to appear everywhere, a club crest hovering above a picture of the Ataturk Stadium. I make no apologies. It had to be done, like. I had to wear a red top for the match for the first time since I was a kid. I'd wanted the mighty Redmen to walk out onto that pitch and see a load of red there for them, like in Rome '77, when there was a sea of red and white chequered flags waiting to greet Paisley's men. I just had to play my part. I even bought a scarf – a red and yellow bar-scarf with a golden Liverbird either end of it, a pure work of art. I remembered how much I'd wanted to play my part in terms of colour at the Chelsea match, and how boss our support was with all the flags and scarves getting twirled around heads. Fuck it, redded up, the rig-out was complete.

I finished work at 9 p.m. on 24th May, jumped off the train at Bootle Strand and walked along Marsh Lane – Carragher country. Walking the bridge, two big oil drums that look like pints of Guinness to my left, the spire of Christ Church to my right, I was trying to listen to a tune on me headphones but concentrating purely on what lay ahead. Me mind turned to what's for tea: chips, curry and rice from George Gerry's Chippie opposite the Aintree boozer, and then I was in ours, getting me scran down me neck whilst reading the *Echo*.

I was getting picked up at about four bells, so an early night was in order. I fired off a few texts to people, letting them know exactly what the boys in red would be doing to Milan this time tomorrow, and then jumped in me pit, ready for kip. With what was on the horizon, I'd need it.

Could I fuck kip. The alarm went off on me mobile at about three bells. I'd just been lying there for four hours, eyes shut but me mind going like the clappers. The big day had arrived. I turned off the alarm a millisecond after it started and crept out the room, trying not to wake up my sleeping girlfriend, Jane. I had all me clobber set up in the spare room so I didn't have to disturb her again. I had a nice, long, hot David Gower and remember thinking about what was in store for me over the next forty-odd hours. I threw a T-shirt on to match me Redmen bath towel and went downstairs and had a bowl of Shreddies, while having a quick shuftee on the 'Red All Over the Land' LFC Internet forum. Brian and Christie would be arriving in a taxi soon, so I leathered the last bit of coffee from my LFC mug and tiptoed back upstairs to throw on me clobber. A quick check in the mirror to make sure my little 'Liverpool FC: Scouse and Proud' badge was directly over my heart, and then I waited at the bottom of the stairs for the sound of the car, while stroking our Sadie, me dog. Here they are. Kissed our Sadie goodbye, jumped in the back of the Joey and we were offski.

We had to make a stop in Mossley Hill to pick up Christie's nephew, Lee, and then straight to Liverpool John Lennon Airport. There were fellas outside selling flags, wigs, hats, etc. 'No ta, mate.' I looked like a wool enough; in fact I was only missing the much-reviled jester's hat and I would've looked like an 'Essex Red'. Some lad who was sat in front of me once, Kosice in the UEFA Cup in 1998, had one of them tall jester's hats on – not them tight ones that look like they stop the blood going to the top of your head. Couldn't see a thing. Had to pure rubberneck around this stupid hat just to get a glimpse of the Mighties. After about four minutes I said, 'Do us a favour, mate. Take that fuckin' hat off. I can't see a thing ere.' Soft twat!

Inside the aiport there's Reds everywhere. After getting our photies taken with John Lennon, scarfed up and fezzed up, we met up with the Dixon brothers (Andy and Neil) for a few nerve-settling bevvies at a makeshift bar they had set up by the Starbucks. No one ever misses an opportunity to fleece a football fan. At three nicker a bevvy, we may as well have walked around with 'Fleece Me' tattooed on our foreheads. Plastic cups, as well – not firm ones that you can grip but floppy ones that bend when you grab them, like drinking a bevvy from a condom, as me mate Johno says.

After two or three pints we went into the departure-lounge area, bumping into loads of faces from the match. Christie and Lee were on a different flight to us, so they got in their queue. I had to buzz off Neil. The lad from *Casualty* walked past us, used to play Greg Shadwick in *Brookie*. Next minute Neil's running after him, asking the girl he was with to take a picture of him with Greg. I bet he's got it in a frame on his fireplace now, the mad bastard.

The flight over was sound. I had a good read of the papers: LFC fanzines and Internet articles I'd printed out. It was dead laid-back on our plane. At first I thought it was cos of the time in the morning, but after watching *Granada Reports* when I got back, I saw flights going over early morning with the plane rocking to a load of Reds songs. We must've caught the bores' flight. Plenty of time to go mad later.

When we got to the airport in Istanbul, we were greeted over the tannoy by the first 'You'll Never Walk Alone' of the day. (Actually, it was my second, cos I threw it on when I got out the shower earlier on. Wool as fuck!) Still, it was a nice touch by the Turks. We also got these boss stamps on our passies which said 'UEFA SLFK – UEFA CLFC'. I'll be gutted when me current one runs out in 2010. Hopefully there'll be a few more European Cup-final stamps in it by the time I have to renew.

There was a bit of madness trying to find our coach to take us to our hotel. It was at that moment that me mobile goes off – text from me girlfriend: 'You selfish get. Why didn't you even say goodbye? What if something happens to you and we never even said goodbye to each other?' Here's me thinking I was doing her a favour by being the Tiptoe Kid, trying not to make a sound so she didn't wake at three or four bells in the morning cos she had to be up for a day's work, and I'm getting grief for it. I explained this in a reply. I got another one back telling me how I never think of anyone apart from myself and the Redmen.

Little did she know that waiting for her when she woke up and went downstairs was a load of wrapped prezzies, flowers and wine and that. I felt a bit guilty cos of all the dough it was costing me to go to this game. As a softener, and to get in the good books, I decided to buy a few prezzies. About twenty minutes later the phone goes off again: 'I'm sorry for before. Thanks for my presents. They're lovely.' Ye see, Judies tend to text before they think. Just cos we're pure footy heads and sometimes act like the boys in red come before everything, it doesn't mean we can't turn on the arl romance every now and then when it's needed. No one does romance like a Red. We're the most romantic bastards on the planet. We've been brought up on it following this fucking team. Mills and Boon have got nothing on Shanks and Paisley.

We got to our hotel well later than expected. We were thinking we'd get there about 1.30 p.m. and spend the rest of the day chilling, drinking in Taksim Square, but it was about 3.30 p.m., so we'd only have an hour or two in Taksim before we set off for the stadium. We got our keys, and I went through my hotel-room ritual of throwing me bag on the bed and then turning the telly on and searching through every channel. Having a quick look out the veranda, I saw a fella walking along the shopping street with a sheep. I know the mighty Red Army has attracted a few wools as a result of thirty years of success, but this was the real fucking deal – a proper woollyback swaggering down the street behind a fella. Poor thing was gonna be in some Kopite's kebab later on that night.

We had a rasper of a view outside our hotel. Me and Brian both posed for a pair of photies then went over the road to a little supermarket to get a big bottle of water to lash in the fridge for the morning, when we'd end up having mouths like Ghandi's flip-flop. Right, offski to Taksim to meet the lads. We threw our water in the fridge and went through the pre-match checks: tickets; hotel key; camera; money; scarf. Right, this is it. I had a look around the room. The next time I see that moody red carpet, we'll be European champions. Let's go.

'Which way to Taksim Square, mate?' I asked a fellow Red.

'Fuckin' 'ell, lad. Are ye avin' a laugh? It's fuckin' miles away. Abar twenty minutes in a taxi. It's the other side of the river.'

Fuckin' 'ell. We must've been in Istanbul's version of Birkenhead. Next thing a yellow taxi comes into view, so we give it toes and get in. Sound. We were on our way.

'Fuckin' 'ell, la, it's Rafa!' Our taxi driver was a proper ringer for our manager. Funny as fuck. The lad mustn't have had a jar of glue what I was going on about. He was just nodding, smiling, probably thinking to himself, 'How much shall I charge these English cunts?' Don't these foreigners know that we're not English? We're Scouse.

'Whooooaaahh!' These taxi drivers were off their heads. It must've been rush hour cos the roads were chock-a-block. There didn't seem to be any lanes or anything, like every taxi for himself. How the fuck we never saw a crash, I'll never know. Proper chaos. Taxis everywhere were carrying Reds to Taksim Square or straight to the stadium. We stopped at these traffic lights and a taxi driver in the cab next to us starts offering something to us. Brian reaches over and grabs it. It was an arl Turkish note – 1000 lira or something, probably worth about tuppence. It was in the old currency anyway. The fella had written on it 'Milan 1 Liverpool 3'. 'I hope so, mate. My fuckin' God, do I hope so.'

I started to think about the match for a moment but had to swerve the thought straight from my mind. It wasn't time yet. If I started dwelling on what lay ahead, me head would end up exploding. Nah, need to enjoy myself first, have a good bevvy and a bit of an arl sing-song. Then I'll get down to thinking that my beloved Liverpool Football Club are about to go head to head with AC fucking Milan in the European Cup final.

We went across this bridge with loads of arl fellas fishing over the edge before arriving at Taksim Square. The taxi took about forty-five minutes to get us there, cos of the traffic being that bad. Brian got a reply to his 'Where abouts are youse?' text from one of the lads saying bluntly 'Taksim Square'. Aye aye, lad, could've narrowed it down for us; there were Reds everywhere. There was no way we'd find them here.

Next thing Brian pointed at some lad in a red T-shirt and a pair of beige cargo shorts. 'That's Warren's brother. I'm sure of it.' He was shimmying up this big massive pole (a flagpole like, not someone from Poland!). He had a flag in his hand, with the intention of tying it to the top. Just as he reached the top, he lost his grip on the flag, and it flew out of his hand into the crowd below, who were all buzzin' off this. Next thing he untied the scarf that was tied around his wrist and tied that to the top of the pole instead. Good initiative there.

We found out a few minutes later that his nickname was Tree Boy, and he'd been in all the papers, including being on the front page of Istanbul's equivalent to the *Echo*. I'd read something about Tree Boy in a paper on the flight over as well.

After he slid down, we followed him up this set of stairs, and there were all the boys at the top: Christie, Gavin, Lee, Steady, Tony, Warren, Christian, their dad, Nessie, Nifty, John Power, Daniel, Frankie and Joe. After all the handshakes and let-ons were out the way, we got down to brass tacks. Where were the bevvies?

The response was: 'We just bought these off some fella who was walkin' round sellin' them.' So we had a little shuftee round, seeing if we could find anyone walking round with a crate of this Efes Pilsen, or whatever it's called. Nothing doing at first, but after a bit we managed to buy a few cans each off some fella. Probably paid about ten times over the odds for them, but I needed a bevvy to gulp down while I looked on in awe at the sight in front of me: flags hanging from everywhere possible, including loads of new ones.

Every Tom, Dick and Scally had a flag made for this game.

It's something I've never been into. I can't be bothered with the hassle of carrying the thing round with me, finding somewhere to put it up and then remembering to get it down after the game. Nah, there's plenty of flag takers among our support, so I'll leave it to them. We did take a red, white and green tri-colour with 'Bootle' written down the green section to Wembley once. It got on the telly just as Rushie was waiting to come off the bench. That was the 1996 FA Cup final, though, and one of my worst moments watching the Redmen, so maybe I'm bad luck with regards to taking a flag – Mags and flags don't go. Me favourite was there: 'Scouse Solidarity, Never Forgiven, Never Forgotten', in reference to our boycott of the S*n newspaper, which is going as strong today as it was the week after the Hillsborough tragedy.

The sun (the one in the sky, not the one in the gutter) was cracking the flags, and everyone was in great spirits. Some moody locals knocking round, though. The Istanbul wrong 'uns were out in force. There was this one fella who was standing right behind me, far too close for comfort. 'What's up, mate?' The fella was just standing there with this old can of lager, wanting to sell it to me. 'Nah, you're all right, lad. I've got one 'ere. Thanks anyway.' He wouldn't move, though. I'm trying to have a gab with the lads and take in the scenery, but I've got this paraffin lamp breathing down me lughole. 'Look, mate, fuck off.' I thought them words were universal and even this Turkish tramp would get onto it, but nah, he weren't shifting. Pure in me personal space. It's a good job he chose me and not someone who isn't as easy-going, cos he might've got a right elbow to his bushy muzzie. I started to get a bit parro and moved me dough from me back bin to the front, meaning me pockets were really bulging. I didn't want to get bumped for me ticket and dough by this blert, though. This soft twat thought he was in 'Tax him' Square, not Taksim. After a few confrontational hand gestures Steptoe fucked off to do some other lad's head in. A couple more bevvies got leathered, and then we were offski to the ground.

We were walking down the road singing the Luis Garcia ('He drinks Sangria') song over and over again. On our way down to the bus for the ground: 'Fuckin' 'ell, la, it's Vegard Heggem!' He was just standing there on a street corner, LFC-trakkied up, having a gab with his mates. He looked terrified when we mobbed him, singing songs and taking photies and all that. His face went the colour of boiled shite when Tony got down on all fours in front of him and started kissing his feet.

When we got to the pick-up point, we got split up cos a few of the lads needed a Geoff Hurst and the others dived on the nearest bus. Daft that, we should've all gone together. Them moody green buses were leaving every two minutes.

Me, Brian, Daniel, Lee and Steady got on our bus, back seat of course, singing our heads off all the way there. It was mad. We sung the 'La Bamba' Rafa song for about an hour non-stop. Me voice was proper done in now, though, making all crazy squeaking noises as I was trying to belt out Red anthems. Fuck this for a lark. I had to start miming so I could save a bit of the arl vocal chords for those boys in red. Pure *Top of the Pops*, lad.

On that bus it was like I kept trying to pinch myself. Was this really happening? On me way to see our lads in the European Cup final. This is all I've ever wanted in life. Me mobile was going off every two minutes, texts from people who were here ('Where are youse?') and from people back in Liverpool ('What's it like, la?'). I wish I'd kept those texts now.

These two Turkish lads took exception to our rowdiness on the bus, cos we were banging on the windows and shaking the seats and that. 'Just because you on holiday, it does not mean you can shake seats!' Haha, behave, lad. The cheeky whopper tried to hand us the moodiest, jargest Besiktas top, pointing at one of the lads' Liverpool tops in a swapping gesture. 'Ye fuckin jokin aren't ye?' Haha. Soft cunt!

One of the lads couldn't hold his Geoff Hurst in, so the only option was to try and piss in an empty can of Efes. He missed like Gudjohnsen, though, and as a result there was hit and miss all over the back seats. Needless to say, we were standing for the rest of the journey.

It was off its head the way the people of Istanbul were lining the streets, waving at us, made-up to see us. Imagine if tens of thousands of Turks were going through the streets of Liverpool. At the very least they'd be getting Vs flicked at them. Though I did hear later on that one of the lads had a rock thrown at him through an open taxi window and had a pure cut chin on all his victory photies.

The massive dual carriageway got rammed with yellow taxis and green buses so much that we came to a standstill. Jib this, let's get off and walk the rest of the way. It's got to be close now. 'Fuckin' 'ell, though, gerron these lads ere.' Bus-surfing! There were these lads, on the roofs of the green buses, hopping from one bus to the other. Haha. Mad bastards! We got a bit closer, and it was only our lads who we got split up from earlier. You couldn't miss John Power, like – big curly head hanging out the bottom of an LFC sun hat. Ah, the LFC sun hat. Memories. I used to love the arl Liverpool sunnie. Circa 1986, everyone wore a sunnie, used to turn the back of the hat up and write a small slogan on it with a black marker. Most lads wrote 'Kopite' on theirs; I had 'Red Army' in black block capitals on the back of mine. Sunnies in the summer; bobble hats in the winter. You had to cut your bobble off, though, cos if you were bobbled up, you were a wool, plain and simple. What have they got nowadays in terms of headgear? Steven Gerrard baseball caps and fucking jester's hats. Give me strength!

Being a fanatical lover of the Liverpool music scene, it's mad being with John Power. The lad's a Liverpool legend. The La's, Cast and his solo stuff: all fuckin' raspers. One of my favourite lyricists of all time, and here he is, bevvied, hopping from one bus roof to another, slowly making their way towards the stadium. He was meant to be playing a gig as well. There was some sort of fan-festival type thing arranged just outside the Ataturk, and John was meant to be playing. I remember Christie saying to him just after the bus-surfing, 'You better get a move on. You're meant to be playing.'

John replied, 'I am playing, la. I'm playing with youse.'

We got back on a bus, cos they started moving, but it was

still at the pace of David Unsworth giving Sammy Lee a piggy-back. We thought, swerve this, we'll definitely walk the rest of the way.

What an amazing sight, and this seems to be everyone's most vivid memory of the day: the Red Pilgrimage. What a sight to behold!: the stadium in the distance, with a red river twisting and turning its way towards it. It was like a scene from an arl film, with a volcano in the distance and a narrow sea of lava snaking its way away from it.

The closer we got, the more amazing the sight became. When we reached the top of one particular hill, the true beauty of the landscape was exposed. The red river eventually turned into a red reservoir. Tens of thousands of diehard Reds, all singing, dancing and chanting in the area just in front of the Ataturk. It reminded me of a Tarzan film, when everywhere seems deserted, only for the viewpoint to change to the top of a big hill and you can see at the bottom a tribe of thousands going through some mad ritu-alistic ceremony.

We got down there among our fellow Reds and joined the festivities. Didn't see any live music, though, must've missed it, just a load of Reds up on the stage singing 'We all dream of a team of Carraghers' and 'Ring of Fire' – the songs of the day.

Me and Brian walked back up the hill, cos we heard there were some taxi drivers selling cans from the boots of their cars. There was nothing doing. Some taxi driver said if we gave him the dough, he'd drive to the nearest supermarket and bring our ale back here for us. Yeah, all right, lad.

Ah, fuck it, let's get in the ground. I missed the kick-off at Dortmund cos of the boozer; I'm not gonna let a bevvy get in the way of missing a second of this game.

There was murder trying to get inside. When we walked up to our entrance, there was only a little queue, but this weren't shifting. It turned out the hold-up was due to the barcodes on the tickets they were scanning. In the end they decided to rip the barcode section off, instead of scanning it. That got the queue moving a bit faster, and soon we were in.

Walking up the steps, we bumped into Paddy and his missus, Joanne. Turned out they'd got to Istanbul that early, and were that knackered, they'd had a kip in some park by Taksim Square. Good job the Turkey Taxers never spotted them. They'd have robbed them blind while they kipped.

As I walked forward to make my way down the stairs to find my seat, the pitch appeared in front of me – bit by bit. Glorious green. Istanbul was full of special, vivid images like that – images that will stay with me for the rest of my life.

By this time I was absolutely starving, so I went to the scran gaff to see if I could get a burger or something. Fuck all. Not even a drink. Me belly would have to wait till later.

We went down to our seats and spent some time just looking around in awe, reading all the flags on display. In my mind I was thanking the Lord me arl fella weren't a Blue. Redness: the greatest gift a father can give his son.

Me and Brian were about halfway down the stand behind the goal – similar speck to my middle of the Kop view. Christie and Lee were just a few rows behind us, with Tony nearer the back. This was special. The teams walked out and everyone was twirling scarves above their heads doing the 'Ring of Fire'. It was a pure kaleidoscope of colour and noise. Looking around, you'd think that they'd spiked the Efes with LSD, and I was tripping me tits off.

How could we not win, looking at the Italians, in their colour-coordinated plastic bibs? Beauts! Far too organised, that shit. Not us, though. Lads who wouldn't dream of going the game in anything but a navy Paul & Shark jumper were redded and scarfed-up to the eyeballs! And – is right! This was it, the big one. The league title may be our bread and butter, but the European Cup is the one we seem to closely associate ourselves with. Look at our flags: you hardly ever see images of the league title trophy, whereas eighty per cent of them have images of arl Big Ears on them. Oh, my God, as the whistle blew to start the game, I've never felt happier in all of my life. This was fucking amazing.

Half-time: 3–0 down. What the fuck was going on? Seriously,

what the fuck? Me head was throbbing. I'm just sitting there with me face buried in me scarf, biting it like fuck, digging me fingers into me head, trying to wake myself up from this nightmare. It was real, though. It was horrible. I stood up and looked around. There were fights going off round by where we were sitting. A young lad standing by us had just been punched and was standing there crying. This was the worst I've ever felt as a Liverpudlian: 3–0 down, and now, Red on Red scrapping. What the fuck was going on? Scouse Solidarity? Nah, not today.

I caught Christie's eye from a few rows away, and he was talking to me, shouting, pointing at each finger to illustrate the points he was making. I couldn't hear him, though. I could just see his mouth moving, with me head spinning everywhere. Nothing was making sense.

I sat back down and buried me head in me scarf again and began thinking, 'What the fuck am I doing here? What a fucking prick! You can't afford this. You haven't even got a proper job, you fucking idiot, and you're spending all kinds of dough coming to Turkey to watch this fucking pile of shite. You should've just stayed at home and watched it in a pub by ours, not with all these fucking beauts!'

The crowd was flat. Everyone had the shite knocked out of them by what they'd just witnessed. There was singing going on, but it weren't passion, just people pissed. Fucking nobheads in Liverpool tops. Singing? Pricks! It obviously means fuck all to them if they could stand around singing. What the fuck was going on? I just couldn't get me head round it. We were Liverpool! We don't get beat on occasions like this. This weren't going to plan. I never dreamed for a second that we could actually lose this game and go home empty-handed. We are special. I always thought our X-factor would get us through. After their third goal went in, I was numb. I tried to sing along, but the words weren't making sense. Everything was different.

Some whopper started singing, 'We're gonna win 4–3', and his mates joined in. Shut the fuck up, you fucking tit. Just fucking behave, will you? That's the anthem of the loser. We hear them songs sung in jest at Anfield by shite teams who are getting leathered 3–0. We haven't sunk that low that we're singing stupid fucking jokey songs about miraculous comebacks.

To be honest, I did believe. In fact I'd go as far as to say, deep down, even at half-time, 3–0 down against the mighty AC Milan, I knew we were going home with the Cup. I just didn't know how we were going to do it. I remember turning to Brian and saying this is either going to be about eight or nine nil and the most embarrassing moment in the history of our club, or we're gonna make a comeback and go on to witness the greatest moment in the history of LFC.

And then 'it' happened.

Our anthem, 'You'll Never Walk Alone'. As I said before, earlier on, I was trying to sing along to songs, but the words were no longer making any sense. This made sense, though. This made so much sense at this moment in time it was almost as if Rodgers and Hammerstein knew what lay ahead. This song was written to be performed at the Ataturk Stadium at half-time on 25th May, 2005. It was that relevant. At the end of the storm that was the first half, the golden sky started to appear, and this musical interlude was the ultimate sweet, silver song of a lark. Throughout that first half, we got blasted by the wind and drenched by the rain, and as everyone stood to sing our anthem, it showed that we were ready to walk on. And it was that loud, the team, hidden away, dejected, in their dressing room, were told that they were not alone for this second half and we were gonna walk with them, every step of the way.

I'm not religious or anything, like, but I've always been into this biblical poem called 'Footsteps' or 'Footprints' or something. Me mate, Higgy, his ma had a postcard with it on their living-room wall. The gist of it is this lad says to Jesus, like, 'You know the way you've walked alongside me throughout my life? Well, looking at our footprints, I've noticed that every time I went through a horrible time in my life, there is only one set of foot-prints. What's the score, there, Jesus lad? How come you swerved me and left me on my own when I needed you most?' Jesus just looked at the lad and said, 'That was when I carried you.'

It makes me fill up, that shout. And that's what we, the supporters, did with the boys in red for the remainder of this game. We carried them until they found the strength and belief to get back on their feet and walk on.

Tell you what, though, la. I've sung some special YNWAs in me time, but nothing compares to this one. This was pure passion. This was the big one. I usually hold me hands open when singing YNWA. This was the clenched-fist version. There were veins popping out everywhere, tears rolling down faces, dripping off chins, eyes bulging and drenched. This was the fucking daddy of all YNWAs, and it worked. We did it! The twelfth man got through again, just as we did against Chelsea in the second leg of the semi. Luis Garcia said that the inspiration for the comeback came from the Red Army's singing at half-time. Garcia said, 'We were sitting in the dressing room and we could clearly hear thousands of fans singing "You'll Never Walk Alone". Can you imagine how that felt? We were 3–0 down in the Champions League final, and all we could hear were 45,000 people letting us know they still believed in us. We knew they had endured a long journey and made so many sacrifices to be there. It was at that point we started to believe too.' Yeah, it worked.

For each of our goals that went in, I got a kiss on the bonce from the fella to my left. (He ran up to me in Taksim Square on the Thursday afternoon and planted another smacker on me swede, saying, "I've just gotta kiss this head one more time.") I felt like fucking Barthez. That's about all I remember from that six-minute period where we scored our three goals. I'd love to go on about how I felt as each goal went in, but I'd be lying. It was that crazy, I must've psychologically blacked out for that period and was just on autopilot, jumping up and down and screaming me head off.

I watched the periods of extra-time peering through the gaps in my fingers that were covering my face, nervous as fuck but knowing deep down we'd won. I said to Brian straight after the double-save from Shevchenko, 'We've won it. It's over!'

When Jerzy saved that final pen, there seemed to be a

millisecond of quietness, a tiny moment where every one of us recognised the magnitude of what had just happened. We had done it. Then – pandemonium. The volcano that was the Ataturk erupted ferociously. I remember thinking, what do you do? I mean, I'm screaming, my arms are flailing, but this is how I celebrated Dudek's last-minute penalty save at Pride Park to win us three points about four years ago. How do you celebrate Dudek's penalty save at the Ataturk to win us the European Cup after being 3–0 down at half-time against a team such as AC Milan? Nothing any of us could do would do this victory justice.

Anyway, the party started there. I was just crying me eyes out watching our boys bounce around the pitch with the Cup – champions of Europe. Jamie Carra, from our school, a Savio lad, from by ours – Liverpool player, European champion. Unfuckin'-believable!

Outside we met up and hugged and spent about half an hour putting our hands on our heads, wondering what the fucking hell had just happened. I don't think I'll ever grasp the enormity of it. Maybe I was trying too hard to analyse the situation. I was constantly aware that it was the thing to which the rest of my life will be compared, and I will be reliving it throughout the rest of my life. I wanted to savour every second of this great occasion, and when my time comes and I'm on my deathbed and I look back at my life, the first thing I'll think of is Istanbul 2005.

The chaos that followed with regards to getting back to Taksim Square was both shite and expected. I knew there was gonna be murder getting back, but I just weren't arsed in the slightest. I floated around that car park, getting nowhere. The only real pain in the arse is that we got split up again, so we never got to go back to Taksim mob-handed for a proper celebratory piss-up and sing-song.

We eventually found a coach with three empty seats, so we blagged our way on. It was about 4.30 a.m. by the time we got back to whatever hotel the coach dropped us off at, so we swerved Taksim Square and got a taxi back to our digs.

Back at the hotel we ended up having a good few bevvies

and a good arl sing-song. They showed the highlights of the penalty shoot-out on the arl Roger Mellie, which was sound.

By this time I realised something: I was starving; we all were. I hadn't had a scran since the plane about twenty-odd hours earlier, so one of the lads got the hotel manager, Roman (a dead-ringer for Abramovich), to go out in his motor and get us some scran. He came back about half an hour later with fifteen kebabs and four whole roast chickens.

I remember saying a couple of weeks ago that the tastiest scrans are when you're starving. This was an analogy referring to 2005 being our best European Cup win cos we'd been starved of it for twenty-one years. That scran got killed in about ten minutes.

This was the life. Grubbing on big, fat kebabs in an Istanbul hotel bar, necking back bottles of ice-cold Efes Pilsen, singing glorious Red Army songs and reminiscing about our European Cup win – not from the '70s, not from the '80s, but from 2005, a few hours earlier. It was too good to be true.

Tony had to get his head down in our room, cos his hotel room was commandeered. We had a single and double bed in our room, so him and Brian kipped in the double.

It must've been about six bells when we finally went to bed. Just as I got in me pit, the lad in the mosque over the road got on the microphone and started giving it the bifters. I could've sworn I heard him give it the arl 'Ring of Fire' – 'De de de de de, der de derrrr!' – but I must've nodded off and dreamt that last bit.

Thank fuck we bought some water. It tasted like someone had broke into the room in the early hours, squatted over me kite and done a pure turd into me snoring mouth while I was kipping. Those tasty kebabs from last night (this morning) weren't too tasty now. I got up and glugged some ice-cold water, while looking out the hotel-room window. Another beautiful day in Istanbul – is right! Looking over at Brian's bed, I saw he was alone. Tony had executed his move, the famous De Asha Dusty. See, this is the thing with Tony: the lad never says goodbye. He'll either say he's going the khazi and do one, or just wait till no one's watching and offski out the gaff. He's that renowned for sloping off un-announced when the night is still going strong that it has earned him the nickname Antonio Slopez.

It was at that point when me kebab wanted to make an appear-ance in the digested form. My shouting about our lack of shit roll must've woke Brian up, so we put our gear on and went down to the scranning area to see what was going for a munch. Ah, fuckin' 'ell, one of them Continental bastards: boiled eggs, slices of ham, mad slices of cheese with holes in that had no taste whatsoever and some tomatoes. Oh well, this'll have to do. After we'd had a scran and possibly the most refreshing pure orange juice I've ever had the fortune to neck in me life, I grabbed a handful of hankies off the buffet table and made me way back up the room to get shot of last night's kebab.

It'd turned out that, not only had Tony used up all our khazi roll on his Titanic Tockie Turd, but he'd treated himself to a David Gower as well, using up all our hot water in the process. So it was a trip to Cold Showersville for me and Brian (not at the same time, like).

We gathered our stuff together and made our way down to the hotel reception area. Our flight had been put back a few hours, so we had a bit of time to kill in Istanbul before we had to meet up back at the hotel to get to the airport. Is right, we thought; it'll be chaos at the airport now.

We threw our bags in the foyer with all the others and cabbed it to Taksim Square. It wasn't as mad a journey this time around. When we got to Taksim, it seemed a bit dead there – compared to yesterday, anyway. There was only a handful of Reds there, all wandering around thinking to themselves, 'Did last night really happen?' Mad. We met up with Tony, Steady and Nessie and had a wander round the shops. We'd have to buy presents for our Judies and that. Ah, jib it, we'll sort that shit later; let's have a bevvy. We found a small side street with a few bars in it with front terraces. One in particular had a Liverpool flag flying and 'You'll Never Walk Alone' blasting from the speakers. That'll do for us, then. 'Five large Efes please, *garçon*.' Big fat glasses. Pure

Rovers Return bastards. A few lads that were already sitting there let us have a shuftee at their newspapers. It was the first printed picture I'd seen of Stevie lifting that big-eared bastard high into the Turkish sky, shaking the living shite out of it. What a sight!

I didn't half feel sorry for this fella who sat a few tables away from us. He must've travelled to Turkey on his own to watch his team in the European Cup final. He sits down, orders a bevvy, then pulls out his newspaper from a carrier bag. The S*n! 'What the fuck's going on here, like? Aye aye bollocks, what's goin' on?' Poor fella was from Romania. Didn't have a jar of glue what we were going on about. Steady tried to explain to him: 'We. Don't. Read. That paper.' The fella muttered something in broken English. He threw the rag away and sat there looking upset. Felt a bit bad about that, to be honest, but all Reds must be educated on the boycott of that filthy piece of shite. I loved seeing the news-stands outside the shops, all the papers sold out, all except for shitloads of copies of the S*n. That sight gave me as much pride in my heart as the sight of Stevie lifting that big cup.

We made our way back to Taksim Square. By this time it was heaving. All the banners were back up, and there was one particular bar that was rammed – everyone standing on the tables, drinking, singing. It was boiling, as well – the perfect scenario for the day after a European Cup win.

This is where things started to get a bit hazy. In other words we got absolutely twisted. The memories came back a little when the photies were developed, but from the afternoon to later on in the airport, I was on pure autopilot, and how I made me way back to the hotel to get the coach that took us to the airport I'll never know.

I started to come out of my mad drunken state when we were in a big marquee that was set up for us. I spent about twenty minutes going round asking if anyone had any paracetamol; me head was proper banging. It felt like a lifetime in that marquee and then in the airport departures lounge. No information whatsoever from anyone, just left there waiting for a plane to take us home.

As soon as I sat down on the plane, I was away. I think I only woke up to murder me scran, and then, as soon as that was polished off, back to bo-bo's. The taxi-driver that took us from Speke back to Bootle was definitely a Blue. Not a dicky bird from him. Don't get me wrong, I was made up. I had one of them pure croaky, raspy voices that sound mad when you're trying to talk, so I couldn't be arsed with the whole conversation thing. We had to pull over again while Brian got out to spew. Paddy spewing for the semi, and now Brian.

The taxi dropped me off outside The Aintree. It was half nine in the morning of 27th May. I was proper goosed, almost limping. I was like a soldier returning from a twat of a war. I walked in the shop to get a bottle of orange Lucozade and the papers, and then got hit smack in the face by the front cover of the *Mirror*. It was pictures from last night's homecoming parade: a fucking sea of red outside St Georges Hall. Truly astonishing. One of the best things I've ever seen in my life. The bastards could've waited for the lads who were still out there. Saying that, though, I know where I'd rather have been: Istanbul – no doubt about it.

Tell ye what, though. He doesn't mess around, our Rafa. His first season and he springs that on us. The European Cup in your first season? Like winning a marathon before he taught us how to crawl. Don't know about you, like, but I like to wine and dine first. None of that with Rafa, la; just kecks off and straight down to business with him.

I love being a Red. What I am, who I am and how I am all boils down to my Reducation. Having two season-ticket holders as parents obviously helps, like. All my ethics, morals and values are soaked in LFC history and culture. Istanbul 2005 was one of the greatest lessons in life I have been taught. No matter how bad things seem, never give up hope. A lot of people don't understand, but it's more than just following a team and hoping they win. I know other fans probably think the same way about their chosen team, but I do genuinely think that we, as Liverpudlians, are a breed apart. Special.

Who knows what type of person I'd be now if that Scottish

fella hadn't walked into Anfield on a cold December day in 1959 and started chatting bastions of invincibility. And you just know that Bill Shankly, the king and creator of this empire known as Liverpool FC, was looking down, watching us, his heart bursting with pride as Stevie lifted that cup. *Everything* we have achieved in the last forty-odd years boils down to the foundations laid by that great man: our Hero, Bill Shankly.

Athens, 2007

TONY BARRETT

Champions League Final, 23rd May 2007
Olympic Stadium, Athens
Attendance: 74,000

AC Milan   2–1   Liverpool FC
Inzaghi (45', 82')   Kuyt (89')

Substitutes: Jerzy Dudek, Álvaro Arbeloa, Sami Hyypiä, Harry Kewell, Mark González , Peter Crouch, Craig Bellamy

Manager: Rafael Benítez

AC Milan: Dida (1), Massimo Oddo (44), Alessandro Nesta (13), Paolo Maldini (3, captain), Marek Jankulovski (18), Gennaro Gattuso (8), Andrea Pirlo (21), Massimo Ambrosini (23), Clarence Seedorf (10), Kaká (22), Filippo Inzaghi (9)

Substitutes used: Kakha Kaladze, Giuseppe Favalli, Serginho, Cristian Brocchi, Alberto Gilardino

Manager: Carlo Ancelotti

The moment when Jerzy Dudek stretched out the fingers of his left hand to save Andrei Shevchenko's penalty in Istanbul was undoubtedly the greatest of my life so far. It was the moment when twenty years of being on the outside looking in on the magic of the European Cup came to an end. And, for the latest generation of Liverpool fans, it was the moment when we finally got to drink the same intoxicating brew of Continental success that the previous generation had got drunk on in Rome, London and Paris. But had I known the hangover that lay ahead, I don't think I would have indulged quite so much – because the harsh truth is that the 'Istanbul effect' turned Liverpool Football Club into a bloated version of its former self and succeeded only in taking it further away from many of the supporters who helped make it what it is.

After Istanbul, when the world looked on in awe at the magnificent display of colour, loyalty and noise put on by the 40,000-strong Red Army, it seemed all of a sudden everyone wanted to be a Liverpool supporter. From Southampton to Strathclyde, Singapore to South Africa, and from Sydney to Stravanger, there were people who were desperate to have a part of what we had.

There was nothing new in this, of course. Ever since the late, great Bill Shankly set off on his one-man mission to turn Liverpool into 'a bastion of invincibility', the club has been collecting new fans with each and every trophy. Those lovable Evertonians have long loved joking about it – pointing out that our support isn't local and they are the club of the people. In their eyes we are a Scouse Man United, attracting the ephemeral loyalty of 'fans' who have to travel by easyJet and bring a 'Learn Yerself Scouse' book with them whenever they want to see the team in action at Anfield.

For those of us who grew up within a John Arne Riise's throw of the Kop, we see this ribbing for what it is. It's a way of diverting attention from the continual shortcomings of their own club by highlighting something they think will wind us up. When you follow a team that's been to just one more cup final than Tranmere Rovers over the last two decades, you can't talk about trophies, can you?

But, like most stereotypes, there is a grain of truth to their rantings. As a successful club with a huge profile, Liverpool have attracted the support of national and international glory-hunters who think that buying a red shirt with 'Justice for the 96' on the back makes them an honorary Scouser. Not all of them can be accused of this, of course. There are tens of thousands of Liverpool supporters in England and beyond who are the real deal: Norwegians who have left their homeland to live on Breck Road and never, ever miss their team in action; Irish lads who have remortgaged their homes to finance their devotion to the club; people from Devon who drive hundreds of miles for home games against Grimsby in the Carling Cup on a miserable Wednesday night. Their commitment is never in question. They are the kind of out-of-towners that any club would welcome, and they are a credit to Liverpool whenever and wherever they play.

It is the jester's-hat-wearing brigade that gets me. And, after Istanbul, their numbers grew like never before. Carrying their copies of the *Sun* under their arms and having honed their finest Harry Enfield 'calm down, calm down' impression for weeks beforehand, they arrive at Anfield hell-bent on little else but having their picture taken on the Kop while the crowd sings 'You'll Never Walk Alone', so they can show off to their mates when they get back to Truro. Post-Istanbul, the number of eye-dazzling flash-bulbs going off while DJ George played Gerry Marsden's finest over the tannoy told its own story: Anfield was being taken over by the jester's-hat brigade.

For traditional supporters the sheer scale of the new influx has been hard to take, and as we began to feel more and more like outsiders in our own ground – with *Soccer AM*-style chants like 'easy, easy' becoming more and more prevalent – it became clear that something had to be done. The answer came in the 2006–07 season with the formation of a new group called Reclaim the Kop, which was set up in a bid to wrestle control back from the day-trippers and the glory-hunters. The only problem was, the newcomers had a secret weapon that no one had counted on, and it was one which put them on an almost equal footing with the diehards: the fan card.

Introduced by chief executive Rick Parry, the fan card is Liverpool's way of recording the number of games supporters attend each season. Anyone can buy one for just three quid. It doesn't matter if you've never been to a match in your life or if you've only started supporting Liverpool in the last couple of years; if you buy one of these plastic cards and go to a few games each season in the right competition, you can have a ticket for a cup final.

It was these little cards that would come back to haunt life-long Liverpool fans when the team made it through to the Champions League final against AC Milan. As soon as it became clear that UEFA would only be giving the finalists a disgraceful and paltry 17,000 tickets each, everyone knew it was game on in terms of getting their hands on a ticket. But just how difficult it would prove only became clear when Parry announced that, after those who had attended an away game in the Champions League that season had had first dabs, the remaining tickets would be doled out in a ballot in which both season-ticket holders and fan-card holders who had been to six Champions League home games during 2006–07 would be included. Basically, if you'd been to just six games in your entire life, you were being given as much right to a ticket as someone who'd barely missed a game at Anfield in decades. So not only was the Istanbul effect changing the nature of Liverpool's fan base, it was actually being endorsed by the club. Still, the glory-hunters are always going to spend money at Liver World on replica shirts, half-and-half Liverpool and Chelsea scarves and jester's hats, so what else should we expect?

A protest against Parry and his ticket arrangements for the

final was held before the last game of the season, against Charlton at Anfield, but once the banners had been put away and the voices of anger had died down, far, far too many good Reds were left facing the same problem: exactly how were they going to get a ticket for the final?

It is one of the irrefutable truths of football that Liverpool supporters can get in anywhere – and I mean anywhere. Whether it's jibbing on a train all the way from Lime Street to Termini in Rome and back or slipping a bent security guard a few euros so he'll turn a blind eye while they slide into the players' after-match party and swig champagne out of the European Cup, it's as if bunking-in is ingrained in Scouse DNA.

It's a skill which has been honed over decades of European conquest. Speak to the veterans of Rome in '77 and they'll tell you stories of daring deeds that common sense should tell you are scarcely possible, but you know that they are because the same kind of things are still happening today. Whether you approve of it or not isn't really the point; even the sternest critics of those who indulge in this particular pastime can't help but be impressed by their ingenuity.

Take the semi-final first leg at Stamford Bridge in May 2007. A measly total of 3000 tickets was never going to be enough for a game of this magnitude, and the sight of hundreds upon hundreds of ticketless Reds at Trafalgar Square meant only one thing: it was going to be another of those nights when an eye for an open gate or a cheeky disguise was as likely to get you into the ground as a forty-five-pound ticket. It was only when we arrived at the ground that it became clear just to what lengths the jibbers had gone.

Six lads turned up with Channel 4 media passes. These hadn't been forged; they were the real McCoy. No doubt one of them knew someone who knew someone at the TV channel who could get their hands on these priceless passes wrapped in plastic. The six of them calmly walked to the press area and showed their passes. The fella on the desk looked them up and down, and you could tell he had his doubts, but they had passes. He was dying to question them, but he also knew his own boss would no doubt have murder with him if it turned out he'd been making life difficult for a TV crew, so he waved them on.

The fact that Channel 4 doesn't even cover the Champions League didn't matter to this gang. This was all about having the bottle to go through with the blag and holding your nerve when it looked like it might be about to come on top. Once inside the stadium they could have gone and found some seats in the Liverpool end or just blended into the crowd, but that's never really been the Liverpool way. The concoction of raised confidence and cheek makes for a heady brew, and this particular gang of six was never going to settle for just getting in. So they headed into the media lounge, where the post-match press conference would be held with Rafa Benítez and José Mourinho, and mingled with the good, the bad and the ugly of Her Majesty's press.

One of them immediately spotted the magnificent buffet that Roman Abramovich had laid on for his media friends and fought his way through the hordes to fill his boots. He started on the sandwiches, before tucking into the cakes and pastries. While he was dining, he turned to a journalist from one of the nationals, and, despite the fact that he had half a croissant in his gob, blurted out in the strongest Scouse accent you've ever heard, 'Cracking spread this, isn't it, lad?' before pulling a Tesco bag out of his coat pocket and filling it with whatever he could get his hands on.

While this was going on, his five mates had discovered the free bar and were busily topping up their bellies, which had been on an alcohol-free diet since they'd left Trafalgar Square to bunk on the tube an hour earlier. I looked at them and thought it'd only be a matter of time before they were rumbled. It would only have taken an eagle-eyed Chelsea steward to spot that not only were they 'working' for a TV company that didn't have accreditation for six for this particular game, their passes were also two years out of date!

At one point it looked like their luck had run out. Within

seconds of leaving the media zone and heading into the stand, they were pulled by a steward. There was a short conversation, which ended with all of them, including the yellow-jacket-wearing steward, falling about laughing. It turned out that the 'steward' was another ticketless Red who had conned his way in by donning a fluorescent coat and putting on a Dick Van Dyke-style cockney accent! Like I said, you don't have to agree with it, but the brazen ingenuity is something even an MI5 agent would struggle to match.

It was the same at PSV a month earlier, when another tiny ticket allocation made it inevitable that the only way for some Liverpool fans to see the game would be if they bunked in. But on that occasion it was easier than ever, as the investigation skills of a Huyton teenager led to the discovery of a door in the stadium souvenir shop that led right into the ground. The Scouse Sherlock Holmes was through the door and up the stairs into the stand before the Dutch security staff even knew what was going on – and he was followed by at least a score of his mates.

So the form was very much in the book. Liverpool fans are among the most ingenious in the country when it comes to getting into grounds without tickets, and the Olympic Stadium in Athens was going to be the next nut for them to crack. With tens of thousands desperate for a ticket, thanks to UEFA continuing their policy of looking after their own and forgetting about the real football supporters, the fear was there could be chaos at the ground if too many tried to bunk in. All the soundings from the Greek authorities, though, were that they had everything under control.

While half of the city was scrambling around trying to get a final ticket, I just had to pop along to Anfield and collect mine. In my case having a season ticket, a fan card and having been to all the Champions League home games and four aways – at PSV, Galatasaray, Barcelona and Chelsea – meant I was one of the lucky ones, and I qualified for a ticket automatically.

Arriving at the Anfield ticket office, I was asked what price ticket I wanted. For anyone who regularly goes to away games in

Europe, this is one of the easiest questions you ever have to answer. 'The cheapest one,' I told the girl, in the knowledge that it would be a case of sitting anywhere in our end, as always happens at big European aways. Why anyone would ever consider paying a hundred and fifty quid when you can get one for forty-three quid is beyond me. The seats are just the same, and the shoddy way games abroad are organised means you've always got a chance of ending up in a posh speck even if you've only paid for a cheap one.

In the same way that the lads who bunk in have built up an encyclopaedic knowledge of grounds, tickets and security, those of us who pay our way have long since realised that you only ever pay as much as you have to – in simple terms, expensive tickets are for mugs. Luckily the johnny-come-latelys aren't wise to this, so they swallow up all the expensive ones, leaving the rest of us to snaffle all the cheap ones.

With a (comparatively) cheap ticket in my hand, I should have been buzzing. What better feeling is there than to have a ticket for one of the biggest games of your whole life? The only problem was I knew far, far too many lifelong, loyal Reds who hadn't been quite so lucky, and their plight totally took the shine off what should have been my moment of glory. It seemed like every two minutes my mobile phone was going with desperate lads asking if I'd heard of any spares. They just wanted to see their team in the European Cup final, but the combination of UEFA's scandalously low allocation and Liverpool's misguided distribution system meant they had been excluded from the party.

My own problem was much more trivial: how was I going to get from Liverpool to Athens without breaking the bank? All the organised trips were ridiculously expensive, with the going rate for a couple of nights in a Greek fleapit coming in at around eight hundred pounds a pop. Just as they had done in Istanbul, the rip-off merchants masquerading as travel operators were having a field day. They knew they could cash in on the desperation of the Liverpool fans to make it to Athens, and they were going to milk the occasion for all it was worth. This was to be no buyer's market. We all knew it would be this way, but there's something so obscene about paying just shy of a grand for a couple of nights in a two-star hotel in Europe that I held back from booking.

It wasn't that I didn't have the money or couldn't, at least, get hold of it. I simply couldn't give them the satisfaction of ripping me off just because I'm a football fan. The only alternative, or so I thought, was to come up with some weird and wonderful trip through Europe using the kind of airlines that don't even rank as 'budget'. That meant scouring the Internet in the hope that CheapoAir or someone would come up with flights that would cost considerably less than the month's wages an organised trip would come in at. Booking a hotel room was not even a consideration. All the rooms in Athens had long-since been sold, and anyway, you can always sleep on a mate's floor or even grab a couple of hours here and there in an all-night bar if needs be.

But flights were proving almost impossible to come by – unless I fancied stumping up around five hundred pounds to go via Warsaw – and by this time most people had booked on organised trips, so I was faced with either swallowing my pride and joining them or catching a flight from Manchester to Istanbul or one of the Greek islands and using public transport to complete the rest of the journey.

Or so I thought.

Perhaps the best thing about my job – I'm a feature writer with the *Liverpool Echo* – is that if there's a major football match somewhere in Europe, the paper will need someone to go over and cover it. I'd already done Turin and Istanbul in 2005, and the FA Cup final against West Ham in Cardiff the year after, so I didn't really expect to be given the nod for Athens. But I must have done something right on those occasions, because I was called in by the news editor and asked would I be prepared to cover the fans at the Champions League final. It's the media-industry version of working your passage. You get to go to an event you're desperate to go to, but you have to work your arse off while you're there.

I knew it would be a hard job, because the fact that tens of thousands of ticketless fans were travelling over made trouble inevitable. Everyone knew that, regardless of what the Greeks were saying. But the choice between being paid to go and having to work incredibly hard and paying for a couple of days in Athens out of my own pocket wasn't even a choice. I snatched the opportunity that had been presented to me before it could be offered to anyone else. There can't be many jobs where you get paid to go and follow the team you love and your brief is to go everywhere the fans go. It is an absolute privilege. Apart from being a Liverpool footballer, there literally isn't a better job. Not in my eyes, anyway.

The only problem this time was that such was the shortage of flights to Athens and the almost total non-existence of hotel rooms in the Greek capital that even the *Echo* were having trouble sorting out travel packages. If it was like that for us, then God knows how difficult it was for the ordinary fans who don't have anything like the same wealth of contacts as one of the country's biggest regional newspapers. After a week of trying to sort something out a decision was taken that I would have to fly to Athens with the Liverpool team. What a burden.

Could there be anything better than being on a plane with the very same players that I'd followed around this country and beyond all season? Again, the only word that does it justice is privilege. Most Liverpool supporters would gladly have walked to Athens to see the team in the Champions League final, and there was me being told not only would I be being paid to go out there, I would also be accompanying the Reds on their pursuit of a sixth European title.

But, and this is a big but, whilst I should've been buzzing like a seven year old at Christmas, something was nagging away at me that meant I just couldn't get excited. Half of my mates didn't even have tickets for the game, so I couldn't exactly get carried away with my own good fortune, could I?

The week before the Champions League final was ridiculously busy at the *Echo*. As well as producing the usual daily paper, we were also bringing out a Cup-final special called 'Clash of the Titans', which would give fans the ultimate guide to Liverpool's most important game since, well, the last one. It was all hands to the pump, and I was seconded to sport to give the lads on there a hand as they dealt with the kind of workload which, fortunately, only ever comes round when games of this magnitude are about to take place.

The tickets furore was refusing to die down, as more and more supporters realised they would not be getting their hands on one for the final. We received literally thousands of phone calls and emails calling on us to challenge Liverpool to reveal exactly where the club's allocation of 17,000 tickets had gone. To be honest, it was a question I wanted answered as much as anyone. The ballot had been and gone, and it seemed far too many genuine fans had missed out. Everyone was calling for transparency, but, at this stage at least, the club was not prepared to offer it.

As the calls and emails continued to flood in, we knew we had to challenge the club on the fans' behalf. At the very least they deserved to have their questions put to the people who matter at Anfield. After a succession of phone calls I finally managed to get hold of Rick Parry, and, realising this was an issue that was not going to go away, given the mood of the fans, he agreed to see me immediately. I jumped in a cab and headed straight to Anfield. For someone who doesn't really suffer from stress, I was feeling under plenty of pressure at this point, because I knew people were counting on me to extract the information they had been asking for.

When I arrived at the ground, Parry took me into a meeting room in the club offices in the Kop stand, and we sat down. He looked worn out, as if the fuss over the tickets had really got to him. I interviewed him for more than twenty minutes, but despite asking him on four separate occasions to reveal exactly where the tickets had gone, he refused to play what he called 'the numbers game', and I left the meeting frustrated and disappointed. It wasn't a professional disappointment, either. It is extremely rare to interview anyone and get all the answers you are looking for, and, apart from a breakdown of the numbers, Parry had otherwise been as forthright as you would expect from the chief executive of a leading Premiership club.

As I sat on the 27 bus home, I realised that my frustration was because I hadn't been able to get the fans the answers they deserved. And I knew that most of them would be wondering why the club felt they were not in a position to be open. I had the feeling it was club policy to keep details like that private, but I knew that many people would come up with conspiracy theories, and, in the absence of any proper information, who could blame them? The whole build-up to Liverpool's most important game of the season was being clouded by the tickets controversy. There was simply no getting away from it.

The following day I was back at Anfield for the media day that the club arranged to allow journalists from home and abroad to fill their boots with interviews ahead of the team leaving for a training camp in Spain. Rafa Benítez and most of the first team were put up for interview, and they were all good value. Most importantly they all seemed relaxed and in good spirits, with just a week to go before the final.

Steven Gerrard kept making the point that lifting the European Cup in Istanbul hadn't quenched his thirst for success. He was desperate to follow Emlyn Hughes into the history books by becoming only the second Liverpool captain to lift ol' Big Ears twice. Jermaine Pennant was confident that his improved form over the season would stand him in good stead if selected for the final. Xabi Alonso told English journalists his teammates had what it took to beat Milan for a second time in three years, before being buttonholed by a female reporter from Spain, who seemed more content to gaze into his eyes than ask him any searching questions.

As usual Jamie Carragher was in the mood to have some fun at someone else's expense. Spotting my *Echo* colleague Dominic King, who usually covers Everton, at the doors to the Trophy Room, he calmly informed him, 'You haven't half been writing some shite lately, haven't you? Where have you been getting all this stuff about "the Grand Old Lady" and "the Holy Trinity" from?' It was typical Carragher. Taking the piss in a light-hearted way but also making sure he'd let a journalist know he was watching him. If Dom ever ends up covering Liverpool, he'll probably give Carra man of the match every week just to make sure he doesn't get another tongue lashing!

From interviewing the players about the forthcoming final, my next task was to speak to Merseyside Police's top football man, Chief Superintendent Dave Lewis, about how plans were proceeding for the big game. Dave was as honest as ever, telling me about his own concerns and recognising the potential for trouble caused by the sheer number of ticketless fans expected to make the trip to Greece. He'd been over to Athens to see the Olympic Stadium and to examine the security measures the Greek authorities had put in place. Worryingly, although he never actually admitted it, he seemed far from impressed – and with good reason.

It turned out there were precious-few turnstiles at the ground, and the so-called 'ring of steel', intended to keep those without tickets from getting anywhere near the ground, was nothing but a five-foot-high fence that wouldn't put many people off, never mind a Liverpool supporter who had travelled thousands of miles in the hope of seeing his or her team in a Champions League final.

All the indications were bad. There was an inescapable feeling that this match was going to be plagued with problems.

I don't know why, but there just wasn't the same excitement at reaching the Champions League final in 2007 that there had been just two years earlier. 'Ballot-gate', as the ongoing ticket farce became known, was one of the reasons for the lack of a buzz, as many people felt there would be a big party going on in Athens, but they hadn't been invited. The UEFA suits had looked after their mates as they always do, and the overriding feeling was that the fans were just an irrelevant sideshow in their corporate eyes.

But there was something else behind the lack of excitement

that I just couldn't put my finger on. Maybe it was that in 2005 there was twenty years' worth of hunger and a desire for redemption bursting out at the Ataturk Stadium; maybe it was a feeling that this was our stage, where we rightfully belonged, so there wasn't too much to get excited about; or maybe it was the fact that many fans had only just finished paying for Istanbul and were having to face up to producing another grand for Athens. Whatever it was, this time just felt different.

The first time I noticed it was during the second leg of the semi-final against Chelsea at Anfield. Don't get me wrong, the atmosphere that night was special, and it did come close to matching that created in the same fixture two years earlier. The home crowd again played a key role in inspiring their team to defeat the nouveau-riche West Londoners, and the ground was bouncing. But it was as if the possibility of facing Man United in the final had taken the shine off the whole thing. Everyone at Anfield knew that reaching the final could turn into the most poisoned of chalices if our friends from the other end of the M62 were to knock out AC Milan the following night.

It wasn't so much that we feared being beaten by our most-hated rivals, although that was an unpalatable enough thought; it was the fact that everyone fully expected there to be murder should the two tribes meet on neutral territory on the Continent.

So, from the very outset, the vibes just weren't good about this one, and for twenty-four hours the joy every Liverpool supporter should have been experiencing was undermined by the prospect of sharing the Athens stage with Gary Neville and Co. Everyone was crossing their fingers, saying their prayers and just hoping against hope that United would come unstuck in Milan so we could get on with the job of looking forward to another big European final in May.

The Liverpool players didn't care who they met. Rafa Benítez had instilled a belief in them that they could beat anyone in Europe thanks to a combination of their own ability and his tactical acumen. That night they went out and celebrated reaching the final at the swanky Sir Thomas Hotel in Liverpool city centre, a regular haunt for Merseyside footballers and other celebrities. Knowing the owners and a couple of the bouncers, I'd managed to talk my way into the players' party with a couple of my mates.

Pretty much the entire first-team squad were there – with Carragher, Gerrard, Alonso, Pennant, Fowler, Hyypia, Agger, Finnan, Bellamy, Gonzalez, Kuyt and Crouch leading the celebrations. As is always the case at such events, a load of celebrities had come to join the party, with the likes of Jude Law, Jennifer Ellison and Clive Owen also in attendance. But, despite star quality, they were never going to steal the limelight on this occasion. All eyes were most definitely on the Liverpool players as they proved that they knew how to party just as well as they knew how to play football.

Local lads Carragher and Gerrard were, to use that well-worn football cliché, over the moon. They sat in the VIP section, still wearing their club tracksuits, and just milked the moment. No one in that part of the bar was paying for their ale – every time bottles ran empty, the Scouse pair were sending down to the bar for buckets full of ice-cold lager at fifty quid a time. They didn't know half of the people they were partying with, but that didn't matter. This was their do, and they wanted everyone who was lucky enough to be there to enjoy it.

As the night wore on, the classy music being played over the speakers in the trendy bar was drowned out by the full range of Kop classics. 'The Fields of Anfield Road', 'You'll Never Walk Alone', 'Scouser Tommy' and 'Ring of Fire' were all belted out. All the players were joining in except on 'Campione', the song that was created on a forum on the Liverpool fans' website 'Red All Over the Land', which only Carragher seemed to know all the words to. Well, most of them, anyway.

By four in the morning the party was winding down, and among those who remained conversation had shifted from Liverpool's success in reaching the final to admitting hoping for an AC Milan win later that day. Even after a do like this one, the players were still thinking as footballers, though. Gerrard and

Carragher both told anyone who asked them that they didn't care who they met in Athens; they would be confident of bringing the Cup back home. But you just felt that in their heart of hearts, they, like the rest of us, didn't even want to contemplate what it would be like if United made it through.

Thankfully Milan made all such thoughts academic that night when they demolished Sir Alex Ferguson's side with a performance that instantly made them favourites to beat Liverpool in the final, in the bookies' eyes, at least. Even if Milan were favourites, and even if they would come with revenge on their minds, and even if they did have the mercurial Kaka, at least we could go and enjoy the game and the trip without the fear of open warfare on the streets of Athens. Knowing his friends and family would be among those travelling out to Greece, Steven Gerrard celebrated all three of Milan's goals over a few pints at The Grapes in Formby. Like everyone else he knew the 'dream' meeting of Liverpool and United could so easily have turned into an absolute nightmare.

At households throughout Merseyside the cheers which greet any goal against United had an extra edge this time – it didn't matter how good Milan were; the only way we were going to be able to enjoy this trip was if the Italians were waiting for us when we got there. We always love to see United lose, no matter what. Some of us even go as far as supporting Everton when they meet. But this time seeing them on the receiving end of a Milanese hiding gave us as much relief as enjoyment. If I'd known then what a shambles Athens would turn out to be, those feelings of relief would have been a hundred times more powerful. Liverpool against Manchester United on that setting would have been simply unthinkable. It probably isn't too far-fetched to suggest that had United got through, English clubs would now be banned from European competition for years to come. It really would have been that bad.

With just over a week to go before the final I still had nowhere to get my head down in Athens. That's nothing particularly new for me, or for most, on a European trip. The idea has always been to get yourself to the town or city where the game is taking place, and sleep will take care of itself. Or so the theory goes, anyway.

But this time I was on the official trip as a member of Her Majesty's press. Surely the organisers had got it all boxed off well in advance so the media would have a hotel in the middle of town? Not a bit of it. I started getting worried when lads who'd been on the official trip to Istanbul told me they'd had to check out of their hotel as soon as they got there because it was that bad. Having stayed in more than my share of dumps in countries like Holland, Turkey and Italy, such thoughts didn't bother me. All I wanted to know was that I had a room and it was situated somewhere at least close to central Athens. In the end my wishes at least partially came true.

Word came through that we had a hotel that was classed as two star on the Internet, but we were told to dismiss that because it was really a four star that would probably pass for a three star in this country. So far, so good. Then came the killer line – in this case the devil was most definitely in the detail.

The hotel was a forty-minute drive from downtown Athens.

It would be like working in Liverpool but staying in Manchester, only worse. Athens isn't exactly commuter friendly, and having already got word of the fourteen-hour-long rush hour that brings the roads into the city to a standstill each and every day, I knew we could not be staying anywhere much worse. Why didn't they just send us to Crete and give us our ferry fare every morning? It would've been easier than navigating those rickety roads in the back of one of those yellow taxis each and every time we wanted to head into town. Some journeys took two and a half hours, and when it came to getting back to the hotel of a night, it was even worse. Most taxi drivers we encountered had never even heard of the hotel we were staying at, and those who had immediately clocked our desperation and put the meter on fast forward.

Still, you can't complain. I was one of the very, very lucky ones. At least I had a room, and, better still, I wasn't paying for

it. I'm used to being a member of the great unwashed, or one of
the plebs, as comedian John Bishop put it to me on the night of
the game, and here I was on an official trip with the team.

We flew from Liverpool John Lennon Airport on the Monday
before the final. It was all new to me, and after arriving at the
airport it took me ages to realise that the official flight isn't listed
on the departures board; you basically have to use a few code
words and a couple of funny handshakes to get on. It was only
when I spotted Rafa Benítez's wife, Montse, handing her bags over
at check-in that I realised where I needed to go. So I headed
straight over and told Montse I hoped she'd be on for another
new watch off Rafa when she got back. She just looked at me
and smiled, no doubt thinking, 'He's about the fifty-eighth fella
to say that to me today.'

In the departure lounge word got around that the Liverpool
players were to make an appeal on behalf of Madeleine McCann,
the little girl who went missing in Portugal whilst on holiday with
her parents just a matter of weeks earlier. Although I was about
to get onto a flight, technically I was still working, so I rang the
office and told them what was going on. Obviously this was a big
story for us. You've got the Liverpool squad heading off for their
seventh European Cup final, which is big enough on its own, but
throw in an appeal for a missing three year old who'd captured
the nation's hearts and you're talking splash material.

The only problem was I didn't know what form the appeal
would take at that point. There were rumours of Steven Gerrard
saying a few words, and there was talk that the players would
unfurl a banner with Madeleine's picture on before getting onto
the plane. It was only when club spokesman Ian Cotton told
me the banner rumour was correct that I was able to let the
office know the score. Gerrard led the players off the team plane
– they were already on board before everyone else, having been
driven straight to the aircraft steps on the team bus – and they
unfurled this massive banner which read 'Please bring Maddie
home'.

Cynics might argue that this was little more than a PR stunt, but how many other clubs would have taken time out from planning for a European Cup final to remember the plight of a family who were going through a nightmare? And anyway, after getting back to their seats, several of the players were still talking about Madeleine, saying they desperately hoped she would be found soon. There was an undoubted empathy.

I boarded the plane from the front, having been told that was were the players would be sitting. I had a load of copies of the *Echo*'s Cup-final special with me to hand out, and the players lapped them up. God knows if they even looked at them, though. Most of them spent the entire flight playing on their PSPs or listening to their iPods. There was hardly any banter. This was where the business of winning the Champions League final really began, and the entire Liverpool party was focusing on the job in hand. I looked around the plane and imagined what it would be like to be accompanied by the European Cup on the way back. No doubt things would be quite a bit livelier on the return trip – or so I hoped.

We landed at Athens airport and were greeted on the runway by scores of photographers, most of whom seemed to be Italian. The players were whisked away to their hotel on a luxury coach without having to go through arrivals. Hopefully the security checks will have been done on board, because you never know what impostors might have sneaked in. Maybe even Bolo Zenden.

After picking up our bags we were taken to our hotel by bus. On the way we passed goats, sheep and packs of wild dogs – pretty much all the things you wouldn't expect to find in a built-up, modern European city. The hotel was so bad I've wiped its name from memory. It had a swimming pool that hadn't seen water for about a decade, a building site outside and it was in the middle of nowhere. And I mean nowhere. Worst of all, from my point of view, it had no Internet access, no Wi-Fi and no mobile-phone coverage. I shouldn't have been surprised, though; it was in the Greek mountains, after all. Somehow I was going to have to file copy from there; otherwise I would have to spend almost every single minute in town trying to bunk into the lobbies of posh hotels so I could use their Wi-Fi.

There was literally no point in sticking around at the hotel, so I decided to head into town to see where all the Reds were gathering. At reception I was told I would have to wait an hour for a cab, because taxis didn't operate in that area and they had to come all the way from town. Patience not being one of my better qualities, I jibbed it and started walking down a steep hill in the vague direction of Athens. After walking for twenty-five minutes my phone kicked into action. It was a message from my mate Boydy, a fanatical Liverpudlian who follows the team everywhere. It read, 'All right, Tony, any tickets going over there? I still need two.' Even in Athens – well, on a Greek mountainside, at least – there was no escaping the issue. Tickets, or rather the lack of them, were going to be the story of this final.

Go to any European footy trip and the reality is that the day before the final is often better than the day of the game itself. The real tension is still to kick in, you get to have a good look around the town before the Red hordes and the accompanying legions of police arrive, and you get to meet up with your mates and all the other familiar faces as they start turning up.

At this stage it's all about establishing yourself. It's about working out where the main action is going to be and finding somewhere else. And, if you're lucky, it's about stumbling upon a bar where the ale is cheap and in plentiful supply, and the owners don't mind serving until well into the small hours and putting up with a load of Scouse lads proving we can't all sing like Lennon and McCartney.

The day before the European Cup final in Athens was different, though. It seemed as if half the world's population had made its way there – and they were almost all wearing red. This was the Istanbul effect in all its full-blooded, gory Technicolor. If anyone was looking for a sign that Liverpool's fan base had become too big and too international to be manageable, it was in Syntagma Square in the heart of the city.

In a space of only a couple of hours I came across a group of eight Pakistani Reds from Johannesburg who were over for their first game, huge gangs of Norwegians and, probably most surprising of all, plenty of Yanks who all wanted to be a part of the Liverpool Reds.

Throw in the usual big turnout of cockneys, Welsh lads and woollyback Reds and this was the most visible evidence of Liverpool's national and international pulling power that I've ever seen. Scousers were undoubtedly in the minority at this stage, as most were coming in on day trips on the day of the game. Many of those who were already there felt marginalised, and there were plenty talking bitterly of having their tickets, culture and birthright taken away from them by a crowd of extras from *Soccer AM*.

Syntagma Square was a seething mass of humanity. The only problem was it seemed half of this seething mass had no tickets, as fans took to wearing sandwich-board-style notices appealing for spares – and there were clearly precious few of them about. Touts selling tickets set up base outside McDonald's – where else were the English going to eat? – where they were charging anything up to three thousand euros for a sixty-euro seat. The odd foreign lad with far too much dough to spare paid the asking price, but most lads just looked at the touts disdainfully. They were definitely taking the piss.

One thing you can guarantee when this happens is that it won't be long before a Liverpool lad who's had a few pints takes exception to the rip-off taking place in front of his very eyes and does something about it. And so it proved, as a Scouser giving away height, weight and reach advantage had words with a Greek tout before catching him flush on the chin with a beauty of a right hook, putting him on his arse before he knew what the fuck had hit him.

As the clobbered tout was still seeing stars and counting his teeth, the lad went through his pockets, pulling out a fistful of tickets, which he whacked out to his mates. He also got a grip of his ill-gotten gains, but there was no chance of him sharing the dough out – that was his spoils of war, and he was going to celebrate with it as only an Englishman can: 'Can I go large with that Big Mac meal please, love?'

Football violence may largely be a thing of the past, and the match is undoubtedly a safer and a better experience for it, but there's still something great about seeing a tout, a parasite who feeds on the desperation of others, getting his comeuppance. That Greek fella will no doubt rue the day he ever tried to rip off a load of Scousers.

Just as in Istanbul, there was hardly any sign of Milan. Italians never travel particularly well, but surely they'd turn up in their numbers after what happened two years earlier? Surely they would have seen what a positive effect a travelling army can have on a team and want to emulate it? At this point they were outnumbered by about ten to one, and quite a few of the Italians we came across were actually supporting Liverpool.

There were loads of Greek police about, and all of them looked like they would put up more of a fight than their touting countrymen. But then you always do look hard when you're carrying a baton and a gun. They made sure their presence was noted in and around Syntagma Square, where the majority of Reds had gathered, with most of the fans establishing themselves on the steps that led down to the square from the Greek parliament building. They stood there pretty much all day and well into the early hours, singing Liverpool song after Liverpool song.

Even when the heavens opened and the rain poured down in a way that made Manchester look drought hit, most of them still stayed where they were. Those who couldn't take being drenched legged it to the nearest shelter. More often than not, that meant going to McDonald's. But some tried to get into the nearby Grande Bretagne Hotel, only to be knocked back by a team of burly security guards. It turned out all the UEFA bigwigs were staying at this five-star gaff, and you can't have soaking-wet fans mixing it with the freeloaders as they hammer their expenses, can you?

There is something about this 'us and them' mentality of UEFA that really gets to me. Who do they think makes football what it is? Who do they think creates the wealth that finances their five-star suites and three-hundred-euro meals? Who do they think pays for their first-class travel and the chauffeur-driven limos at their beck and call? The thing is they know quite well who it is, but their arrogance means they will never acknowledge it, and they will never share their ill-gotten gains with us. We're on the outside looking in, getting soaked to the skin, while they quaff Bellinis in a hotel positively dripping with opulence.

Looking through the windows of the Grande Bretagne and seeing these clowns having the time of their life while the great unwashed were not even allowed into the building really got to me. This was the most symbolic evidence I'd ever seen of what football has come to. Something inside my head was telling me I had to get in there, to expose what was going on behind those closed doors. But those very same burly security guards were still in place, and my T-shirt, shorts and flip-flop combo was never going to impress them, especially if I opened my mouth and they heard my guttural Scouse.

There was only one thing for it – I was going to have to bunk in. The only problem was that about a hundred lads were having the same thought, and this was definitely one of those cases when too many cooks could so easily have spoiled the broth. There is a strength in numbers in these situations, but the key is to let others do all the legwork while you just stand to one side, clocking what's going on and looking for an opportunity. A gang of a dozen lads were telling the bouncers that they were meeting their mates inside and they had to let them in. It's an old line that never usually works, and this occasion was no different. The bouncers knocked them back, but the lads refused to go. There was only one thing for it – they had to be physically removed.

A scuffle ensued, and in the melee I shot in, like Roadrunner after a pile of Acme birdseed, and headed straight for the sanctuary of the bar. Not surprisingly, I was the only one in there without a suit. Not that I stood out, though. Shorts, flip-flops, T-shirt and a shaved head – could I have looked any more Scouse if I'd tried? Undeterred by my inability to blend in, I grabbed a seat that allowed me to keep an eye on everyone as they came and went, and it also let me see what the bouncers were up to. The first known face I saw was Michael Laudrup's. Then I saw Phil Neal. Then Gerard Houllier. Then former UEFA head honcho Lennart Johansson (good to see they don't strip you of all your freebies when you get binned from the top job, eh, Lenny?). Next I clapped eyes on Chelsea chief executive Peter Kenyon. Obviously, being a professional, I should have contained myself, but I defy anyone not to have a sly dig at this fella if you ever come across him. 'Hello, Peter, what are you doing here?' I asked politely. Before he could answer, I butted in, 'José did tell you you got knocked out in the semis, didn't he?' It wasn't a killer line, by any means, but the look in his eyes before he turned on his heels told me I'd got to him. One–nil to the plebs.

Next on the conveyer belt of UEFA freeloaders was the top man himself, Michel Platini. Being UEFA president means you're not allowed to go anywhere without a trail of sycophants, and the former France star was barely visible as he walked towards the foyer surrounded by a ten-strong group of sharp-suited clip-board carriers. It was only his perm that gave him away. 'This is too good to be true,' I thought. I simply had to challenge him over the tickets shambles that had left so many good Liverpudlians with little hope of seeing a game they should have been able to see as of right.

But I also wanted a picture to mark this iconic meeting of scally and Gallic minds, and I didn't have a camera with me. So I rang my mate, Paul Rogers, who was still in the square. Paul takes his camera everywhere he goes, and I also knew he'd be one of the few people with the confidence and the swagger to evade security and get into the hotel. Within two minutes he was there, camera in hand and ready to go. I jumped up from my seat, put my arm around Platini's shoulder and asked, 'Any chance of a photo, Michel?'

Seeing as he had nowhere to go, and no doubt conscious that rejection could have caused a scene, Platini agreed. As soon as Paul had pressed the button, and before the glare of the flash had cleared from my eyes, I was on him. 'So, then, Mr Platini, are you satisfied with the way tickets have been distributed for the final?'

Platini: 'No comment.'

Me: 'There has been a lot of criticism from Liverpool fans about the way tickets have been distributed. Does that concern you?'

Platini: 'No comment.'

Me: 'Mr Platini, are you aware there are thousands of ticket-less fans outside this hotel? Do you have any spares for them?'

Platini: (Laughs) . . . 'No comment.'

I hadn't managed to get any answers from him, but at least I'd asked him the questions that so many Liverpool supporters wanted to confront him with, and I walked out of the Grande Bretagne feeling like I'd got the scoop of the century, simply because of how hard it was to get near enough just to be able to speak to Platini. But no doubt within seconds of our impromptu meeting he'd forgotten all about it as he was whisked away to his next corporate meeting in a chauffeur-driven limo. It must be a hard life being the top man at European football's governing body.

When I left the hotel, Syntagma Square was heaving again. The rain had stopped, and the fans had returned, this time in even greater numbers than before. I'd arranged to meet with a few mates, and, seeing as they had Liverpool legend Jimmy Case with them, I gave the square a swerve and headed off to see them in a bar in nearby Pláka.

When I got to the bar, they'd already been there for a couple of hours, and the owner, a crazy fella called Babbis, was keeping them well entertained with his tales of watching the great Liverpool sides of the '70s and '80s on a bad television with a crackly reception. He loved Dalglish and Rush, of course, but most of all he loved the fans, who he insisted were the most fanatical he had ever seen. Seeing as he was in the presence of a dozen or so hardcore Reds, he could hardly have said anything else, though, could he?

We stayed there for an hour or so before deciding to head back to the square. It should have only taken ten minutes on foot, but when you've got Jimmy Case with you this is never going to be likely. Every few yards we walked, Jimmy was mobbed, and 'Oh, Jimmy Jimmy, Jimmy Jimmy Jimmy Jimmy Case' rang out like it was 1977 all over again. Jimmy didn't mind. In fact he loved it. Thirty years on and his status as a Kop cult hero was still intact. He even showed he hadn't lost any of the old ability when one lad launched a ball in his direction and he caught it with the sweetest volley ever seen on the streets of Athens.

When Jimmy and the rest of the lads decided to call it a night halfway to Syntagma, myself and a mate of mine called Andy Kelly, an Ulsterman who moved to and settled in Liverpool mainly out of devotion to his team, decided to continue to the square to see what was happening. When we got there, the scene was a mad mix of bladdered lads stumbling about or sleeping on chairs and fellas for whom the night was still young – they were still singing and drinking as strong as they had been twelve hours earlier. A crowd of locals had gathered just to see them in action, and they weren't disappointed, with pretty much every single Kop anthem, even the less-well-known ones such as 'Underneath the Floodlights' and 'Bill Shankly from Glenbuck', being given an airing. But the all-day party was definitely coming to an end, and having told Andy of the splendour of the Grande Bretagne, he wanted to see for himself where the UEFA bigwigs would be getting their heads down that night.

This time getting in was much easier, probably because Andy's one of those lads who always tries to look smart – I think he even wears a suit jacket for bed – so the hotel security no doubt thought he fitted in there. Still clad in shorts and T-shirt, I let him lead the way to the bar, but it was quiet in there, and one of the waitresses told us that hotel guests were welcome to attend the rooftop party that was going on. You don't need a second invitation, do you? We jumped in the lift and went up to the eighth floor. When the lift doors opened, we were greeted by the kind of scene you only usually see in Hollywood movies.

There were waitresses dressed like Greek goddesses serving cocktails, celebrities everywhere you looked and a panoramic view of Athens that could not possibly be bettered. The first thing we did was look for a familiar face so we could blend in. The only problem was although we recognised them, we couldn't really go and stand with Jamie Redknapp, Didi Hamann, Ruud Gullit, Paulo Rossi or the actor Clive Owen without them wondering who the hell we were. And I wouldn't stand by Andy Gray if you paid me. Thankfully we spotted a mate of ours called Julian Flanagan, who owns the Sir Thomas in town, and he called us over and handed us a bottle of lager each. Seriously, I've been to some cracking parties, but this was something else. We stayed for an hour, but in the end sheer exhaustion got the better of us, so we decided to call it a day and headed back to our hotel in the hills. Unfortunately, the first group of taxi drivers we came across had never heard of the place (or claimed they hadn't – you're not likely to get a fare back from a mountain retreat at four o'clock on a Wednesday morning, are you?) and the only one who had wanted a hundred euros to take us. Seeing as he was the only show in town, we agreed. Anything to get us back in time to have a few hours before the day of the European Cup final.

When you wake up on the threshold of a European final, you don't need reminding what day it is. If it's not the knot in the stomach that tells you, it's the spring in the step that biology suggests you shouldn't have after a day and night on the ale. You can see it in your mates' eyes. There is a feeling that runs through every single one of you like electricity. Your FA Cup finals are one thing, but unless you've been to a European Cup final, you just can't imagine what that feeling's like.

Two of the lads I go the match with, Philly and Paul Smart, had arrived in Athens at 6 a.m., and as soon as I got up, I gave Philly a bell to see what he was up to. Despite having nothing booked, he'd managed to sweet-talk the charming lady owner of a back-street hostel to let the pair of them get their heads down there. As usual, once he was asleep it was almost impossible to shift him, but a bit of gentle persuasion – along with the usual abuse and threats of violence – convinced him to come and meet me, Dave Kirby and Nicky Allt at Syntagma Square.

As soon as I got there, I realised all was not right with Nicky. He actually looked like he'd seen a ghost. I asked him what was wrong, but he stayed quiet. Dave was trying not to laugh, but his giggles soon gave him away. 'Come on, Nicky, what's up?' I asked.

'I've just been attacked in my room by a bird,' he stuttered. With that answer all sorts of things went through my mind. But, as is usually the case with Nicky, fact was stranger than fiction. He continued: 'I was closing the bedroom window, and this fuck-off big bird flew at me. Honest to God, it was fucking massive. I've never seen anything like it. I shit myself.'

Here he was, a one-time Annie Road skinhead, admitting to having the shit scared out of him by a mate of Emu's. Dave was in bulk, and the rest of us were just bewildered. True to form Nicky recovered himself before any of us had really had a chance to take the piss. 'You know what it was like,' he continued. 'It was like that big massive bird out of *Harry Potter*, and if I see it again I'm deffo going to grab it and make it fly me into that ground tonight, because I haven't got a ticket.'

The last bit of that conversation was being repeated thousands of times in and around Syntagma Square. It actually seemed like there were more people there without tickets than with them. And half of those who had them only had the phoney ones that someone had obviously run off on their Commodore 64 at home. Most of the blags carried the name 'Robert Bernard Ryder', which, as any proper Red will tell you, was Robbie Fowler's name as a teenager. Even when they're making forgeries, there's something in Scousers that makes them do it with a cheeky flourish.

Dave and Nicky had arranged to meet Bill Shankly's grand-daughter, Karen Gill, outside McDonald's, so we headed down there. But just as we got there, another downpour started. The 'restaurant' was full, so all we could do was shelter outside as everyone else went scurrying for cover. Karen told us the weather had been great before the Liverpool fans had turned up in Athens – now I'm not one for omens, but there was something about what she said that made me wonder if this trip was fated to turn into a damp squib.

The downpour lasted for more than an hour, but that didn't stop the party in Syntagma Square. If anything the singing became even louder. It was a show of defiance that even the elements could not stop Liverpool in their tracks. One lad who climbed one of the highest trees in the square hadn't taken the slippy conditions into account, though, and he promptly plummeted to the deck before dusting himself down and carrying on with his drinking. Another fella was pelted with (full) cans of lager as he clambered on top of an enormous plant pot. Despite the entertainment it was becoming increasingly clear that the square was not the place to be. It was as if there'd been a conscious effort to recreate the atmosphere of Taksim Square in Istanbul, and it all felt too forced. Most of the Scouse Reds had given up on it hours earlier and set up base in bars in the back streets, so we did the same.

With five hours to go before kick-off, just about everyone I spoke to was in confident mood. They were confident that Rafa Benítez would get his tactics right, they were confident that the team would win and they were confident that they would get into the ground – whether they had tickets or not. After spending a couple of hours at a bar where the ale was half the price it had been in Syntagma Square, we decided to make our way to the Olympic Stadium, in the knowledge that getting in could be lively, given the number of lads with fake tickets and no tickets at all.

In the days leading up to the game the Greek authorities had been at pains to tell us to get the bus to the ground because the underground was for Milan fans only. Having seen the rush-hour traffic in Athens, there was no chance of any of us following those orders. So we headed down to the station at Monastiraki Square and got straight on a train, no problem at all. God knows where the Milan fans were, because all I could see were Reds. The train was absolutely chocka – it looked like one of those rattlers from Mumbai to Delhi, with people packed in like sardines and hanging

out of the windows. It didn't smell too good either, but what else
would you expect from a carriage load of fellas who'd been on
the ale all day? You can only imagine what the locals thought as
their daily commute home from work was taken over by thousands of characters straight out of Scouse central casting.

Seeing as everyone's vocal chords had been well oiled, the
singing didn't stop from Monastiraki to the stadium. The forty-
minute-long journey was anything but comfortable, and the longer
we were on the train, the more energy levels sapped. But the
singing kept on going. The locals seemed to like 'Campione' and
'You'll Never Walk Alone', but they were less sure about 'Kopites
are Gobshites', which the Annie Road old-timers belted out at
every opportunity. A piss-taking chorus of 'There's Only One Rick
Parry' rang out, which some of the out-of-towners genuinely
seemed to believe was being sung in his honour. The irony was
definitely lost on them. At least they got the joke when my mate
Philly sang 'Bolo, Bolo Zenden' to the tune of 2 Unlimited's 'No
Limit' non-stop for about fifteen minutes. He even did a Russian-
style dance to go with it.

By the time the train got to the ground, everyone was done
in, and we emerged into the sunlight looking like zombies in a
1970s horror flick. Thankfully the riot police were there to offer
us a traditional Greek welcome, complete with guns, batons and
shields. No doubt those attending the Olympic Games a few years
earlier were given the same welcome – and if you believe that,
you'll believe anything. As soon as you saw them, you just knew
there were going to be problems. Whatever happened to sending
riot police onto the streets when there's an actual riot?

Apparently their job was to sort those with tickets from those
without. How you do that with a baton, I'll never know. Not
surprisingly the riot police proved themselves to be totally shite
as stewards but top class when it came to meting out beatings to
anyone with a genuine ticket who just wanted to see the game.
Who'd have thought it?

Outside the ground it was like a scene from *The Warriors*, as
you literally had to run the gauntlet of the turbo-charged robo-

cops just to get through the checkpoints they'd set up. And, as if that wasn't bad enough, there were twats snatching tickets off fellow Reds. Now I can live with UEFA treating us like shit – I've come to expect that. Foreign police forces being badly organised but handy with the baton is nothing new either. But seeing these rats picking their marks, usually older fellas or kids, and stealing their tickets sickened me. You may be able to explain away bunking-in by arguing you're only 'stealing' from money-bags UEFA, but how can you possibly justify stealing from your own? In all my time following Liverpool at home and abroad it was this scene that shocked me most. Maybe I'm naïve and it's been going on for years – I actually did see it happen sporadically before the FA Cup final at the Millennium Stadium a year earlier – but the sheer scale of it in Athens was unbelievable. Every other minute you'd see a chase scene straight out of *Benny Hill*, as someone legged it after a low-life who'd just snatched their ticket.

And what were the forces of law and order doing while this was going on? They were just stood there, looking on as one theft after another took place under their very noses. Obviously they didn't give a shit. Maybe they didn't want to break ranks, because that would've weakened them for the big battle they were so obviously spoiling for. So the vultures were having a field day, picking off their prey at will and leaving those who they'd targeted clearly sickened and distraught. Whatever the shortcomings of UEFA and the Greek police, they could not be blamed for this. No one will ever convince me that this was the fault of anyone but the parasites who were stealing from their own. Even if you were left feeling bitter because UEFA's scandalously low ticket allocation had cost you a place at the final, you just don't do that.

The mad thing was you didn't even need to have a genuine ticket to get in. Lads were walking through the checkpoints holding up blag tickets, pieces of blue card, lap-dance flyers, even a packet of Regal King Size, and they were all getting in no bother. The 'ring of steel' was basically just a load of riot police who had no idea what a real ticket looked like. You may as well have had Ray Charles on the door checking them. The organisation was so bad that there were even lads who'd turned up at the ground with no intention of bunking-in who ended up seeing how easy it was to do so and just waltzed through. It was like that old archive footage of the White Horse Cup final when every man and his dog got into Wembley whether they wanted to or not.

For those who take pride in their bunking skills, there was no challenge in this. Where's the fun in defeating the authorities if they're not even doing anything to stop you? Some were still pulling the old stunts, though, as lads wearing yellow fluorescent steward's bibs appeared in the press box and even in the directors' box. Others found themselves still in possession of whole tickets when they got into the ground and simply passed them back to their ticketless mates at the final checkpoint just in case. It really was that easy.

The problem was it was far too easy, and when I got through the final checkpoint and walked into Gate 1, I soon realised just how big a problem it had become. The whole Liverpool end was rammed – and this was more than an hour before kick-off. There were already three people to every two seats, and the stairways were packed with people who had either bunked in or who simply couldn't make their way to their seats because of the congestion. I stood at the top of the steps and looked behind me. There were thousands outside still to come in. If ever the arguments in favour of bunking-in have been shot down in flames, it was here. Usually seen as a bit of a laugh and a chance to get one over on the authorities, on this occasion it was shown up to be nothing more than a high-risk game of chicken which could have gone terribly, terribly wrong. If the odd few manage to bunk in, then hardly anyone bats an eyelid. But if thousands do it, then the risks to everyone's safety are there for all to see.

Our end was uncomfortable, such was the volume of people in there, and the fact that the Greeks clearly had no way of counting the number of people entering the stadium is something that should send a chill down the spine of anyone who has ever read the Taylor Report. Crowd control had broken down spectacularly. There were no systems in place to root out forged tickets (save for the odd ultraviolet scanner that was all too easy to avoid), no systems in place to stop people from bunking in, and no systems in place to ensure all those with tickets got into the ground safe and sound.

This was a UEFA operation, all right. Before the game they'd made all the usual noises about security being tight and how the organisation was better than ever, but in reality their words were as hollow as their commitment to fans. Those inside the Olympic Stadium were the lucky ones. As kick-off approached, there were still thousands outside, and an announcement was made telling them that the ground was full and they would not be allowed in. Now I don't know about you, but if I'd paid thousands of pounds and travelled thousands of miles to see a game I'd legitimately bought a ticket for, this kind of announcement wouldn't exactly make me happy. The majority of those locked out had genuine tickets, but they were destined to become the innocent victims of an organisational farce of the highest order.

Many refused to budge. They had tickets, and they had done nothing wrong: why should they be denied access? The morals of the argument didn't matter, though. The Liverpool end of the ground was already dangerously full, and the decision had been made that they wouldn't be getting in. A couple more minutes passed, and in this time the crowd outside had swelled, as more and more ticket holders arrived. There was a bit of a crush, and the riot police panicked, indiscriminately setting off pepper spray and baton-charging anyone who dared to stand their ground. People were sent scattering in all directions, many in tears as the pepper spray took effect. And these, don't forget, were people with tickets.

Some stood their ground, but others fled. They weren't hooligans looking for a battle – some were actually players' wives and friends – they just wanted to see their team on the biggest stage of all. The brutality of the police was in marked contrast to the restraint of the fans, although some did attempt to force their

way into the stadium amidst the mayhem. The Greek police soon
got worn out, though, and those who'd stuck around were able
to take advantage of their flagging energy levels and managed to
get into the ground after kick-off. By the time they got there, the
Liverpool team was already on top of a Milan that was looking
a pale shadow of the side that had racked up a three-goal lead by
half-time in Istanbul just two years earlier.

Pre-match, the Milan *tifosi* had unfurled a banner saying 'Only
You'. Did it mean only victory over Liverpool and no other side
would remove the pain from Istanbul that was still eating away
at their souls? Was it a show of devotion to their own club? Or
had The Platters' hit from the '50s become the Rossoneri's own
version of 'You'll Never Walk Alone'? Whatever it was we still
don't know, despite the fact that it was one of the main talking
points in our end when the game got under way.

The other one was Bolo Zenden. Everyone knows that in
Benítez's vision of what makes a good team the sum is always far
more important than the individual parts. It is all about finding
an absolute balance between attack and defence, keeping things
tight in defence and midfield and pretty much squeezing the life
out of your opponents. Because of the way he sets up tactically,
Benítez is able to find room in his team for players who wouldn't
get anywhere near the starting eleven for the likes of Man United
or Chelsea. When arguments about the greatest manager of all
time are put forward, surely the man who has won a European
Cup with Djimi Traore, Igor Biscan and Josemi as key members
of his squad must be worth a shout.

Despite having seen Benítez work like this since his arrival
from Valencia in the summer of 2004, there were not many Reds
who agreed with his selection of Zenden in Athens. This was
despite the fact that the Dutchman had played a key role in the
semi-final win over Chelsea, with a tactically astute display which
won him plaudits from fans and the media alike. Zenden does
play for the team, not for individual glory, but there was a
consensus, albeit not one shared by the Liverpool manager, that
he was the main weak point of the side, that he could not hurt

Milan in any way. So when Zenden's name was read out in the starting line-up, there were audible groans in the Liverpool end – even their belief in Benítez and their devotion to him couldn't change their view that a player who was to be discarded by the club the following day should not be starting in a European Cup final.

The general view was that the manager had got it wrong. He had also got it wrong in Istanbul when he omitted Didi Hamann from his starting line-up – a mistake Milan exploited to the full as they ran rampant in the first half. Benítez was able to rectify that mistake at half-time, and most of us were hoping this would happen again here (without having to go three goals down!). We were also acutely aware that Rafa's ability to confound his critics with his tactics is one of the things that marks him out as a top manager. But still, the selection of Zenden pleased hardly anyone in the massed ranks of Liverpudlians, and many of us articulated our fear that even if we got on top of Milan it would be difficult to hurt them, given the lack of pace down our left-hand side.

And Liverpool did get on top – mainly thanks to the solid platform given to them by Javier Mascherano and Xabi Alonso in central midfield. The Argentinian was suffocating the brilliant Kaka, tracking his every move and depriving him of possession in threatening positions. Alonso, meanwhile, was doing what he does best: getting hold of the ball and spreading it to Pennant on the right or looking for the runs of Gerrard, who was playing as a split striker just behind Dirk Kuyt. For forty-four minutes everything worked well. Half-chances came and went, but at least we were creating them, and Milan had hardly featured as an attacking force – they looked totally unable to shake off Benítez's tactical straitjacket and were making uncharacteristically sloppy mistakes.

But just as referee Herbert Fandel was about to blow for half-time, he spotted one of those fouls which are only ever given in European combat. Alonso lunged into a tackle and won the ball, but he also caught Kaka – the kind of challenge which you see every week in the Premiership and for which a free-kick is rarely, if ever, awarded. But we knew the score in European football –

we have seen enough of it over the years – and no one was particularly surprised when Fandel gave a foul. What happened next
must have been predicted by every single Liverpool fan in the
Olympic Stadium and back home. You just knew that, after doing
fuck all for the entire half, Milan would score. And they did, with
a goal which, had it been scored by us, would have left Evertonians
muttering darkly about pacts with the Devil. Pipo Inzaghi was
doing nothing more than following Andrea Pirlo's free-kick into
the box when the ball hit him and ricocheted wickedly past the
already committed Reina. As lucky goals go it was right up there
with Lou Macari's against us for the Mancs at Wembley in '77.
It was a name-on-the-cup goal, and most of us knew it.

At half-time the Liverpool fans tried (and failed) to recreate
the spirit of Istanbul. The chorus of 'You'll Never Walk Alone'
which rang out was so predictable it sounded and felt passionless.
It was as if we'd all dipped into the A–Z of how to be a Liverpool
fan and come up with an identikit solution to the team being a
goal behind. In Istanbul the Rodgers and Hammerstein classic
had sounded emotionally raw and passionate. In Athens it simply
sounded like any other football song. We may as well have been
Man City singing 'Blue Moon'. Maybe it was all the problems
getting in, or maybe it just came down to the fact that the situation was nowhere near as desperate as it had been in Athens,
but the fact was this Liverpool crowd was lacking in passion and
spontaneity. We were still supporting our team, of course, but, on
this occasion, we certainly could not claim to be having a positive impact on the outcome of the game.

When Inzaghi added a second in the second half, the game
was well and truly up. Two-goal deficits have been overcome
many, many times before, but there was something about the way
this Liverpool side was set up that suggested it wouldn't be
happening this time. It wasn't a negative line-up, but it wasn't
positive either. The substitutions came too late to make a real
difference, and Milan were coasting to their seventh European
Cup with what must rank as one of their worst performances in
a major final. It just wasn't going to be our night. The gods who

had smiled on us so willingly in Istanbul were wearing the red and black of Milan in Athens. This was their night, and good luck to them.

Even when Kuyt pulled a goal back in the dying moments, no one even dreamed there would be another miracle. Pretty much all that strike did was make the Milan fans (and the Evertonians and Mancs watching on TV at home) shit themselves. But in our hearts we knew the game was up. We'd been taken on yet another wonderful magical mystery tour of Europe, but Athens was to be our final destination. The only question now was how would we react to defeat.

Had you not seen what actually happened at the end of the game and only taken note of the UEFA smear campaign that followed, you would be forgiven for believing the Liverpool fans went on the rampage, smashing up the Olympic Stadium and the rest of Athens and filling in any Italians and Greeks who crossed their path. Unfortunately for UEFA, and particularly for William Gaillard, the Redmen reacted to defeat with a spontaneous display of support and sportsmanship that should have seen them showered with plaudits. Only a nasty spin on events stopped this from happening, as UEFA used their vast media machine to rewrite history and absolve themselves of all blame for the pre-match problems outside the ground. All of a sudden all the talk was of ticketless hordes smashing their way into the stadium, leaving the poor Greek police powerless and the governing body's perfect planning in tatters.

We all know their version of events was bollocks. They were doing what major organisations always do when they've fucked up so publicly: shift the blame to save their own arses. We've seen it with South Yorkshire Police in '89 and with UEFA after Heysel. They know that if they throw enough mud then it'll stick, and it ends up being us who carry the can. Smears do work. Ask any neutral what their abiding memory is of the fans at the 2007 Champions League final and their response is likely to be the Liverpool supporters causing mayhem before the game.

In actual fact their real abiding memory should be of the

Liverpool fans to a man staying in the stadium to applaud Milan for winning the trophy. Two years earlier the Milan fans had cleared their end well before Steven Gerrard had got his hands on the European Cup, and understandably so. The pain of defeat is enough to send even the least passionate of fans heading for the exit doors, so you can't really knock anyone who decides they don't fancy sticking around while their opponents dance and celebrate on the pitch right in front of them with the cup they so desperately wanted to win. But, just as they had done the previous March when Benfica knocked their team out of the Champions League at Anfield, and on countless other occasions, the Liverpool supporters simply swallowed their disappointment and sportingly clapped Paolo Maldini and Co. as they danced and cavorted with the trophy we now knew would not be coming back to Merseyside.

The thunderous applause was enough to elicit a reaction from Milan boss Carlo Ancelotti, who ordered his players to return the compliment. Such moments are so rare they border on the unique, and it was no surprise when the following day the splash on one of the leading Greek national newspapers was headlined 'Milan win the cup, but Liverpool win our hearts'. The positive image of the Liverpool fans in Greece had also been boosted by a pilgrimage to the memorial at the Olympiakos ground that saw more than a hundred Reds pay tribute to the twenty-one Greek fans who lost their lives in a stadium disaster in 1981. They brought scarves and flowers and spent hours at the ground, mixing with victims' families and honouring the dead. This tribute went unnoticed in the UK, but in Greece it forged a bond between Liverpool's fans and the native population that is unlikely to be replicated by any other set of supporters anywhere in the world.

Similarly, the fact that so many Liverpudlians had turned Syntagma Square into a carnival of colour and noise, both before and after the game, with hardly a hint of trouble despite the huge numbers involved, created an impression amongst many Greek people that Liverpool fans are well behaved. The only problem was that all these undeniable positives, which were clocked up over a three-day period, were wiped out in the eyes of the bulk of the British media from the moment UEFA decided to scapegoat us for their own failings at the Olympic Stadium. The minority of Reds who let the side down with their behaviour gave UEFA an opportunity to point the finger, and they grasped it. But make no mistake about it, not only was what happened outside the ground a product of desperate fans taking advantage of gross organisational failings, it also painted a misleading picture of the overall behaviour of the Liverpool fans in Athens.

At the end of that match I was as proud to be a Red as I've ever been. It's easy to support a team when they win, but to stick with them when things go wrong and still have the decency to hail your conquerors is something special. Maybe one day, when the lurid national-newspaper headlines have been forgotten, someone will look back in history, and the performance of those who travelled thousands of miles and paid thousands of pounds just to follow Rafa Benítez's team will be viewed a lot more kindly.

When it comes to presiding over an organisational shambles, UEFA are in a league of their own. It's as if they've come up with a foolproof method of ensuring that anything that can go wrong does go wrong. Before every European Cup final they ensure the supply of tickets is always grossly exceeded by the demand. They fill the best seats with the bastard members of the 'UEFA family' and leave the rest of us to fight it out for the crumbs from their ever-expanding table. Then they sit back and wash their hands of the problem when inevitability takes its course and ticketless fans who have been denied a place at the biggest stage of all turn up at the setting for the final out of sheer desperation to see their team.

And how many more times are they going to select a stadium which is not fit for staging such a major event? They did it at Heysel, a crumbling dump of a ground, which became a death-trap as soon as trouble broke out. They did it at the Ataturk but got away with it because the Liverpool fans and the players who took part in the game turned it into one of the greatest sporting spectacles of all time. But our great memories of that night should not make us forget that that ground was a soulless bowl on a lunar landscape in the middle of nowhere, with precious few facilities.

There were 40,000 Reds in the Ataturk that night – around about the same amount that travelled to Athens. It seemed the only difference was that the UEFA family didn't fancy making their way to somewhere so inhospitable, and we filled their seats. It looked to me that the Olympic Stadium was a different kettle of fish, though, as they obviously fancied a nice little jaunt to Athens, and all of a sudden the tickets that were flying around in Istanbul had been grabbed by UEFA's sons, daughters, brothers, sisters and cousins twice removed.

Liverpool fans saved the Champions League final in Istanbul. By turning up in our usual huge numbers, we stopped the prestigious occasion from being an unmitigated flop, played out in front of a half-full stadium. But by doing so we made the Champions League sexy again, and UEFA made sure the next time we were in town only a limited number of us were granted access to their party. This is the main reason why Athens turned into such a shambles – like the most evil of drug dealers, UEFA had given us a big enough 'hit' to become addicted, only to withdraw the supply when we needed it most.

It has always been like this, though. From 1977 in Rome to 2007 in Athens we have been treated like shit, and there is no sign of things changing for the better. If they hadn't learned the lessons from Heysel twenty-two years earlier, what chance is there of them learning the lessons of Athens?

Having lost the night before, the flight home was never going to be the dream trip I'd hoped it would be. I'd visualised myself sat there, with the players proudly wearing their medals around their necks, champagne being sunk by the crate-load and the European Cup being passed around the plane until I could get my own hands on it and sit it down beside me. But in the event flight BD7964 was not carrying the European Cup home; it was carrying a load of broken-hearted footballers who were struggling to come to terms with their defeat.

Don't let anyone ever tell you that all modern-day footballers don't care about winning and losing. You only had to see the dejected looks being worn by the entire Liverpool squad to realise that they care all right. The players were accompanied on the trip home by the WAGs, but even being surrounded by some of the most stunning women you'll ever see in your life wasn't enough to lift their spirits.

Steven Gerrard looked absolutely gutted. The only time he raised a smile on the four-hour trip from Athens was when his then wife-to-be, Alex Curran, grabbed tight hold of him during a nasty bout of turbulence. Jamie Carragher, a man who lives and breathes Liverpool FC, made small talk but was far from his usual sparky self. Robbie Fowler, who'd missed out on the subs bench the night before, was obviously devastated at not having been given the opportunity to say his final farewell on the biggest stage of all. The squad had something to cheer 'God' up, though, as he was presented with his shirt from the final, which had been signed by every single player. He was undoubtedly grateful for their gesture, but the pain he was suffering at not getting onto the pitch and having had to watch the team he is hopelessly devoted to being beaten was clear for all to see.

Me? I was every bit as disappointed. And for a time I was as sick as the players. But that only lasted until I thought of what a wonderful journey we've been blessed to travel on. Back in 1976 a European Cup final was still a dream for us. The likes of Bayern Munich, Real Madrid, Ajax, Celtic and even Man United had all had their name carved on that wonderful trophy. We'd pocketed a couple of UEFA Cups, but the big one had always eluded us. That was until 25th May, 1977, when Bob Paisley's men made all our dreams come true in the Olympic Stadium in Rome.

Since then we've been in an incredible six more European Cup finals, and in total we've won five of the seven. It is a record to be proud of and which only Milan themselves can match over the last thirty years. There was no shame in losing in Athens; we gave it all we had and came up short, but only after knocking out the likes of Chelsea and mighty Barcelona on the way. And, anyway, we can always content ourselves in the knowledge that we've got our very own European Cup in permanent residence at Anfield.

Defeat may be hard to take, but when your past is as glorious as ours is, the pain can only last so long before all those wonderful memories come flooding back.

Hopefully it won't be too long before we can again go gathering cups in May.

THE BOOK OF LISTS: FOOTBALL

STEPHEN FOSTER

'Some people think football is a matter of life and death. I am disappointed with that attitude. I can assure you it's much, much more important than that.' Bill Shankly

This is the ultimate collection of football facts and trivia from around the world, featuring: The 7 Fastest Goals, 11 Amazing Hat-Tricks, 10 Fishy Facts about Grimsby Town, 10 Trophy-Winning Smokers, 10 Ex-Footballers in Politics and many, many more!

'Fascinating' *Maxim*

'A football trivia utopia.' *Irish Times*

'I guarantee you will find yourself quoting from this utter gem of a book.' *Sun*

£8.99

ISBN 978 1 84195 761 6

ONCE UPON A TIME IN ENGLAND

HELEN WALSH

By the prize-winning author of *Brass*

It's the coldest night of 1975, and a young man with shock-red hair tears through the snowbound streets of Warrington's toughest housing estate. He is Robbie Fitzgerald, and he is running for his life – and that of his young family. In this unbending northern town, he and his Tamil wife Susheela must face up to prejudice and poverty; but now Robbie has seen a way out, and he's sprinting to his date with destiny . . .

Helen Walsh plunges us into the Fitzgeralds' lives and loves over two decades, showing herself to be a brilliant chronicler of our people and our times. In the Fitzgeralds, she has created a family who will stay in your heart long after the final page.

'She will knock you sideways.' *Guardian*

£14.99

ISBN 978 1 84195 868 2

THE RULES OF THE GAME

NEIL STRAUSS

The follow-up to the Number One bestseller *The Game*

The Rules of the Game is the book Neil thought he would never write. 'The Stylelife Challenge' is the ultimate guide to landing the woman of your dreams; taking it one day at a time, the challenge is to confront your insecurities and overcome them through rigorous self-examination and field missions.

In the second part, Neil journeys into the dark side of the Game. 'The Style Diaries' is a series of tales of seduction and sexual (mis)adventure. From finding the perfect woman during a night on the tiles in Reykjavik, to a threesome with a musician's granddaughter; from conducting a keenly felt relationship over email, to the stress of the '30-day experiment', 'The Style Diaries' takes you further into the seduction underworld than ever before.

'It is informed by a sound and pithy knowledge, not just of romance but of the human condition.' *Arena*

'The ultimate self-help manual for shy and awkward blokes . . . Essential stuff, for him and her.' *Daily Mirror*

£16.99

ISBN 978 1 84767 250 6

THE GAME

NEIL STRAUSS

The Number One bestseller

The Game recounts the incredible adventures of a shy man who transforms himself into Style, a character irresistible to women. But just when life gets better than he ever dreamed (he uses his techniques on Britney Spears, moves in with Courtney Love and is officially voted the World's Number One Pickup Artist), he falls for a woman who can beat him at his own game. Jaw-dropping and hilarious, *The Game* reveals the truth about sex, love and relationships, and getting exactly what you want.

'One hugely entertaining story. I loved every page.' *Esquire*

'A narrative of daredevil sexuality.' *Guardian*

£7.99

ISBN 978 1 84767 237 7